RECENT TRENDS IN MEANING-TEXT THEORY

STUDIES IN LANGUAGE COMPANION SERIES (SLCS)

The SLCS series has been established as a companion series to STUDIES IN LANGUAGE, International Journal, sponsored by the Foundation "Foundations of language".

Series Editors

Werner Abraham
University of Groningen
The Netherlands

Michael Noonan
University of Wisconsin-Milwaukee
USA

Editorial Board

Joan Bybee (University of New Mexico)
Ulrike Claudi (University of Cologne)
Bernard Comrie (University of Southern California)
William Croft (University of Manchester)
Östen Dahl (University of Stockholm)
Gerrit Dimmendaal (University of Leiden)
Martin Haspelmath (Free University of Berlin)
Ekkehard König (Free University of Berlin)
Christian Lehmann (University of Bielefeld)
Robert Longacre (University of Texas, Arlington)
Brian MacWhinney (Carnegie-Mellon University)
Marianne Mithun (University of California, Santa Barbara)
Edith Moravcsik (University of Wisconsin, Milwaukee)
Masayoshi Shibatani (Kobe University)
Russell Tomlin (University of Oregon)
John Verhaar (The Hague)

Volume 39

Leo Wanner (ed.)

Recent Trends in Meaning-Text Theory

RECENT TRENDS IN MEANING-TEXT THEORY

Edited by

LEO WANNER
University of Stuttgart

JOHN BENJAMINS PUBLISHING COMPANY
AMSTERDAM/PHILADELPHIA

The paper used in this publication meets the minimum requirements of American National Standard for Information Sciences — Permanence of Paper for Printed Library Materials, ANSI Z39.48-1984.

Library of Congress Cataloging-in-Publication Data

Recent trends in meaning-text theory / edited by Leo Wanner.
    p.   cm. -- (Studies in language companion series, ISSN 0165-7763 ; v. 39)
   Includes bibliographical references and indexes.
   1. Semantics. 2. Grammar, Comparative and general. I. Wanner, Leo. II. Series.
P325.R345   1997
410'.43--dc21   97-47268
ISBN 90 272 3042 0 (Eur.) / 1-55619-925-2 (US) (alk. paper)   CIP

© Copyright 1997 - John Benjamins B.V.
No part of this book may be reproduced in any form, by print, photoprint, microfilm, or any other means, without written permission from the publisher.

John Benjamins Publishing Co. • P.O.Box 75577 • 1070 AN Amsterdam • The Netherlands
John Benjamins North America • P.O.Box 27519 • Philadelphia PA 19118-0519 • USA

Authors

David Beck
Department of Linguistics
University of Toronto
Toronto, ON M5S 3H1
Canada

Aravind Joshi
Department of Computer and
Information Science
Moore School
University of Pennsylvania
Philadelphia, PA 19104-6389
USA

Igor Boguslavsky
Institute for Information
Transmission Problems
Russian Academy of Sciences
Ermolovoy 19
Moscow 101 447
Russia

Elena V. Paducheva
Institute of Scientific and
Technical Information
Russian Academy of Sciences
Usievixa 20a Moscow 125 219
Russia

Marie-Christine Escalier
CISI–Ingénierie/
Méthodes Avancées
1, rue le Corbusier
SILIC 232 94528 Rungis Cedex
France

Alain Polguère
Département de linguistique et
de traduction
Université de Montréal
C.P. 6128, Succ. "Centre Ville"
Montréal, QC
Canada H3C 3J7

Corinne Fournier
Dassault Aviation
78, quai Marcel Dassault
92214 Saint-Cloud
France

Owen Rambow
CoGenTex Inc.
840 Hanshaw Road, Suite 11
Ithaca, NY 14850
USA

Petr Sgall
Faculty of Mathematics and
Physics
Charles University
Malostranske namesti 25
CS-118 00 Prague
Czech Republic

Jean St-Germain
Département de linguistique et
de traduction
Université de Montréal
C.P. 6128, Succ. "Centre Ville"
Montréal, QC
Canada H3C 3J7

Contents

Preface   xi
Leo Wanner

Meaning-Text Semantic Networks as a Formal Language   1
Alain Polguère
    1   Semantic Networks: One of the Languages of Linguistics . .   1
    2   Definition of Nine Basic Semantic Concepts   3
        2.1   General Presentation of the Taxonomy of Linguistic1 Meanings   3
        2.2   The Key Concept of MEANING   6
        2.3   Concepts Belonging to the Specification of the Semantic Structure of MT-Networks   8
        2.4   The case of PRESUPPOSITION: A Concept Belonging to the Specification of the Communicative Structure of MT-Networks   12
    3   Specification of the Formal Language of MT-Networks . . .   15
    4   Conclusion   20

Towards a Notional Representation of Meaning in the Meaning-Text Model: The Case of the French SI   25
Marie Christine Escalier and Corinne Fournier
    1   Introduction   25
    2   Types of Paraphrases and Expression of Causality   26
    3   The Information in the ECD   28
    4   The Relation of Causality and Description of Fr.SI_{conj} in the ECD   29
        4.1   Is *SI* a Logical Connective?   29
        4.2   Nature of the Definition Zone in Lexical Entries . . .   31
        4.3   Analysis of *SI:* Nine Different Lexemes   33

		4.3.1	De Cornulier's Description of *SI*	33
		4.3.2	Problems Raised by the Definition of *Si X, Y* as *'Dans le cas où X, Y'*	35
		4.3.3	Temporary Description: Modal Analysis of *SI*	35
		4.3.4	Insufficiency of the Four Basic Values: The Role of Contextual Elements	37
	4.4	Description of *SI*1 in the extended ECD		40
		4.4.1	Iordanskaja's Tests	40
		4.4.2	*SI*1: Speech Act and/or Descriptive Content	45
		4.4.3	Representation of Supposition in Terms of 'Asserted Content' and 'Presupposed Content'	46
		4.4.4	Conclusion	47
5	Notions and the Notional Dictionary			48
	5.1	Some Characteristics of Notions		48
	5.2	Theoretical Status of Notions		50
	5.3	Advantages of the Notional Representation		51
	5.4	Relations between a Notional Dictionary and the ECD		54
	5.5	Notional Representation of the Meaning of Sentences		55

Verb Categorization and the Format of a Lexicographic Definition (Semantic Types of Causative Relations)   **61**

Elena V. Paducheva

1	Introduction	61
2	Non-intentional (Non-controlled) Causation	64
3	Intentional (Controlled) Causation	68
4	Partial Control	69
5	Guaranteed Causation	70
6	Conclusion	72

Semantic Communicative Structure of Verbal vs. Conjunctive Causative Expressions ([*to*] *kill*/[*to*] *cause to die* vs. [*to*] *die because P*)   **75**

Jean St-Germain

	1	Introduction		75
	2	Verbal vs. Conjunctive Causative Expressions: Specification, Thematization and Focalization		79
		2.1	Specification	79

	2.2	Thematization	83
	2.3	Focalization	84
3	Lexical vs.Syntactic Verbal Causative Expressions: Unitarization		87
4	Conclusion		89

Theme, Rheme, and Communicative Structure in Lushootseed and Bella Coola   93
David Beck

1	Introduction		93
2	Subject and Predicate		94
	2.1	The Canonical Clause	95
	2.2	Verbless Sentences	98
3	Theme, Rheme, and Syntactic Structure		103
	3.1	Wh-Questions	104
	3.2	The Lushootseed Existential Negative	106
4	The Communicative Structure of the Verbless Sentence . . .		108
	4.1	The Syntactic and Semantic Representation of Deixis	109
	4.2	Sem-Theme, Sem-Rheme, and the DSyntR	118
5	Conclusion: Towards a Communicative Typology of Language		129

Scope of Generic Noun Phrases and Its Correlation with the Verb Meaning in Russian   137
Igor Boguslavsky

1	Introduction	137
2	Predicates of Change and Conservation of State and the Problem of Coreferentiality	138
3	Coreferentiality of Generic Noun Phrases	140
4	Scope of the Genericity Quantifier	143
5	Conclusion: Lexicographic Implications	147

Valency and Underlying Structure: An Alternative View on Dependency   149
Petr Sgall

1	Introduction	149
2	Dependency Syntax and Underlying Structure	150
3	Topic-Focus Articulation	154

	4	Status of Underlying Structure	157
	5	Lexical and Grammatical Information	160
	6	Specification of Underlying Representations	161

A Formal Look at Dependency Grammars and Phrase-Structure Grammars, with Special Consideration of Word-Order Phenomena 167

Owen Rambow and Aravind Joshi

1	Introduction		167
2	Dependency, Phrase Structure and the Lexicon		169
3	Formal Aspects of Word Order Variation		177
	3.1	Computational Properties of Dependency Grammars	177
	3.2	Word Order Rules and Non-Projectivity	178
	3.3	Embedded *Wh*-Words in English	179
	3.4	Embedded Clauses in Dutch	182
	3.5	Localizing Syntactic Rules	183
4	Conclusion		187

Subject Index 191

Name Index 201

Preface

Leo Wanner

The present collection of articles is the second in the series on recent work carried out in the framework of the *Meaning-Text Theory* (MTT). The first, (Wanner, 1996), was dedicated to one single prominent topic within MTT—the representation of restricted lexical co-occurrence by means of *Lexical Functions*. The present collection is broader in the sense that it addresses several topics in MTT and related issues—although, again, there is a focus identifiable. Most of the articles address the problem of semantics, semantic representation, and relation of semantics to surface in MTT.

In the age of new linguistic theories and formalisms, MTT is already a theory with tradition: it was launched by I. Mel'čuk and A. Zholkovsky in Moscow in the sixties (Žolkovskij & Mel'čuk, 1965, 1967, 1969),[1] becoming more and more known in the West during the following decades—especially in Canada, France, and Germany. Mel'čuk's move to Montreal certainly constituted a major push to the "missionary work" for MTT in the West.

In the last few years, MTT gained importance in several areas of linguistics and computational linguistics. Thus, features of MTT have been directly integrated into other theories (cf., for instance, the integration of Lexical Functions into Pustejovsky's (1995) Generative Lexicon by Heylen *et al.*, 1994). MTT also influenced the design of grammar formalisms (Rambow *et al.*, 1995). Further active research is continuously carried out in MTT on a number of topics (of which this volume is a convincing example). Therefore, we can expect that MTT will become even more attractive across the borderline of linguistic theories for both theoreticians and practitioners building NLP-systems.

The basic principles of MTT are well-described in several monographs (among them Mel'čuk, 1974, 1982, 1988; Mel'čuk & Pertsov, 1987) and articles (for example, Mel'čuk & Žolkovskij, 1970, Mel'čuk, 1981, 1988b). Thus, we refrain from giving an overall introduction to MTT in this preface

---

[1] "Zholkovsky" is the English spelling of the name, "Žolkovskij" is the Russian spelling. We use the latter to refer to the author's work carried out in Russia.

and proceed directly with the outline of the volume.

The volume consists of eight articles. As already mentioned above, most of them deal with semantics—either with the Semantic Representation (SemR), as Polguère's contribution, or with one or several structures of the SemR (in MTT, the SemR consists of three structures: the Semantic Structure (SemS), the Semantic Communicative Structure (SemCommS), and the Rhetorical Structure (SemRhetS)), as, e.g., Beck's and St-Germain's contributions. The latter group of articles can further be divided into those that address one of the structures as a whole (thus, Beck discusses the SemCommS) and those that discuss a concrete instantiation of one of the structures—be it for classes of phenomena or individual expressions (for example, Paducheva discusses the SemS of causative relations, Escalier & Fournier describe the semantic decomposition of the French conjunction SI 'if').

It is remarkable that an increasing number of works addresses the Communicative Structure, which is a part of the SemR. This tendency is also identifiable in the present volume: five out of eight articles refer, at least to a certain degree, to the SemCommS.

One article addresses a topic within the Semantic Component, which establishes the correspondence between the SemR and the Deep-Syntactic Representation (DSyntR)—the article by Boguslavsky on the relationship between semantics and morphosyntax.

Two contributions in this volume go beyond the scope of the Meaning-Text Theory in that they present works done in other schools of linguistics and relate them to MTT. These are the articles by Sgall and Rambow & Joshi. Sgall discusses the relevance of communicative dimensions (such as Theme and Focus) developed by the Prague school of linguistics. He argues that Theme and Focus naturally fit into the dependency grammar framework adapted in MTT. Rambow & Joshi compare the realization of certain non-projective constructions in the *Tree Adjoining Grammar* formalism (TAG) and in MTT, and show that MTT would profit from adapting the realization pursued in TAG.

In what follows, each of the articles is briefly presented.

Polguère. Polguère addresses the problem of a rigorous specification of semantic networks as a means for meaning representation. The main focus is, thereby, on definitions in the *Explanatory Combinatorial Dictionary* (ECD)—the dictionary used in MTT.

The article begins with an introduction of nine basic concepts needed for the characterization of Meaning-Text (MT) semantic networks: MEANING,

FUNCTOR, ACTANT, OPERATOR, QUANTIFIER, PREDICATE, ARGUMENT, OBJECT NAME, and PRESUPPOSITION. All but Presupposition belong to the Semantic Structure of MT-networks.

Presupposition belongs to the Communicative Structure. An important distinction with respect to Meaning is in Polguère's presentation the opposition 'U-meaning' (utterance meaning) vs. 'L-meaning' (lexical meaning). Five of the concepts from above are placed in a taxonomy as descendants of L-meaning, i.e., as specific L-meanings: Functor and Object Name as its direct descendants and Operator, Quantifier, and Predicate as specializations of Functor.

After the introduction of the basic concepts, Polguère discusses them in more detail. First comes the presentation of the concepts U-meaning, L-meaning, and one distinguished kind of L-meaning—the dominant L-meaning around which the internal structure of a specific U-meaning is centered. Then, concepts that belong to the Semantic Structure of MT-networks are elaborated on. Finally, the presentation of Presupposition (as an element of the SemCommS) is given. As in the case of Meaning, Presupposition is further divided into an 'L (lexical)-presupposition' and 'U (utterance)-presupposition'.

With the introduced terminology at hand, Polguère proposes a formalization of MT-networks that shall avoid, amongst others, the problem of current MT-networks: complexity and bad readability. Polguère argues that the opacity of most MT-networks is usually due to a lack of precision in the formal specification of the representation language.

The formalization of MT-networks is aimed at an explicit representation of (i) the formal properties of each element of the representation, (ii) the semantic dependency links, and (iii) the internal organization of the represented L-meaning. In order to allow an intuitive access to the described L-meaning, Polguère suggests the use of a linear representation in a pseudo-language as a supplement of the (graphical) formalized representation.

An example in the appendix (the definition of the French lexeme REPROCHER1.a '[to] reproach') illustrates the approach proposed.

Escalier & Fournier. Escalier and Fournier investigate one specific aspect of the Semantic Representation in MTT,: the use of sememes in the Semantic Structure for describing causality. They start with a concrete task: how to account in the ECD for semantic equivalence of a set of specific French lexical and syntactic causal constructions. An analysis shows that present means available for representing meaning in the ECD fall short of modelling the meaning of the conjunction SI 'if'. Which means are required is discussed in the remainder of the article.

The discourse on SI begins with an informal analysis of the properties of SI, which is based on De Cornulier's (1985) grouping of the uses of SI into thirteen different cases. Escalier and Fournier reject De Cornulier's proposal to treat the meaning of all SI-cases as encoding sufficient condition: *Si X, Y* 'If X, Y' = *Dans le/les cas où X, Y* 'In the case(s) of X, Y'. They argue that this proposal does not account for modal meaning components that are available in some of the uses of SI. After discussing and also rejecting one possible modal analysis of SI, they come up with nine different senses of SI.

A deeper analysis of the concessive sense of SI (in the article referred to as SI1), which includes an evaluation of Iordanskaja's (1992) parameters for describing conjunctions, shows that the present apparatus of the ECD does not provide a satisfying means to represent 'SI1'. As consequence, Escalier and Fournier suggest to describe SI1 in terms of the metalinguistic concept of *notion* (with the notion "*causalité*(X,Y)" standing for the meaning of *Si*1 *X, Y* 'If X, Y').

Escalier and Fournier state that notions allow for a representation of lexemes that are difficult to describe in terms of semantemes, as well as for a direct representation of the equivalence between lexical and non-lexical realizations. Notions avoid, thus, the need to postulate the presence of a semanteme where the corresponding lexeme is absent. Furthermore, notions facilitate an abstraction of semantic shifts between non-strictly equivalent meanings and an abstraction of different orientations between conversive lexemes (such as BUY and SELL).

Having introduced the concept of notions and the idea of a "notional dictionary", i.e., a dictionary that makes use of notions in Semantic Structures, Escalier and Fournier conclude by discussing the relationships between such a notional dictionary and the ECD.

Paducheva. While Escalier and Fournier discuss causative meanings in order to demonstrate the need for an extended theoretical apparatus in the ECD, Paducheva focuses on causative meanings themselves. Her article addresses the problem of causative verb categorization and adequate formats of lexicographic definitions for their representation. It suggests a correlation between a taxonomic category of a verb and its lexicographic definition. According to Paducheva, verbs that belong to different taxonomic categories should possess different formats of lexicographic definitions, while those that belong to the same category should possess the same format.

Before going into detail with respect to causative verb categorization, Paducheva presents the principle formats of different taxonomic categories.

Her verb categorization follows the tradition of Wierzbicka's work, which establishes a relationship between causation and Vendler's aspectual classification. However, it takes Wierzbicka's work further in that it introduces the following global types of causation: (i) non-intentional (non-controlled) causation, (ii) intentional (controlled) causation, (iii) partial control causation, (iv) guaranteed causation. The distinction between controlled and non-controlled causation is determined by the type of the Causer argument in the causative relation: verbs of non-controlled causation take an event or a state as Causer; verbs of controlled causation take the activity of their Subject as Causer. Partial control and guaranteed control are further specializations of controlled causation. Each of the causation types is discussed in a respective section, where also further several more delicate distinctions are introduced.

St-Germain. St-Germain's article addresses semantico-communicative oppositions between the following two pairs of causative phrases:

(i) the verbal causative 'X killed Y by P-ing Y' and the conjunctive causative 'Y died because X P-ed Y', and
(ii) the lexical causative 'X killed Y by P-ing Y' and the syntactic causative 'X caused Y to die by P-ing Y'.

It is important to note that St-Germain speaks of above phrases as being 'homosemous' (rather than 'synonymous') because they possess the same 'situational' meaning but different Semantic Communicative Structures (while their synonymy would require identical SemCommSs).

Before going into detail, St-Germain introduces the communicative notions he uses to contrastively characterize the phrases discussed. These are: (i) SPECIFICATION (with the values *given*, *new*, and *parameter of interest*), (ii) THEMATIZATION (with the values *theme* and *rheme*), FOCALIZATION (with the values *focalized* and *non-focalized*), and (iv) UNITARIZATION.

The notions along which verbal causative expressions are contrasted to conjunctive causative expressions are Specification, Thematization, and Focalization. Lexical causative phrases are contrasted to their syntactic counterparts in terms of Unitarizaton. Each of the concepts is elaborated on in much detail, examples are provided, and SemRs are discussed.

Beck. Beck's article too deals with the SemCommS of the SemR, although it does not focus on concrete phrases, but presents a study dedicated to the realization of the communicative structure in two languages. The languages under investigation are the two most distantly related representatives of

Salishan (a language family spoken in the North West of the American continent), Bella Coola and Lushootseed. Beck notes that these languages reveal in the sentence building process an overwhelming predominance of SemCommS over lexical categories. In other words, in Bella Coola and Lushootseed, SemCommS appears to be the primary organizing principle of syntactic constructions. This is argued to be especially true for verbless sentences, i.e., sentences with non-verbal predicates as heads.

Before Beck sets out to discuss the SemCommS and its semantics, he presents a brief grammatical outline of the canonical clause and of the syntactic organization of verbless sentences in Bella Coola and Lushootseed. The insights from the presentation of the syntactic organization of verbless sentences let Beck identify a requirement available in both languages under consideration, namely that the Subject correspond to a discourse topic.[2] This means that there is an alignment between the communicative and syntactic organization. To further demonstrate this alignment, Beck discusses *Wh*-questions in Bella Coola and Lushootseed and the Existential Negatives in Lushootseed. (Existential Negatives are negatives that deny the existence of an entity or the truth of a statement in its entirety.)

From the SemCommS concepts introduced in MTT, Beck brings in two, COMMUNICATIVE DEPENDENCY and THEMATIZATION, to account for the syntactic structure of all kinds of verbless sentences in Bella Coola and Lushootseed. The SemCommS, as a part of which these two concepts are represented, plays a significant role in the process of syntacticization, i.e., during the translation of semantic networks into dependency trees of the DSyntR. To this end, Beck proceeds first with some of the subsidiary issues of syntactic and semantic representation in Salishan, and in particular, the representation of deixis in Semantic and Deep-Syntactic Structures. Deictic elements serve as *Communicative Dominant Nodes* in the SemCommS and as syntactic heads in the Deep-Syntactic Structure. This means that there is a linkage from Communicative Dominance to the selection of a syntactic head during syntacticization.

Having established these basic relationships, Beck examines the effects of the SemCommS on the process of syntacticization and the procedural rules for the selection of the "entry node"—the node of the SemS that will appear as the syntactic head (Polguère, 1990).

Boguslavsky. Boguslavsky addresses the problem of how the meaning of sentence elements combine to the meaning of the sentence. The focus of

---

[2] For Beck, *Topics* are elements that are thematic or directly related to Themes over a given stretch of discourse.

his paper is on words with an *inner scope*. A word is considered to possess an inner scope if its valency is filled by word meaning components rather than by complete word meanings. For instance, a negative particle such as *not* (or *ne* in Russian) affects only the assertive part of a word meaning and possesses, thus, an inner scope. In contraindication, a quantifier such as *every* does not possess an inner scope. According to Boguslavsky, not all quantifiers lack an inner scope, though. He puts forward two claims, which are central to his article:

(i) generic noun phrases possess a quantifying meaning component (so-called *meaning of genericity*), i.e., they are generic quantifiers,

(ii) unlike quantifiers of *every*-type, generic quantifiers possess an inner scope.

After a brief introduction, Boguslavsky discusses Russian 'change and conservation of state' (CCS) predicates, as, for example, *perestavat'* '[to] stop', *brosat'* '[to] give up', and *prodolžat'* '[to] continue', with respect to coreferentiality. In abstract terms, the Semantic Structure of CCS predicates can be described as
'I. before time T, X is in the state S;
II. after time T, X is either still in the state S or in the state ¬S'.
Boguslavsky states that if X is a generic NP (as, for example, *studenty* 'students' or *anglijskie koroli* 'English kings'), the elements denoted by the NP in I and II may be either identical or different; cf. *Studenty perestali interesovat' sja politikoj* 'Students lost interest in politics'. The students who were interested in politics before T do not need to be the same who lost interest in politics.

According to Boguslavsky, this does not mean, however, that there is no referential identity between referential NPs. Rather, he argues, the character of the referential identity may be different—either *generally coreferential* or *distributively coreferential*. In the case of the first, the elements referred to in I and II do not need to be identical. In the case of the second, they do. This difference may be motivated by the lexical meaning of the predicates involved, or by the scope of the generic quantifier.

Concluding, Boguslavsky touches upon the problem of specifying the correlation between verbal meaning and the meaning of genericity in the lexicon.

Sgall. Sgall's article does not address a specific topic within the Meaning-Text Theory as the previous articles do. Rather, it discusses the assets of the notion of dependency with respect to the representation of functional concepts of language, citing constituent and phrase structure as being not well-suited for this task. Two of these concepts are addressed in the article: VALENCY FRAME (grid) as the central part of the *Underlying Structure*, and TOPIC FOCUS ARTICULATION (TFA).

A valency frame should, in Sgall's view, contain a specification of the functional type of the head's complements (such as Actor, Appurtenance, General Relationship, etc.), as well as indications of the relationship of a complement to the head (inner participant or free adjunct) and its obligatoriness (obligatory *vs.* optional). Apart from the valency frame, an Underlying Structure, which corresponds to a combined Semantic and Syntactic Representation in MTT, contains a lexical part and values of grammatical categories.

TFA is described in terms of an ordering of complements on the scale of *Communicative Dynamism*, from *topic proper* (= what the sentence is about) to *focus proper* (= the core of the new information). The basic ordering, called *Systemic Ordering*, is language-specific. For instance, for English, the Systemic Ordering is Actor–Addressee–Objective–Source–Effect–Manner–... Czech differs from English in that it shifts Objective and Effect to the right after most of the adverbial complements.

After discussing TFA, Sgall turns again to the topic of Underlying Structure. Against the background of different TFAs for syntactic constructions that are very close in their meanings, Sgall argues that it is doubtful that strictly synonymous syntactic constructions exist, and concludes that it is questionable to differentiate between a semantic structure and a (deep-)syntactic structure. Instead, he suggests to consider a single Underlying Structure that is opposed to the extra-linguistic Cognitive Structure.

In the last two sections of his article, Sgall describes the lexical and grammatical information specified in a lexical entry of a Prague school lexicon, and a generative procedure for the specification of the Underlying Structure.

Rambow & Joshi. As Sgall, Rambow and Joshi contrast dependency-based theories to phrase structure-based theories. Referring to Sgall's observation that in dependency theories, lexical information plays a central role while in phrase structure-based theories it does not, Rambow and Joshi argue that this is not coincidental, but a property of underlying formalisms, and that an attempt to lexicalize the phrase structure formalism leads to what is known as the *Tree Adjoining Grammar* (TAG) formalism. To buttress their argumentation, Rambow and Joshi provide analyses of sample fragments of a context-free phrase-structure grammar and a *Tree Substitution Grammar* (TSG). It turns out that in order to be lexicalizable, a phrase-structure grammar must provide the operation of tree substitution (as in a TSG) and, additionally, the operation of tree adjunction. Both operations are characteristic of a TAG.

Rambow and Joshi show that a TAG and a dependency grammar reveal a series of resemblances, but also a series of deviating features. Against this background they discuss the realization of non-projective constructions in both theories. They point out that there are two potential problems with non-projective constructions in a dependency-based theory as adapted in MTT: (i) in the worst case, the parsing time of a non-projective construction is exponential to the length of the input string, and, thus, not quite suitable as a model for human language processing; (ii) the syntax of non-projective constructions cannot be expressed in terms of the notion of *syntagm* as projective constructions are—which is linguistically unmotivated. After elaborating on these problems, Rambow and Joshi address the realization of two types of non-projective constructions in TAG and MTT: embedded *Wh*-words in English and embedded clauses in Dutch. Then, they present a proposal rooted in TAG for handling certain types of non-projective constructions using syntagms. They conclude by stating that important findings in TAG can be transferred to MTT in order to improve MTT with respect to some evidently problematic aspects.

Acknowledgements

Most of the articles have been read and commented on by two other contributors to the volume. Additionally, Lidija Iordanskaja, Igor Mel'čuk, Richard Kittredge, Alexander Nakhimovsky, Tanya Korelsky, and Elke Teich reviewed all articles. Bruce Jakeway, Igor Mel'čuk, and Alain Polguère did the proofreading. I would like to express my heartfelt gratitude to all of them.

Bibliography

Cornulier De, B. 1985. *Effets de sens*. Paris: Editions de Minuit.

Heylen, D., K.G. Maxwell & M. Verhagen. 1994. "Lexical Functions in Machine Translation". *Proceedings of the 15th International Conference on Computational Linguistics*. 1240–1244.

Iordanskaja, L. 1992. "Communicative Structure and its Use during Text Generation". *International Forum on Information and Documentation*. 17.2:15–27.

Mel'čuk, I.A. 1974. *Opyt teorii lingvističeskix modelej "Smysl—Tekst"*. Moscow: Nauka.

Mel'čuk, I.A. 1981. "Meaning-Text Models: A Recent Trend in Soviet Linguistics". *Annual Review of Anthropology*. 10:27–62.

Mel'čuk, I.A. 1982. *Towards a Language of Linguistics*. Munich: Wilhelm Fink.

Mel'čuk, I.A. 1988a. *Dependency Syntax: Theory and Practice*. Albany: State University of New York Press.

Mel'čuk, I.A. 1988b. "Semantic Description of Lexical Units in an Explanatory Combinatorial Dictionary: Basic Principles and Heuristic Criteria". *International Journal of Lexicography*. 1.3:165–188.

Mel'čuk, I.A. & N. Pertsov. 1987. *Surface Syntax of English*. Amsterdam: John Benjamins.

Mel'čuk, I.A. & A.K. Žolkovskij. 1970. "Towards a Functioning Meaning-Text Model of Language". *Linguistics*. 57:10–47.

Polguère, A. 1990. *Structuration et mise en jeu procédurale d'un modèle linguistique déclaratif dans un cadre de génération de texte*. PhD thesis: Département de linguistique, Université de Montréal.

Pustejovsky, J. 1995. *The Generative Lexicon*. Cambridge, Massachusetts: The MIT Press.

Rambow, O., K. Vijay-Shanker & D. Weir. 1995. "D-Tree Grammars". *Proceedings of the 33rd Meeting of the Association for Computational Linguistics*. 151–158. Cambridge, MA.

Žolkovskij, A.K. & I.A. Mel'čuk. 1965. "O vozmožnom metode i instrumentax semantičeskogo sinteza". *Naučno-Texničeskaja Informacija*. 5:23–28.

Žolkovskij, A.K. & I.A. Mel'čuk. 1967. "O semantičeskom sinteze". *Problemy kibernetiki*. 19:177–238.

Žolkovskij, A.K. & I.A. Mel'čuk. 1969. "K postroeniju dejstvujuščej modeli jazyka Smysl ↔ Tekst". *Mašinnyj Perevod i Prikladnaja Lingvistika*. 11:5–35.

Wanner, L. (ed.). 1996. *Lexical Functions in Lexicography and Natural Language Processing*. Amsterdam: Benjamins Academic Publishers.

Meaning-Text Semantic Networks as a Formal Language

Alain Polguère

1 Semantic Networks: One of the Languages of Linguistics

The object of the present discussion, Meaning-Text semantic networks, is not a formalism but is, rather, one of the languages of linguistics described in (Mel'čuk, 1982:13). This means that the term *semantic network* does not refer only to a given formal language, but also to the structured set of concepts which forms the basis of this formal language. Mel'čuk, (1982:13–14) defines four types of languages of linguistics:

(i) Type I languages for representing linguistic1 utterances ,[1]

(ii) Type II languages for representing (rules of) linguistic2 models,

(iii) Type III languages for representing procedures for the activation of linguistic2 models,

(iv) Type IV languages for representing concepts which are involved in the three other types of languages.

In the present article, I will study one of the Type I languages involved in the Meaning-Text approach, namely, the language of semantic networks.

Specifying the language of semantic networks is not only a problem of formalization, it is a prerequisite to any rigorous work on the semantic level of linguistic2 modeling. I will make use here of the standard Meaning-Text terminology; I presuppose that the reader is familiar with this terminology as well as with the Meaning-Text approach in general (for an introduction, see Mel'čuk, 1981, 1982). Since Meaning-Text Theory makes use of only one network formalism—semantic networks, I will use the term MT-*network*

---

[1]Reminder: in Meaning-Text terminology, *linguistic*1 means 'relative to language' and *linguistic*2 means 'relative to linguistics'.

(= 'MEANING-TEXT NETWORK') to refer unambiguously to Meaning-Text semantic networks.

Two important points must be noted before starting the study of MT-networks. Firstly, as indicated in (Mel'čuk, 1982:14), Type I languages are involved in the specification of Type II languages. MT-networks will therefore be used in contexts other than the semantic representation of utterances. They are present in the semantic component of linguistic2 models. More specifically, they are used:

(i) in the entries of EXPLANATORY COMBINATORIAL DICTIONARIES (ECDs) (Mel'čuk & Polguère, 1987); see, for instance, the definition for Fr. REPROCHER1a '[to] reproach' in the Appendix;

(ii) in grammatical rules describing the correspondence between the SEMANTIC REPRESENTATION (SemR) and DEEP-SYNTACTIC REPRESENTATION (DSyntR) of utterances, as illustrated in Figure 1.[2] For a study of this latter type of rules, see (Polguère, 1990) and (Mel'čuk & Polguère, 1991).

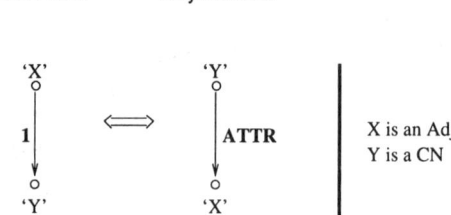

Example: *They live on a blue[X] planet[Y]*

Figure 1: *Sample (simplified) SemR $\Longleftrightarrow$ DSyntR correspondence rule for English*

In the context of a more thorough study, it would be necessary to consider separately the two usages of MT-networks: (i) as a simple Type I language, and (ii) as a component of Type II languages. I will focus here on only one particular case of this latter usage, namely, MT-networks that are used in ECD definitions.

Secondly, and this is implied by the above-mentioned specification of linguistic2 languages, the elaboration of the fourth type of language (linguistic2 terminology) is needed for the elaboration of any other type of

---

[2] I cannot enter into the detailed description of this type of rule. Notice that the underlined node, on the left-hand side of the rule, is communicatively dominant.

language. Mel'čuk (1982) mainly defines the terminology that is required for the morphological level of linguistic2 modeling, and we lack precise definitions for some concepts involved at the semantic level. Therefore, my first step will be to define the minimal terminology (Type IV language) which will be needed in order to characterize MT-networks (Type I and II languages) in this paper. The nine concepts whose definitions are necessary are MEANING, FUNCTOR, ACTANT, OPERATOR, QUANTIFIER, PREDICATE, ARGUMENT, OBJECT NAME, and PRESUPPOSITION.

Before defining these concepts, let me stress that the present paper by no means pretends to be definitive in its formalization of the language of MT-networks. The following should be regarded as an attempt to formalize part of this linguistic2 language. Many definitions are missing here, and most of the definitions or graphical conventions presented would need to be reformulated in the context of an exhaustive and methodical study.

2 Definition of Nine Basic Semantic Concepts

2.1 General Presentation of the Taxonomy of Linguistic1 Meanings

Although the following definitions are approximate and call for some refinements, they are sufficient to provide a basis for a formal specification of the language of MT-networks in the present paper. Apart from the concept of presupposition, which is linked to the COMMUNICATIVE STRUCTURE of MT-networks, all concepts defined below belong to the specification of the SEMANTIC STRUCTURE of MT-networks. They are centered around eight core concepts which are introduced in the taxonomy of linguistic1 meanings shown in Figure 2.

Figure 2 distinguishes between two sub-classes of linguistic1 meanings: U-meaning and L-meaning. We will see below that L-meaning refers to meanings which are expressed by lexical units of natural languages, whereas U-meaning refers to meanings of linguistic1 utterances. Later in this section, I will explain why I am using the term *utterance* here. (Notice that the above taxonomy could be developed and refined; e.g., by specifying subclasses of U-meanings.)

The distinction between functor and object name, based on concepts which are linkages vs. concepts which are not, calls for some justification. Take for example a semantic predicate such as 'red', the meaning of RED$_{adj}$; it is impossible to do anything with it—at least, it is impossible to define it—without considering at the same time another L-meaning which depends semantically on it. Thus, writing 'red' is in fact necessarily a shortcut for '(X is) red'. On the other hand, an L-meaning which is an object name can

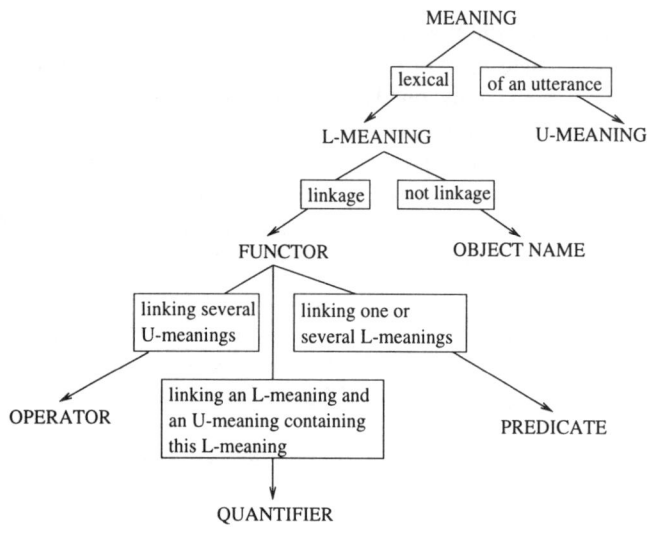

Figure 2: *Taxonomy of linguistic1 meanings*

always be considered in isolation. In some sense, it is autonomous because its interpretation is not relative to other meanings. It is therefore justifiable to say that some L-meanings are linkages since they carry the expression of one or more semantic links which hold between them and other meanings. Object names are not linkages because they do not carry the expression of such links.[3]

The two concepts of *semantic link* and *semantic dependency* (which is an oriented link) will be considered as being "too primitive" to be defined in the following discussion: they cannot be defined uniquely in terms of other linguistic2 concepts. As a consequence, no definition for these concepts will be proposed. Note that semantic dependency should be treated in roughly the same way one usually deals with syntactic or morphological dependencies: there is no operational definition other than procedures for the determination of these links based on a list of operational criteria; cf. (Garde, 1977). It is not the right place to analyze and justify this distinction between two types of definitions for linguistic2 concepts; rather, as an illustration, let us take a look at the definitions of two related linguistic2 concepts, given by *The American Heritage Dictionary* (1981):

---

[3] As noticed by I. Mel'čuk, the term *functor* can in fact be ambiguous between (i) a certain class of semantic units (i.e., a class of sememes—see Mel'čuk, 1988:54), and (ii) a function of a semantic unit in an MT-network ('s_i' is a functor of 's_j'). It is of course the first meaning of the term that is considered here.

allophone (...) *Linguistics* Any of the variant forms of a phoneme (...)

phoneme (...) *Linguistics* One of the set of the smallest units of speech that distinguish one utterance or word from another in a given language. (...)

The point here is not to decide whether these definitions are good or not. (For instance, some may prefer to define these concepts the other way round: i.e., PHONEME in terms of ALLOPHONE.) At least, they avoid circularity: ALLOPHONE is defined in terms of PHONEME, which in turn is not defined in terms of ALLOPHONE or any other concepts which may contain this one. What should be noticed in the above definitions is that the first one is a simple decomposition of an abstract linguistic2 concept in terms of other linguistic2 concepts. The second definition, on the other hand, is more than that. It not only makes use of other linguistic2 concepts (*unit of speech*, *utterance*, etc.) but also contains some sort of directions for identifying the denotation of the concept. Even though the "directions for use" are approximate, we recognize in the definition for PHONEME the methodology based on the use of minimal pairs for distinguishing between sounds which do or do not belong to the same phoneme.

All systems of linguistic2 terminology need these two types of definitions if they are to be conceived of as tools for describing natural languages. The operational definition of the concept of semantic dependency will not be used here, even though such definition has already been proposed:

Let 'X' stand for the meaning of unit X, and the symbol 'X_n(...)' for a predicate X with n arguments (in semantic or logical sense of the term **predicate**). In a sentence, wordform w_1 directly depends semantically on wordform w_2 if and only if the meaning of lexeme $L(w_2)$ is described (in the language's dictionary) by a predicate '$L(w_2)_n$(...)' and in the sentence in question the meaning '$L(w_1)$' is an argument of this predicate: '$L(w_2)_n$(..., $L(w_1)$, ...)'. (Mel'čuk, 1988:116)

The above definition is not compatible with the definitions I propose for other related concepts: it defines semantic dependency in terms of ARGUMENT and PREDICATE, whereas I need to refer to the former in order to define the latter. Of course, the system of semantic concepts I present here will not be completed until a non-circular operational definition of semantic dependency has been proposed.

In the remainder of this section, I make use of definitions already presented in such texts as (Mel'čuk, 1981, 1988b; St-Germain, 1988). These definitions will be completed and adapted according to the three following criteria:

(i) they must be compatible with the Meaning-Text approach to linguistic2 definition (found in ECD entries), which is the one adopted in (Mel'čuk, 1982) for the definition of linguistic2 concepts themselves;
(ii) they must reflect the taxonomy proposed in Figure 2;
(iii) they must cover all basic concepts whose descriptions (even approximate) are required in order to establish a formal specification for the language of MT-networks.

2.2 The Key Concept of MEANING

As previously stated, the term *meaning*, as used in Meaning-Text linguistics, is ambiguous; it refers to at least two distinct but related concepts: U-meaning and L-meaning.

Definition of U-MEANING and L-MEANING:

1. *U-meaning of (utterance)* U = Invariant of linguistic1 paraphrases of the utterance U; i.e., the only property shared by all utterances which have the ⌜same meaning⌝ as U.

2. *L-meaning of (lexical unit)* L = component of the meaning of all utterances containing the expression of one of the linguistic1 signs associated with the lexical unit L.[1]

In these definitions, *utterance* refers to any grammatical construction which can be uttered in isolation. In other words, an utterance can be a sentence or any part of a sentence which can function autonomously. The definition for U-meaning is an adaptation of a standard Meaning-Text definition for the concept of meaning (Melčuk, 1988b); it is here explicitly restricted to the particular case of utterances. The definition for L-meaning seems to be both necessary and operational for at least three reasons: (i) it is consistent with the definition for U-meaning, (ii) it reflects the fact that a lexeme (or a phraseme), while being a set of linguistic1 signs, is associated with ONE meaning, and (iii) it does not interfere with the concept of SIGNIFIED of a linguistic1 sign—the meaning of a lexeme is conceptually distinguished from the signified of the linguistic1 signs this lexeme contains.

The dichotomy U-meaning/L-meaning can be very directly connected to the following remark by A. Wierzbicka:

The object of semantic analysis is the content of human thought, as expressed in speech. This means that semantics cannot limit its interests to the meaning of lexical items as such—nor to the meaning of grammatical categories as such. In actual fact, neither lexical items nor grammatical categories have any meaning: only utterances have meaning, because only utterances express thoughts. To speak about the meaning of lexical items or grammatical categories is elliptical: strictly speaking we can only talk about the contribution that particular elements make to the meaning of the whole utterance. (Wierzbicka, 1977:164)

This characteristic of the concept of meaning noted by A. Wierzbicka is reflected in the above definitions for U-meaning and L-meaning. Note that while L-meaning is defined by means of U-meaning, a U-meaning as such is always made up of at least one L-meaning. More precisely, the following constraint on the structure of U-meanings will play an important role in the formal specification of MT-networks:

Any U-meaning 'u' virtually contains a DOMINANT L-meaning around which all the internal structure of 'u' is centered. In more precise terms, all U-meanings have an internal (communicative, etc.) structure from which a set of possible dominant nodes can be computed.

The problem of associating a dominant node to a given U-meaning is beyond the scope of the present paper (for a presentation, see Polguère, 1990 and Mel'čuk & Polguère, 1991). The above remarks, of course, do not define the concept of U-meaning itself, but rather, they characterize its anatomy. Such constraints on the structure of U-meanings allow us to adopt the convention for their graphical representation as shown in Figure 3.

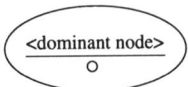

Figure 3: *Standard graphical representation of U-meanings in MT-networks*

A (non-decomposed) L-meaning is usually represented in an MT-network by means of a labeled node. Therefore, a U-meaning will necessarily be represented by means of a sub-network—a circled set of nodes—in which a dominant node has been singled out by means of any well-specified graphical convention (underlined, in bold characters, etc.). This graphical representation of U-meanings is in fact an over-simplification. An

MT-network that is the SemR of a set of paraphrastic utterances does not contain the specification of one dominant node. Rather, it possesses an internal structuring (sub-networks for Communicative Structure, etc.) from which different dominant nodes can be inferred. On the other hand, a given utterance can be associated with a more restricted network containing the specification of one dominant node, which roughly corresponds to the lexeme which will be the top-node of the DSyntR for this utterance. I cannot enter into the study of this problem here; for more information, one should refer to (Iordanskaja & Polguère, 1988; Polguère, 1990; and Mel'čuk & Polguère, 1991).

2.3 Concepts Belonging to the Specification of the Semantic Structure of MT-Networks

Definition of FUNCTOR:

Functor = L-meaning on which at least one U-meaning or L-meaning depends.

This definition is general enough to be applicable to particular cases such as operators, quantifiers and predicates (see below). It is specific enough to distinguish between a functor, which is an L-meaning with a corresponding system of semantic dependencies, and an object name, which is an "isolated" meaning. The concept of functor goes together with the concept of (semantic) actant, which will be involved in the definition of other concepts denoting classes of L-meanings.

Definition of ACTANT:

Actant of (functor) F = U-meaning or L-meaning which depends semantically on the functor F.[4]

Actant refers to the semantic dependent of any functor, whether it is an operator, a quantifier, or a predicate. We will see later that *argument* is more specific.[5]

Definition of OPERATOR:

Operator = Functor whose actant(s) is/are U-meaning(s) and which expresses a logical or para-logical operation performed on this(these) actant(s).[2]

---

[4] An actant of a functor which is the L-meaning of a lexical unit L is called a *semantic actant* of (the lexical unit) L.

[5] In this paper, *actant* refers to semantic actants only; no mention will be made of the concept of SYNTACTIC ACTANT. On this latter concept; cf. (Mel'čuk, 1993).

MT SEMANTIC NETWORKS AS A FORMAL LANGUAGE 9

Operator is preferred to *connector* as operators are not, strictly speaking, connectors. For instance, the linguistic1 negation does not connect two U-meanings but is applied to a U-meaning in order to produce a more complex one. As in logic, operator refers here to symbols which are expressing an operation (conjunction, disjunction, negation, etc.): an operator is what expresses/represents an operation. Not all linguistic1 operators are logical ones, so the definition of this concept cannot be based on a truth-value semantics. The relevant criteria are (i) the characterization of the dependents of this particular class of functors, and (ii) reference to logical or para-logical operations. Because of the wide range of functors which can be considered as operators, the above definition is vague and has to remain vague (i.e., it contains no precise specification of what is expressed by a linguistic1 operator).

Their dependents being necessarily U-meanings, operators should graphically be represented in the way shown in Figure 4.

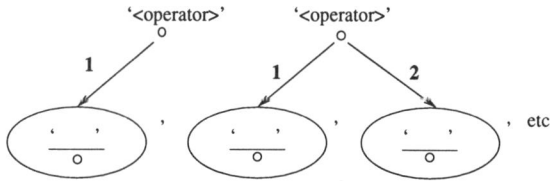

Figure 4: *Graphical representation of operators in MT-networks*

Notice that in this figure the arcs should not be pointing directly to the dominant nodes of the utterances for at least two reasons:

(i) it is the utterances themselves, and not any of the nodes they contain, which are the actual actants of the operators;

(ii) utterances can have several virtual dominant nodes, which are computed from the MT-networks's communicative and semantic structures: there is no reason to select any of them at the level of semantic representation.[6]

Definition of QUANTIFIER:

Quantifier of A_1 in A_2 = Functor whose first actant A_1 is an L-meaning and whose second actant A_2 is a U-meaning containing A_1, and which expresses the quantification of A_1 in A_2.

Example: 'All$_{Quant}$ [mynahs$_{A_1}$ need calcium]$_{A_2}$'.

---

[6]Remember the last paragraph of Section 2.2 above: the underlined nodes in my representations stand for the set of all possible dominant nodes.

As with operators, it is preferable to build a relatively vague definition for the concept of quantifier, using the more primitive concept of QUANTIFICATION. Quantifiers are first characterized as functors, based on the specification of their actantial structure. They have two actants: the first one being an L-meaning and the second one a U-meaning containing the first actant. They express a quantification of their first actant, in the sub-network which is their second actant. This corresponds to an MT-network modeling of the logical concept of SCOPE OF A QUANTIFIER. From the above definition, we can infer that the formal graphical representation of a quantifier in an MT-network should encode both the specification of the quantified element—a node in the MT-network, and the specification of the scope of the quantifier—a sub-network in the MT-network (more precisely, a U-meaning). Figure 5 shows the general pattern for representing quantifiers in MT-networks.

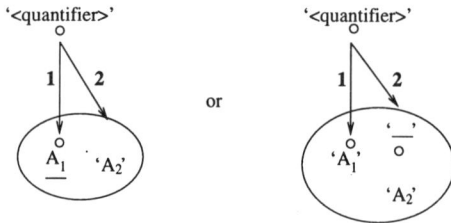

Figure 5: *Graphical representation of quantifiers in MT-networks*

Note that Figure 5 envisages the two possible configurations for quantification: (i) the quantified element is the dominant node of the U-meaning (which corresponds to the scope of the quantifier), or (ii) the quantified element is not the dominant node. Woods (1975:73–75) makes some interesting remarks on network representation of quantifiers. One can see in Figure 5 that quantifiers are a very special type of functors—a case of *higher operators* according to W. Woods—whose formal manipulation in MT-networks could be rather complex to handle.

Definition of PREDICATE:

Predicate = Functor whose actant(s) is/are L-meanings.

Predicates are sometimes defined as 'meanings which are neither operators nor quantifiers', but the distinction between U-meanings and L-meanings allows for a more adequate definition, based on positive rather than negative criteria. A predicate is neither an operator nor a quantifier because none of its arguments is a semantic "block" corresponding to an utterance. The concept of predicate is linked to the concept of argument, whose definition follows.

Definition of ARGUMENT:

Argument of (predicate) P = L-meaning which is a semantic dependent of the predicate P.

This definition is appropriate as it would be misleading to extend the concept of argument to the semantic actants of any type of functor. In fact, argument is often used as a synonym for actant, whereas it is a more specific concept: compare *?argument of an operator/quantifier*. The more general concept of actant may be sufficient and argument superfluous; but in case this latter has to be introduced, it seems to me that it is preferable to stick to the traditional meaning of 'dependent of a predicate'.

According to the above definition of predicate, the actants of a predicate can only be lexical meanings. But let us consider a predicate such as 'want' or 'decide':

(1) a. *Adèle wants to have a mummy.*
 b. *Adèle has decided to look for her mummy.*

Cases like (1a,b) force us to consider that the second actant of 'want' or 'decide' is something more complex than a lexical meaning. We could say that 'have' or 'look for' are here lexical meanings, thus being consistent with the predicative nature of their semantic governor: both actants of the predicate being L-meanings; but it is clear that they are at the center of a semantic constellation that functions, as a whole, as an argument of 'want'. We cannot describe this constellation of meanings as a U-meaning for a very simple reason: it would be absurd to say that the utterances *Adèle has a mummy/Adèle is looking for her mummy* have been produced when one utters (1a) and (1b). So, what can be said about predicates such as 'want' and about the special type of arguments they take? Clearly, there are different types of predicates, depending on the exact nature of their arguments.

It seems obvious that predicates should be allowed to take as arguments, in MT-networks, subnetworks which strictly speaking are not lexical meanings, thus calling for a refinement of the definition given for the concept of predicate. As a result, Figure 6a will be considered a better semantic structure for the SemR of (1a) than Figure 6b:[7]

---

[7]The numbering 'have²1a' is taken from *The Longman Dictionary of Contemporary English*, (1987). As indicated, Figures 6a and 6b only display Semantic Structures.

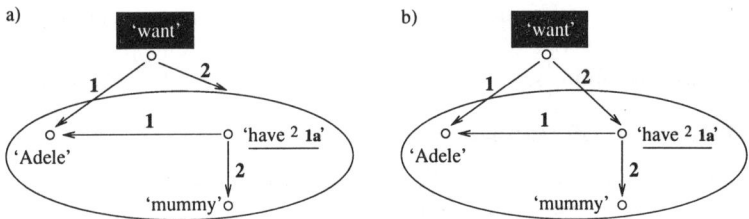

Figure 6: *Two semantic structures for the SemR of* Adèle wants to have a mummy

One can see that the MT-network in Figure 6a makes 'want' look almost like some sort of quantifier. It is not a quantifier nevertheless, as its purpose is not to express a quantification for its first argument within the scope of its second argument. But it remains that the predicate 'want' possesses a quantifier-like structure and should be characterized as such. I do not pretend to offer here any definitive solution to this problem. On the contrary, my goal is to raise a question in order to demonstrate that the problem of formally classifying linguistic1 meanings is not a trivial one and far from being solved in the present study.

Definition of OBJECT NAME:

Object name = L-meaning which cannot have a semantic dependent (U-meaning or L-meaning).

This definition is self-explanatory. According to it, object name is some sort of antonym for functor, which reflects quite well the taxonomy in Figure 2. Of course, in MT-networks, object names are represented as nodes from which no arc of semantic dependency originates.

All basic concepts associated with the Semantic Structure of MT-networks have been introduced. I will now examine one concept associated with Communicative Structures: the concept of PRESUPPOSITION.

2.4 *The case of PRESUPPOSITION: A Concept Belonging to the Specification of the Communicative Structure of MT-Networks*

The Communicative Structure of an MT-network representing a given message roughly corresponds to what encodes the attitude of the Speaker towards this message, and controls grammatical and lexical choices in the

---

Full-fledged SemRs should contain, for instance, the specification of a Communicative Structure.

expression of the Semantic Structure of the MT-network. The Communicative Structure can be subdivided into at least five components which are five systems of conceptual oppositions (compare Mel'čuk, 1988:58, 1997):

(i) *Theme* vs. *Rheme*,
(ii) *Given* vs. *New*,
(iii) *Foreground* vs. *Background*,
(iv) *Assertion* vs. *Presupposition*, and
(v) *neutral presentation* vs. *emphatic presentation*.

The present description is limited to only one of these components: the presuppositional structure, which is a component implied in ECD definitions.

The presuppositional structure of MT-networks presents one or more systems of the opposition 'assertion/presupposition'. There are two types of presuppositions, those appearing in MT-networks that correspond to lexical definitions and those appearing in SemRs of utterances. I will illustrate this point by means of examples. Let us consider (2a), for which (2b) is a presupposition:

(2) a. *Hyper-active mynahs need calcium.*
     b. $\Longrightarrow$ 'There exist hyper-active mynahs'

The inclusion of (2b) in the meaning of (2a) results from the interaction of many inter-related parameters: syntactic role and determination of *mynahs*, grammatical mode of the main verb, etc. As such, this type of presupposition could be considered as some sort of "grammatical presupposition". The situation is quite different in the next example:

(3) a. *This vet knows that my mynah needs calcium.*
     b. $\Longrightarrow$ 'My mynah needs calcium'

The presupposition (3b) clearly originates from a particular lexical unit found in (3a): 'X knows that Y 'presupposes' Y takes or took place/exists'. Even though the syntactic structure of (3a) plays an important role in the activation of the presupposition (*knows* is the main verb, etc.), it is possible to state that (3b) is a "lexical presupposition", which originates from the meaning of the lexeme TO KNOW.

These observations justify the introduction of two related but distinct concepts: presuppositions of utterances (U-PRESUPPOSITIONS) and lexical presuppositions (L-PRESUPPOSITIONS). The following definitions are based on the concept of '(utterance) U presupposes (U-meaning) M'.

'U presupposes M' will not be defined in terms of other concepts, but rather by means of criteria for its identification (compare once again, the discussion of the two types of definitions for linguistic2 concepts in Section 2.1 above). O. Mørdrup has proposed an elegant definition for this concept, based on such criteria:

> P présuppose Q si et seulement si à chaque fois que P est affirmée, niée ou mise sous forme de question le locuteur ne peut pas nier que Q sans se contredire
> 'P presupposes Q if and only if each time P is asserted, negated or questioned the speaker cannot deny Q without contradiction'. (Mørdrup, 1988:128)

The above criteria apply to the determination of both lexical and grammatical presuppositions; consider:

(4) a. *Hyper-active mynahs need calcium and hyper-active mynahs do not exist.*
    b. $\implies$ CONTRADICTION

(5) a. *The vet knows that Birden needs calcium, but Birden doesn't need calcium.*
    b. $\implies$ CONTRADICTION

Once the concept 'U presupposes M' has been described with the above operational criteria, it is relatively easy to write the definitions for the two concepts of presupposition:

Definition of PRESUPPOSITION:

1. *U-presupposition of (utterance)* U = U-meaning that is presupposed by the utterance U.
2. *L-presupposition of (lexical unit)* L = L-meaning which is a U-presupposition of all utterances whose dominant L-meaning is 'L'.

There is no problem with the definition for U-presupposition. The definition for L-presupposition calls for three comments:

(i) This second definition is based on the fact that an L-presupposition is in fact some sort of potential U-presupposition.

(ii) The notion of dominant L-meaning is needed here in order to account for the fact that a lexical unit does not presuppose anything by itself; it is the utterances where its meaning is dominant which express its presupposition.

(iii) The L-presupposition of L will be expressed by any utterance where 'L' is the dominant L-meaning. But this does not entail that the same presupposition cannot be expressed by an utterance where 'L' appears as a more peripheral L-meaning.

Presuppositions should be graphically represented in MT-networks as sub-networks which are clearly distinct from assertions. For this purpose, I propose to use shaded sub-networks (as shown in Figure 7).

Figure 7: *Graphical representation of presupposition in MT-networks*

As for the graphical representation of utterances, subnetworks representing a presupposition contain the specification of a dominant node. As a rule, any subnetwork in an MT-network should contain either the specification of a dominant node, or the specification of an internal sub-partition which could be used to compute one or more possible dominant nodes. Due to space limitations I cannot enter here into a detailed study of the concept of dominant node.

Herewith the series of definitions for the nine basic semantic concepts is finished. In Section 3, I will use this terminology in order to specify a higher level semantic language: the language of MT-networks.

3 Specification of the Formal Language of MT-Networks

In the work done within the Meaning-Text framework, MT-networks are not used very much as a tool for building linguistic2 descriptions. They could almost be considered as some sort of innocuous but rather useless appendix of the Meaning-Text approach. Even for the lexicographic work on the French ECD (see Mel'čuk et al., 1984, 1988, 1992) MT-network formalism is not used as a tool for representation and description. Three factors can explain this situation.

Firstly, the SemR $\Longleftrightarrow$ DSyntR correspondence has often been conceived of as based almost exclusively on the application of lexical rules (mainly, lexical definitions) to establish a correspondence between a lexeme (a node in the DSyntR) and its semantic decomposition (a sub-network of the SemR). No actual semantic correspondence rules have been considered. This approach, which disconnects the level of SemR from grammatical description, necessarily makes MT-networks less functional than the other formal languages used by Meaning-Text theory at the more superficial levels of linguistic2 description: they are used primarily for illustrative purposes. Somehow, MT-networks do not "function". Of course, a more grammatical approach to the description of the SemR $\Longleftrightarrow$ DSyntR correspondence, based on the type of rule presented in Figure 1, allows for a more active participation of the MT-networks in the linguistic2 models.

Secondly, MT-networks corresponding to definitions of lexemes are figures which are too difficult to read if one wants to use them as a basis for lexicographic reasoning or discussion, as opposed to the trees representing syntactic structures of utterances (which are extensively used in the construction of Meaning-Text models; cf. Mel'čuk & Pertsov, 1987).

Finally, it is in fact easier to manipulate a linear description of the meaning of a lexeme than the corresponding graphical description. Of course, this last observation is a direct consequence of the preceding one. In order to illustrate this problem, I give below the definition presented in (Dostie *et al.*, 1992) for the French lexeme REPROCHER1.a '[to] reproach', together with the very unclear network in Figure 8, which was proposed in this article.[8]

REPROCHER1.a *X reproche Y à Z =*

X étant convaincu que Y, dont il croitII Z responsable, a eu ou a lieu, Y ou les conséquences de Y affectant négativement l'état émotionnel de X, X a présent dans sa conscience que X n'excuse2 pas Z pour Y, et aussi X croitII que Z doitII.1 être conscient du caractère relativement mauvais de Y.
Approximate English gloss: X reproach Y to Z = X being convinced that Y, which he believes Z is responsible for, took or is taking place, Y or the consequences of Y negatively affecting the emotional state of X, X has in his mind that X does not excuse Z for Y, and also X thinks that Z must be aware of the relatively negative nature of Y.

I will focus on the particular case of MT-networks representing lexemic definitions, and see "what is wrong" with graphical representations such as Figure 8. There is no reason why the graphical representation of a decomposed L-meaning should be harder to interpret than a linear para-formal

---

[8]I can be nasty as I am the one who drew the original network.

MT SEMANTIC NETWORKS AS A FORMAL LANGUAGE 17

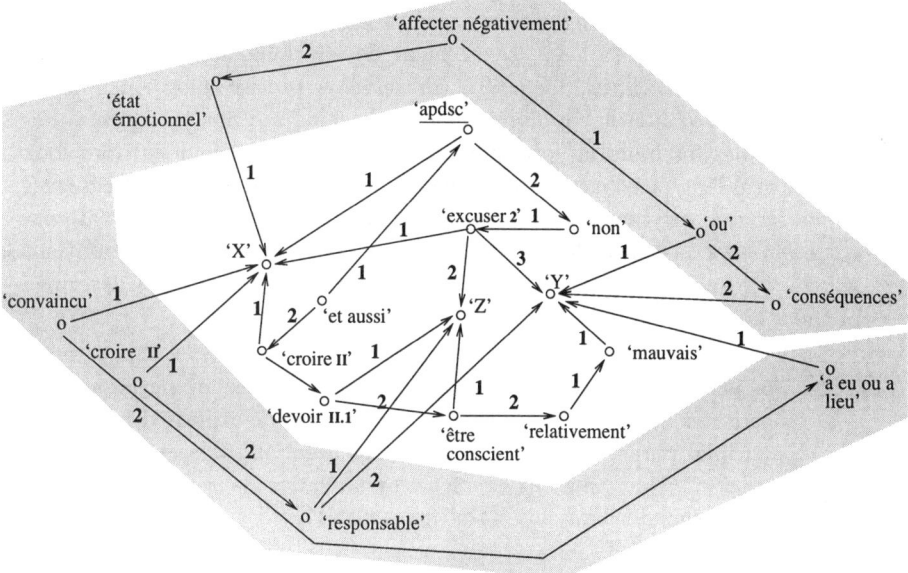

Figure 8: *Linear/graphical definitions of Fr.* REPROCHER1.a *in (Dostie et al. 1992); 'apdsc' stands for 'avoir présent dans sa conscience'*

representation based on the syntactic and morphological tools of the natural language being described. The opacity of most MT-networks is usually due to a lack of precision in the formal specification of the corresponding representational language.

Graphical representations should make the internal structure of L-meanings explicit.

In order to make such structure explicit, it is not sufficient to simply specify a few communicative sub-networks and dominant nodes for these sub-networks. Such an approach, which has been used for instance in (Polguère, 1990), does not make MT-networks fully operational. On the other hand, standard MT-networks for lexical definitions are semiotically weaker than the corresponding linear representations written in a constrained natural language (see below), but it would be inappropriate to base our formalism for representing linguistic1 meanings on natural language itself. The semantic description of lexical units is supposed to give us access to something that natural language expresses but does not represent.

Natural language is not meant to represent the meanings that it expresses; this is the reason why linguists are using formal languages to encode their descriptions/representations. Even linear descriptions, such as those used in (Mel'čuk et al., 1984, 1988, 1992), must follow precise rules which define a language of semantic representation, and which are not the normal linguistic1 rules for building grammatical utterances. Linear definitions look like natural language but are based on the use of certain grammatical tools which have a very special interpretation in this context. Participial constructions, for instance, are used to identify the components of definitions which correspond to presuppositions; such formal convention is described in the following rule for building ECD definitions:

> The part of the meaning of L that is never affected by negation constitutes either a presupposition, which must be expressed by a participial phrase outside the scope of a negation, or a semantic restriction, which must be expressed by a relative clause modifying the corresponding variable. (Mel'čuk, 1988c:179)

In fact, it would be necessary to formalize, by means of a some sort of Meaning-Text *meta-model*, this type of correspondence between an MT-network representation and a linear representation; for instance as shown in Figure 9.

Figure 9: *Two different ways of formally representing presuppositions*

Figure 9 describes a correspondence, which could be modeled by means of formal correspondence rules; nevertheless, such rules are never used in the process of writing ECDs, because definitions are usually written directly in a linear format. It is possible to envisage the development of new lexicographic methodologies which would make the implementation of the above-mentioned correspondences necessary. Definitions could be written by graphically editing MT-networks on a computer screen, these MT-networks being automatically translated later into a linear representation based on natural language. Such a method should also be coupled with the possibility of directly working on linear representations and automatically generating the corresponding MT-networks. It seems to me that both tools—MT-networks and linear representations—are necessary if one wants to efficiently produce definitions which are well-formed expressions (in the language of semantic representation) and which are, at the same time, descriptively adequate. Such a claim can be justified with the following arguments:

(i) The formalism of MT-networks makes explicit (i) formal properties of each element of the representation: U-meaning, operator, quantifier, predicate (together with its arity), or object name, (ii) semantic dependency links, and (iii) the internal organization of the represented L-meaning by means of the topography of the corresponding MT-network (its partition into sub-networks, etc.).

(ii) The linear representation in pseudo-language allows for the actual intuitive access to the L-meaning which is described.

This last point is extremely important. One should not forget that linear representations will always be needed, not only in order to make the published ECD more accessible to the layman, but for lexicographers as well. Meaning-Text definitions belong to the lexicographic tradition which bases the access to lexical meaning on the notion of paraphrase rather than on formal descriptions whose justification could be found outside natural language itself (cf. Wierzbicka, 1984 for a critique of the definitions based on conditions for denotation and componential analysis). Only a linear paralinguistic1 representation enables the lexicographer to use his linguistic1 intuition in order to make sure that a relation of equality of meaning holds between a lexeme and its semantic decomposition, thus ensuring that the definition is adequate. This corresponds quite directly to the remarks made by A. Wierzbicka on the grammar of the *lingua mentalis* (Wierzbicka, 1977). According to Wierzbicka, a lexicographic definition has to be linear because it expresses the internal structure of thoughts, and thoughts are necessarily organized by means of propositions whose meaning has to be described:

> Semantic representations constructed in the language of semantic primitives are linear. When they are complex (as they usually are) this complexity takes the form of long sequences of linear components, the interrelations between the components of a sequence being determined simply by temporal order. (Wierzbicka, 1977:171)

ECD definitions are quite different from those written by A. Wierzbicka (which are based on semantic primitives, with a maximal level of semantic decomposition, etc.). Nevertheless, the above quotation can enlighten us on an important characteristic of any functional semantic representation: there is no possible access to the intuitive perception of a meaning encoded in a representation, no matter which type of representation it is, without the mediation of some sort of temporal order. Therefore, the crucial notion here is not linearity, but rather the deeper notion of temporal order, which is adequately modeled by means of linear order. The following rule can be postulated:

> A semantic representation can be a non-linear structure as long as it possesses an internal hierarchy which implies a given linear order when the representation is read.

In the particular case of MT-networks, a first reading method has been proposed in (Polguère, 1990), based on the introduction of the concept of COMMUNICATIVE DEPENDENCY and by using a strategy for determining a path through the networks. In the Appendix, I present a re-writing of the MT-network for the definition of Fr. REPROCHER1.a (given above). Although far from being perfect, this new figure makes an extensive use of the concepts, and their graphical counterparts, introduced in Section 2. This sample lexical definition shows how a clear conceptualization of the formal language of MT-networks can help in structuring semantic representations and, consequently, in introducing an internal hierarchy which would graphically model the notion of temporal order. (More on this can be found in Polguère, 1992.)

4 Conclusion

I have examined MT-networks as formal representations for lexical definitions. Two additional problems must be considered when MT-networks are used as representations of the meaning of utterances: (i) representation of thematic structures, and (ii) encoding of grammatical meanings. Only a systematic definition of all concepts which belong to the semantic language, together with a specification of their graphical representation, will make MT-networks truly operational. The most logical way to implement such a language is to integrate it into a general methodology for elaborating ECD entries, based on the automatic processing of graphical representations. The method suggested here seems to be particularly profitable as it would benefit both from the formal validation allowed by the formal language of MT-networks and from the extensive use of the intuitive perception of linguistic1 meanings, through the use of linear representations.

Acknowledgements

This paper is a re-worked English version of (Polguère, 1992) (in French). I have benefited from feed-back by Marga Alonso Ramos, Liesbeth Degand, Eli Goldberg, Lida Iordanskaja, Igor Mel'čuk, Leo Wanner, and two anonymous reviewers. The final version was read by Priscilla Ng, who has slain many Gremlins. Thank you all and don't worry: mistakes and nonsense are mine, as usual.

Endnotes

[1] Two remarks are needed here. Firstly, in Meaning-Text linguistics, a lexical unit is conceived of as a set of linguistic1 signs; for instance, BIRD = {**bird-**, **bird**, **birds**}—elementary root sign and non-elementary signs corresponding to the singular and plural of BIRD. Secondly, in the above definition for U-MEANING, ⌜ ... ⌝ indicates that ⌜same meaning⌝ is a phraseological expression. The definition is not circular, as ⌜same meaning⌝ is truly simpler than the concept of meaning. It is directly connected to the native speaker's perception of a paraphrase relation holding between two or more utterances. In other words, it will be defined by means of the second type of linguistic2 definition mentioned previously.

[2] The terms 'logical' and 'para-logical' are to be taken in a rather narrow sense. A logical operation is an operation which can be characterized semantically in terms of truth-values; on the other hand, a para-logical operation cannot be fully characterized in terms of truth-values.

Appendix: MT-network for the definition of Fr. REPROCHER1.a (from Polguère 1992)

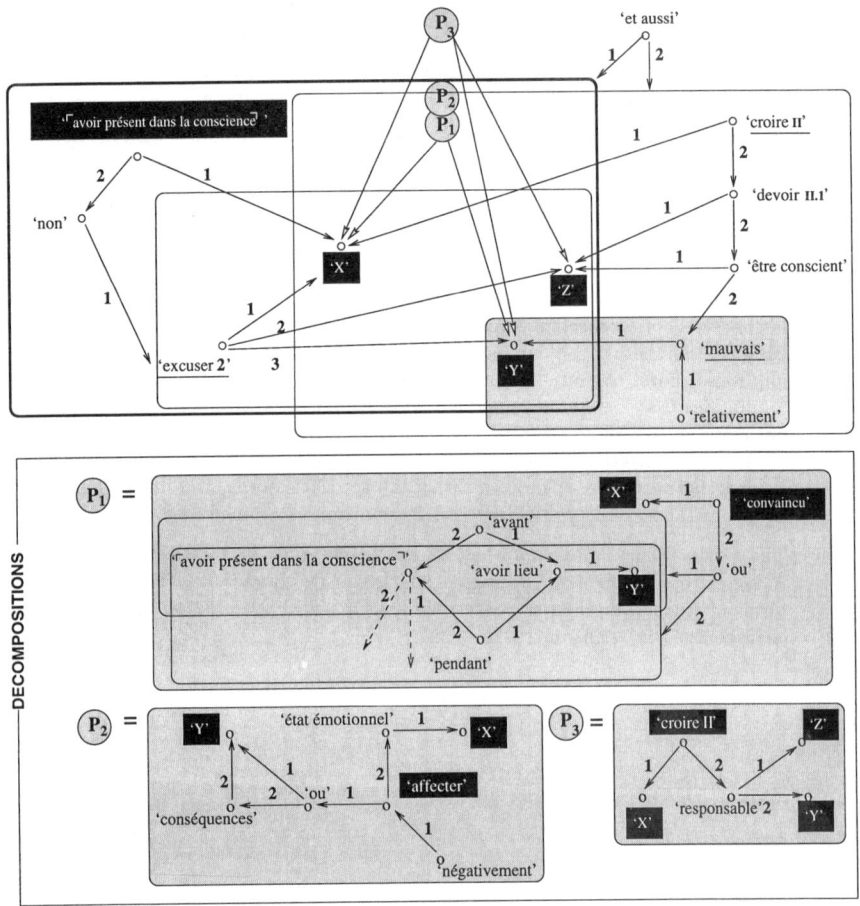

Figure 10: *An alternative network for the definition of* REPROCHER1.a

Bibliography

Dostie, G., I.A. Mel'čuk & A. Polguère. 1992. "Méthodologie d'élaboration des entrées lexicales du dictionnaire explicatif et combinatoire (reprocher, reproche et irreprochable)". *International Journal of Lexicography*. 3:165–198.

Garde, P. 1977. "Ordre linéaire et dépendance syntaxique: contribution à une typologie". *Bulletin de la Société de Linguistique de Paris*. LXXII.1:1–26.

Iordanskaja, I.A. & A. Polguère. 1988. "Semantic Processing for Text Generation". *Proceedings of the International Computer Science Conference '88*. 310–318. Hong Kong.

Mel'čuk, I.A. 1981. "Meaning-Text Models: A Recent Trend in Soviet Linguistics". *Annual Review of Anthropology*. 10:27–62.

Mel'čuk, I.A. 1982. *Towards a Language of Linguistics*. Munich: Wilhelm Fink.

Mel'čuk, I.A. 1988a. *Dependency Syntax: Theory and Practice*. Albany: State University of New York Press.

Melčuk, I.A. 1988b. "Paraphrase et lexique dans la théorie linguistique Sens-Texte". *Lexique*. VI:13–54.

Mel'čuk, I.A. 1988c. "Semantic Description of Lexical Units in an Explanatory Combinatorial Dictionary: Basic Principles and Heuristic Criteria". *International Journal of Lexicography*. 1.3:165–188.

Mel'čuk, I.A. 1993. "The Inflectional Category of Voice: Towards a More Rigorous Definition". *Causativity and Transitivity* ed. by B. Comrie & M. Polinsky. Amsterdam & Philadelphia: Benjamins Academic Publishers.

Mel'čuk, I.A. 1997. *The Communicative Structure in Language*. Technical report: Département de Linguistique et de Traduction, Université de Montréal.

Mel'čuk, I.A. (with N. Arbatchewsky-Jumarie, L. Elnitsky, L. Iordanskaja & A. Lessard). 1984. *Dictionnaire explicatif et combinatoire du français contemporain, Volume I*. Montréal, Canada: Presses de l'Université de Montréal.

Mel'čuk, I.A. (with N. Arbatchewsky-Jumarie, L. Dagenais, L. Elnitsky, L. Iordanskaja, M.-N. Lefebvre & S. Mantha). 1988. *Dictionnaire explicatif et combinatoire du français contemporain, Volume II*. Montréal: Presses de l'Université de Montréal.

Mel'čuk, I.A. (with N. Arbatchewsky-Jumarie, L. Iordanskaja & S. Mantha). 1992. *Dictionnaire explicatif et combinatoire du français contemporain, Volume III*. Montréal, Canada: Presses de l'Université de Montréal.

Mel'čuk, I.A. & N. Pertsov. 1987. *Surface Syntax of English*. Amsterdam & Philadelphia: Benjamins Academic Publishers.

Mel'čuk, I.A. & A. Polguère. 1987. "A Formal Lexicon in the Meaning-Text Theory (or How to Do Lexica with Words)". *Computational Linguistics*. 13.3-4:276–289.

Mel'čuk, I.A. & A. Polguère. 1991. "Aspects of the Implementation of the Meaning-Text Model for English Text Generation". *Research in Humanities Computing 1* ed. by I. Lancashire. 204–215. Oxford: Clarenton Press.

Mørdrup, O. 1988. "Prèsuppositions, implications et verbes français". *Revue Romane*. X.1:125–155.

Polguère, A. 1990. *Structuration et mise en jeu procédurale d'un modèle linguistique déclaratif dans un cadre de génération de texte*. PhD thesis. Montréal: Département de linguistique, Université de Montréal.

Polguère, A. 1992. "Remarques sur les réseaux sémantique Sens–Text". *Le mot, les mots, les bon mots* ed. by A. Clas. Montréal: Les Presses de l'Université de Montréal.

St-Germain, J. 1988. *Etude sémantico-syntaxique des expressions verbales causatives en français contemporain*. Master's thesis. Montréal: Département de linguistique, Université de Montréal.

Wierzbicka, A. 1977. "Mental Language and Semantic Primitives". *Communication and Cognition*. X.3-4:155–179.

Wierzbicka, A. 1984. "Cups and Mugs: Lexicography and Conceptual Analysis". *Australian Journal of Linguistics*. 4:205–255.

Woods, W.A. 1975. "What's in a Link: Foundations for Semantic Networks". *Representation and Understanding—Studies in Cognitive Science* ed. by D. Bobrow & A. Collins. 55–82. Orlando: Academic Press.

Towards a Notional Representation of Meaning in the Meaning-Text Model: The Case of the French SI

Marie-Christine Escalier and *Corinne Fournier*

1 Introduction

An NLP research team at *Dassault Aviation* has been working on Natural Language Generation for the last five years. The first application we worked on was the translation of Prolog rules in a deductive database into French. The second one was the generation of causal explanations of physical systems. For both applications, we chose as linguistic formalism the *Meaning-Text Theory* (MTT). There were two major reasons for that choice. Firstly, MTT is the formalization of a complete descriptive model. As such, it differs from other models that are only concerned with a given phenomenon such as reference or rhetorical relations. Secondly, the paraphrasing power is the foundation of MTT; for this reason, a model that is based on this theory seems the most appropriate in solving the problem of meaning representation, which is crucial for a generation system.

The *Semantic Representation* (SemR) in MTT is complex. It consists of three distinct structures: the *Semantic Structure* (SemS), the *(Semantic) Rhetorical Structure* (SemRhetS), and the *(Semantic) Communicative Structure* (SemCommS). SemS represents the situational meaning, or denotative content, of sentences. SemRhetS and SemCommS represent the Speaker's stylistic and communicative intentions, respectively, that govern the expression of the sentence to be generated. The problems we were faced with in the context of our applications led us to study the following aspects of SemR:

(i) representation of reference;

(ii) conceptualization and role of the SemCommS;

(iii) semanteme-based nature of the SemS.

In this paper we will mainly focus on the last issue. Since we are working on the phenomenon of causality, we will first try to extend present descriptions of the *Explanatory Combinatorial Dictionary* (ECD) to account for the various linguistic means which express causality. Then, we will discuss problems that cannot be solved by this extension. Finally, we will suggest a semantic representation based on notions instead of semantemes.

2 Types of Paraphrases and Expression of Causality

Mel'čuk (1988) defines different types of paraphrases. Non-linguistic paraphrases are based on encyclopaedic and contextual knowledge or require reasoning skill. Linguistic paraphrases may be syntactic or semantic. Syntactic ones involve structural transformations, while lexical units remain unchanged. Semantic paraphrases differ with respect to at least one full lexical unit and may be classified into two sub-classes:

> [...] those which are realized by semantic rules and those which are realized by 'paraphrasing rules'. Paraphrases of the first subclass are generated by different lexical choices. Such paraphrases are deeper than the others. On the other hand, paraphrases of the second subclass are generated by lexical substitutions: they reveal the semantic links existing between lexical units in the lexicon. (Mel'čuk, 1988)

Given these definitions, let us consider the kind of sentences we have to generate and the type of paraphrase they belong to. The following sentences express some kind of causality in a generic context. They are different linguistic realizations that express a law. This law forbids planes whose configuration contains a tank at the fuselage central point from taking off.

(1) a. *Si une configuration comporte un réservoir au point central fuselage, elle est interdite au décollage*
    lit. 'If a configuration contains a tank at the fuselage central point, it is forbidden from taking off'.
   b. *La présence, dans une configuration, d'un réservoir au point central fuselage, entraîne son interdiction au décollage*
    lit. 'The presence, in a configuration, of a tank at the fuselage central point entails its forbidding from taking off'.

c. *De la présence, dans une configuration, d'un réservoir au point central fuselage, résulte son interdiction au décollage*
lit. 'From the presence, in a configuration, of a tank at the fuselage central point, results its forbidding from taking off'.

d. *Une configuration qui comporte un réservoir au point central fuselage est interdite au décollage*
lit. 'A configuration that contains a tank at fuselage central point is forbidden from taking off'.

These sentences are paraphrases for they are intuitively felt as such. The intuition of meaning proximity is a defining feature of paraphrastic relations. See (Mel'čuk, 1988): "The identity or closeness in meaning is only an intuitive judgement made by speakers." Moreover they are linguistic paraphrases: there is no need for encyclopaedic or reasoning skill to establish the equivalence between them. These sentences express laws and the notions of hypothesis, consequence and cause they suggest seem close to the logical relation of entailment. But, whatever the properties of each sentence, the relation between them is neither deductive nor inferential, and in general, does not call for any reasoning. This relation is only supported by meaning proximity of linguistic expressions which they are composed of.

We consider these sentences as semantic paraphrases. The only knowledge needed for the interpretation of the sentences (1a) to (1c) as such paraphrases is the linguistic meaning of the verbs ENTRAÎNER '[to] carry away, [to] lead, [to] entail, [to] involve, [to] occasion'/RÉSULTER '[to] result' and the conjunction SI 'if'. These lexemes are different realizations of one semanteme that expresses a certain kind of causality. (1d) is different in nature; the relative clause is one among the possible expressions of a restrictive relation. The relation that exists between the Subject of a generic sentence and its restricting modifier can always be paraphrased by a conditional clause, as in (1a).[1] We could say that the relative clause in a generic context is a syntactic construction that realizes a semantic relation, namely the causality relation we are interested in. Therefore, (1d) is a semantic paraphrase derivable from a SemR common to (1a) to (1d).

We conclude that the relation between different lexical and syntactic realizations in (1a) to (1d) is that of semantic equivalence. In what follows, we try to account for these paraphrases in MTT, considering two aspects: what definitions we need to include in the ECD (Sections 3 and 4) and how to use these definitions in semantic representations (Section 5).

3 The Information in the ECD

Here are some aspects of the ECD that will be relevant to our purpose:[1]

(i) Lexical Functions (LFs) such as **Syn** or **Conv**, which express semantic proximity between lexemes, are always used for lexemes that belong to the same syntactic category;

(ii) the definition zone in the ECD describes the correspondence between a semanteme, i.e., the semantic content of a lexeme, and a network of semantemes that decomposes this content;

(iii) conjunctions have never been mentioned or described, neither in the dictionary, as entries, nor in the paraphrasing rules, until recently (Iordanskaja, 1992).

The equivalence between *entraîner* in (1b) and *résulter* in (1c) is easy to represent in the ECD by the LF **Conv** as $\mathbf{Conv}_{21}(\text{ENTRAÎNER1}) = \text{RÉSULTER1}$ and $\mathbf{Conv}_{21}(\text{RÉSULTER1}) = \text{ENTRAÎNER1}$. The relation between these two lexemes and the conjunction in (1a) or the relative clause in (1d) seems more difficult to describe. There are two problems:

(i) between ENTRAÎNER and SI there is a double change in orientation and part of speech of the lexemes: ENTRAÎNER and SI are conversives; the first one is a verb and the second a conjunction. So the equivalence cannot be described in the ECD with the LF **Conv** such as $\mathbf{Conv}_{21}(\text{ENTRAÎNER1}) = \text{SI1}/\mathbf{Conv}_{21}(\text{SI1}) = \text{ENTRAÎNER1}$;

(ii) in the case of the relative clause, there is a correspondence between a given semantic content and a particular syntactic construction, not between (the semantic content of) a lexeme and a network of semantemes. So, the equivalence cannot be described in the ECD in the definition zone of a lexical entry.

For the time being, we will make the assumption that these difficulties are not due to theoretical limits of MTT, but only due to a lack of such descriptions in the literature. So we will examine the descriptive tools that are available in the ECD and the necessary extensions needed for solving these problems.

The LF $\mathbf{Adv}_i(C_0) = B$ accounts for the double change in orientation and part of speech; it expresses the transition from any part of speech to an adverbial. For example: $\mathbf{Adv}_1(\textit{to lead}) = \textit{at the head of}$, $\mathbf{Adv}_2(\textit{to lead}) =$

---

[1] For a general introduction to ECDs, see (Mel'čuk *et al.*, 1995); for a detailed presentation of LFs, (Mel'čuk, 1996).

NOTIONAL REPRESENTATION OF MEANING IN MTM 29

under the direction of. The subscript indicates a converse relation between terms and means that the semantic actant i of C_0 will be the governor of B at the deep-syntactic level. Now, can we consider the conjunction SI as an adverbial? If so, given the semantic equivalence between ENTRAÎNER1(X, Y) and SI1(Y,X), we could say that $\mathbf{Adv_2}$(ENTRAÎNER1) = SI1. If not, we can create a new Lexical Function, $\mathbf{Conj}_i(C_0) = B$. So, we would have the following correspondence: $\mathbf{Conj_2}$(ENTRAÎNER1) = SI1. As for the relative clause, another procedure must be used. As we saw before, this kind of semantic information cannot be represented in the ECD. Thus, another type of dictionary could be created and used together with the ECD. This dictionary would represent the meaning of syntactic structures by equivalence rules between a network of semantemes and a syntactic representation.[2] Then, we would have the correspondence as shown in Figure 1.

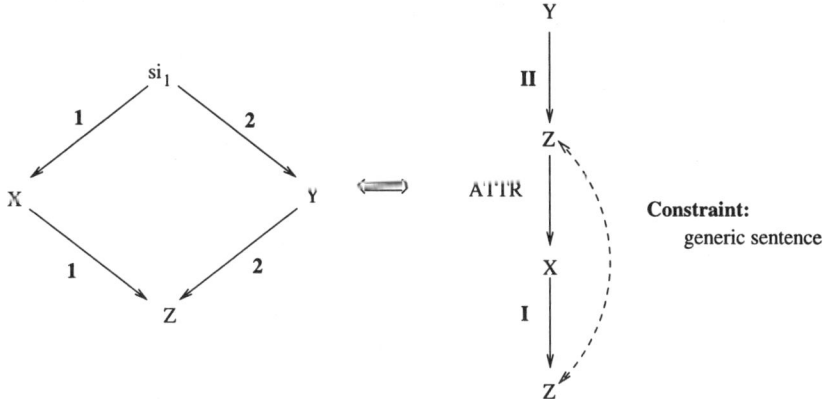

Figure 1: *Correspondence between a semantemic network and syntactic representation*

In this way, we provide and store the descriptions necessary for generation of our paraphrases. Now, let us consider the nature of the semanteme ('si') associated with the lexical and syntactic realizations that express, in the context of (1a) to (1d), this particular kind of causality.

4 The Relation of Causality and Description of Fr. SI_{conj} in the ECD

4.1 Is SI a Logical Connective?

To say that sentences (1a) to (1d) are semantic paraphrases presupposes that the lexemes SI, ENTRAÎNER, RÉSULTER, and the restrictive relative clause are formally different realizations of the same content. The problem is to determine the nature of this content. The entities present in the semantic representations of MTT can either be (classes of) objects or functors. Functors are either predicates that denote actions or relations or logical connectives. Mel'čuk lists the following connectives: ET 'and', OU 'or', SI 'if'. Given the law-like character of our sentences, we will first assume that the lexeme SI and the other realizations in (1b) to (1d) express the logical connective SI. The presence of ENTRAÎNER among the possible realizations seems to confirm this assumption. The French lexeme ENTRAÎNER inherits the feature 'necessary consequence', which is specific of the semantics of entailment, to its second actant when it is not of the 'animate' or 'human' type. Thus, we assume that the functor that appears in the SemR which underlies our paraphrases is the logical connective '$\rightarrow$', or 'logical if'. In this case, the definition zone of our realizations would be confined to this connective. Actually, this hypothesis cannot be sustained. The logical relation of entailment is far more universal than its linguistic realizations; it is referred to for the hypothetic, causal, or consecutive relation. Yet these relations express different meanings in the ordinary use of language. We cannot consider the following sentences to be semantically equivalent, although, in both cases, their logical representation is 'P $\rightarrow$ Q':

(2)   a. *Si Pierre vient, je n'irai pas*
        lit. 'If Pierre comes, I will not go'.
      b. *Je n'irai pas parce que Pierre vient*
        lit. 'I will not go because Pierre is coming'.

Such a difference in interpretation of linguistic and logical semantics is due to the fact that the truth evaluation of simple propositions is a matter of the logical system (i.e., propositional calculus) while that of sentences is given in language. To take an example, let us call 'P' the fact that Pierre is coming. On one hand, the utterance *Pierre vient* 'Pierre comes' holds the fact as true, no matter its reality (whether Pierre really comes or not). Truth in linguistics depends on the modal form of sentences: assertive vs. non-assertive sentences (e.g., interrogative sentences). See (Martin, 1983): "linguistic truth is an asserted truth". On the other hand, the logical proposition that denotes P is true only if, in the real world, it is the case that the fact P occurs. It depends on the state of the world. In fact, logical truth concerns only logical relations between propositions and not simple propositions denoting a fact. The logical system determines values that the propositions related by connectives should have so that their relation be true or false. Then, the logical representation of (2a) and (2b) is identical since the underlying relation between the main clause and the subordinate clause is the same. But facts expressed by clauses are given as occurring in (2a) and not in (2b). This is what opposes linguistic expressions *si* 'if' and *parce que* 'because'. The conditional clause suspends the assertion process.

To illustrate the difference in meaning between conditional clauses and entailment, let us recall Ducrot's (1972) example: a gambler uttering *S'il pleut, le 3 gagnera* 'If it rains the 3 will win' neither loses nor wins his bet if it does not rain, whether number 3 wins or not. Now, if the semantics of the conditional were that of entailment, in any case he would win his bet if it did not rain. The inhibition in classical logics of the modal opposition between *virtualisé* 'virtualized' vs. *actualisé* 'actualized', which is so important in language (see: *hypothesis* vs. *cause, generic* vs. *specific, presupposed* vs. *asserted*), and the difficulties encountered in modal logics when accounting for this distinction lead us to the conclusion that a semantic representation of SI, PARCE QUE and other linguistic expressions of the same type in terms of logical relation (entailment) is not adequate. Such a representation would not account for all the elements of their semantic content. Since the functor realized in (1a) to (1d) is not a logical connective, it must be a predicate and, as such, require a description in the definition zone of the ECD.

4.2 *Nature of the Definition Zone in Lexical Entries*

The ECD offers three possibilities with respect to the organization of the definition zone:

(i) The definition zone is empty. It is a function word which is semantically empty, e.g., the relative pronoun *que* 'which', 'that'.

(ii) There is no description associated with a semanteme. A semanteme is equivalent only to itself. It is a primitive, e.g., *causer* '[to] cause', *temps* 'time'.

(iii) An equivalence is established between a semanteme (*definiendum*) and a semantemic network (*definiens*), so that the definition can be substituted for the definiendum in all sentences.

The notion of the semantic primitive mentioned in (ii) is used to address three different types of object. A semantic primitive is either:

– A fundamental seme necessary for describing a number of semantemes and grammemes. This seme is not decomposable and, hence, not describable in terms of more detailed semes. We may think that no lexical realization corresponds to it.

- A semanteme for which no satisfying description can be given. Unlike in (i) above, this kind of primitive is not indivisible by nature and has a lexical realization;
- A descriptive element which is not related to the semantic content of an utterance but to its characteristics as a message, as an utterance act (e.g., *énoncer* '[to] utter', *locuteur* 'speaker').

Coming back to our realizations we assume that the lexemes ENTRAÎNER1 and RÉSULTER1 are of type (iii). The lexical entries will have the following definition zone in the ECD:

X *entraîne*1 Y: *le fait X a pour conséquence le fait Y*
   'the fact X has as consequence the fact Y'.
X *résulte*1 *de* Y: *le fait X est produit*1 *par le fait Y*
   'the fact X is produced by the fact Y'.

Actually, these lexemes express differently the relation that holds between X and Y. ENTRAÎNER1 identifies a consequence, RÉSULTER1 identifies a cause. However, notions of cause and consequence imply each other reciprocally. So, there is a semantic equivalence between both lexemes (as between ACHETER1 '[to] buy' and VENDRE1 '[to] sell') and the sentences they appear in are semantic paraphrases of the first subclass mentioned above. Now, the conditional clause (and therefore the relative clause) seems to express a different relation: in this case, X is presented as the hypothesis in which Y is realized.[2] To find out what the semantic equivalence between (1b) and (1c) and between (1a) and (1d) is based on, we will examine some of the properties of SI. We will begin with an informal analysis, using restatements and glosses to make obvious the semantic nuances from one acceptance of SI to another (see Subsection 4.3). Then we will examine the definition of SI1 in the "extended" ECD, taking into account some descriptive parameters suggested by L. Iordanskaja for representation of conjunctions (Subsection 4.4). The difficulties raised by this representation will lead us to the conclusion that it is impossible to define SI1 in terms of a semantemic network.

---

[2]In the case of ENTRAÎNER1/RÉSULTER1, the relation is presented differently with conditional and relative clauses. In the case of the relative clause, X is presented as a restriction on the class of objects that is denoted by the Subject of (the clause expressing) Y.

4.3 Analysis of SI: Nine Different Lexemes

4.3.1 De Cornulier's Description of SI

De Cornulier (1985) lists thirteen different values or uses that dictionaries and grammars provide for the description of SI:

1. **hypothetical:**

    1.1 (3) *S'il pleut dimanche, je resterai à la maison*
    lit. 'If it rains on Sunday, I will stay at home'.

    1.2 (4) *S'il n'en reste qu'un, je serai celui-là*
    lit. 'If there is only one left, I will be the one'.

2. **bi-affirmative:**

    (5) *Si la vie et la mort de Socrate furent d'un sage, la vie et la mort de Jésus furent d'un Dieu*
    lit. 'If the life and the death of Socrates were that of a wise man, the life and death of Jesus were that of a God'.

3. **bi-affirmative + modality:**

    (6) *Si je ne me trompe pas, il travaille à Dassault Aviation*
    lit. 'If I am not mistaken, he works at Dassault Aviation'.

4. **bi-affirmative + superlative value:**

    (7) *S'il est un gouvernement insoupçonnable de racisme, c'est bien celui qui nous gouverne*
    lit. 'If there is a government that cannot be suspected of racism, it is the one that governs us'.

5. **bi-negative:**

    5.1 (8) *Si c'est lui le plus fort, moi, je suis le pape*
    lit. 'If it is him who is the strongest, I, I am the pope'.

    5.2 (9) *Si c'était vrai, on le saurait*
    lit. 'If it were true, it would be known'.

6. **causal:**

    (10) *Si je ne vous ai pas salué, c'est que je ne vous ai pas vu*
    lit. 'If did not say hello to you, it is because I did not see you'.

7. **oppositive**:

7.1 (11) *Pourtant, s'il réalise des exploits, il ne peut accomplir des miracles*
lit. 'Nevertheless, if he achieves exploits, he cannot achieve miracles'.

7.2 (12) *S'ils ne prétendaient pas faire des miracles, ils entendaient au moins ne pas subir les événements*
lit. 'If they did not pretend to achieve miracles, they at least intended not to be submitted to events'.

8. **concessive**:

(13) *Marie partira même si Jean reste*
lit. 'Marie will leave even if Jean stays'.

9. **iterative**:

(14) *Si Pierre la regarde, elle rougit*
lit. 'If Pierre looks at her she blushes'.

10. **restrictive**:

(15) *On ira au cinéma si tu finis tes devoirs*
'We will go to the movies if you finish your homework'.

11. **illocutionary**:

(16) *Si tu as soif, il y a de la bière dans le frigo*
lit. 'If you are thirsty, there is beer in the fridge'.

12. **indicates restraint**:

(17) *Il vous ressemble, si ce n'est qu'il est plus petit que vous*
lit. 'He resembles you except he is smaller than you'.

13. **presupposing**:

(18) *Je suis interloqué et, si les informations à ce sujet se justifient, indigné*
lit. 'I am very surprised and, if the information proves true, indignant'.

De Cornulier points out that the form SI would not be interpretable if it had so many literal meanings (i.e., senses). So, he opts for a unitary representation of the conjunction. Whatever the particular nuances suggested by context, the sense of SI remains that of sufficient condition, described as *Si X, Y = Dans le/les cas où X, Y*.[3]

4.3.2 Problems Raised by the Definition of Si X, Y as 'Dans le cas où X, Y'

One must admit that the rephrasing of *Si X, Y* 'If X, Y' by *Dans le cas où X, Y* 'In the case of X, Y'—even expressed in a more natural way with *au cas où*—is rather questionable in cases 2, 3, 4, 7, 9, and 12 from the previous subsection. Furthermore, it neither accounts for the double interpretation of 6 (6.1 and 6.2 in what follows):

6.1 **hypothetical**:

(19) *Au cas où je ne vous aurais pas salué, c'est que ...*
'In case I did not say hello to you the reason is ... '.

6.2 **oppositive**:

(20) [*Il est vrai + certes*] *je ne vous ai pas salué, mais c'est que ...*
'[It is true + sure] I did not say hello to you, but the reason is ... '

nor for a specific semantic nuance in 9; cf.

(21) *On ira au cinéma au cas où tu finis tes devoirs, sinon on n'ira pas*
'We will go to the movies in case you finish your homework, if not, we will not go'.

where logicians (as Tarski) see the expression of a double implication. The definition of SI with *au cas où* is thus appropriate only for cases 1, 5, 13, and for 6.1 introduced immediately above. This is not surprising since the conjunctive phrase *au cas où* expresses a hypothesis, i.e., presents a fact as possible. Thus, *au cas où* cannot be substituted in the examples where in the structure *Si X, Y* X denotes an effective fact that is assumed as certain.

4.3.3 Temporary Description: Modal Analysis of SI

If we want a homogeneous description of the different values of SI, we should make the modal value of the conjunction explicit. *Il se peut que* 'it might be that' and *peut-être* 'maybe' seem good rephrasings of SI insofar as they reflect the double functioning of the conditional conjunction as:

(i) markers of epistemic modality: 'X may be true'; see case 1.1 restated as

[*Il se peut qu'il pleuve/peut-être qu'il pleuvra*] *dimanche. Dans ce cas, je resterai à la maison.*
'[It might rain + maybe it will rain] on Sunday. In this case, I will stay at home'.

(ii) argumentative markers of concession: 'I (the Speaker) concede that X (is true) but ... '; for instance, *Si ça t'arrange, moi pas* lit. 'If this suits you, it does not suit me' restated as

[*Il se peut/peut-être*] (*bien*) *que ça t'arrange, moi pas*
'It might suit you, not me'.

The restatement of *Si X, Y* as *Au cas où X, Y* also has the disadvantage of hiding that there are two possible relations between X and Y: one which shows that X has Y as consequence, and one which shows that X and Y are simultaneously valid. Consider cases 1.1 and 1.2 in Subsection 4.3.1. In 1.1, the Speaker means that if it rains, the consequence will be that he will stay at home. In 1.2, the Speaker means that if it is true that there will be only one person staying, it will also be true that he will be that one. He does not mean that if there is only one person staying, the consequence will be that he will be that one.

The difference between these two types of relations holds when modality is of an argumentative nature as well as epistemic. So we will suppose that there are four different lexemes, SI1, SI2, SI3, and SI4 with the following properties:

SI1

X expresses a modal value, it is a hypothesis
+ The relation between X and Y shows that X has Y as consequence; cf. the cases 1.1, 3, 5.1, 5.2, and 13;

SI2

X expresses a modal value, it is a hypothesis
+ The relation between X and Y shows that X and Y are simultaneously valid; cf. the cases 1.2, 4, 9, and 11;

SI3

X is a speech act (concession)
+ The relation between X and Y shows that X has Y as consequence; cf. the case 7.1;

SI4

X is a speech act (concession)
+ The relation between X and Y shows that X and Y are simultaneously valid; cf. the cases 2 and 7.2.

However, the identification of these four SI is not sufficient to account for the various semantic nuances listed in Subsection 4.3.1.

4.3.4 *Insufficiency of the Four Basic Values: The Role of Contextual Elements*

Let us first consider the case where SI is in a particular structure and co-occurs with other lexemes, and then the case where no other lexeme is associated with SI to take in charge a particular semantic value.

I. *SI* is in a particular structure and co-occurs with other lexemes:

(i) *même si* (concessive):

Y *même si* X   = *Il se peut que* X. *Pourtant, même dans ce cas,* Y
'Y even if X'   'X might happen. Yet, even in this case, Y'

(ii) *si ... , c'est que* (causal):

Si X, *c'est que* Y = X, *puisque* Y = X *rien que parce que* Y
'If X that is Y'   'X, since Y/X just because Y'

(iii) *si ce n'est que* (subtractive):

Y *si ce n'est que* X = Y *sauf que* X
'Y if not X'   'Y except that X'

II. No other lexeme is associated with SI to take in charge a particular semantic value; see, for instance, the restrictive SI and the iterative SI.

In case I, De Cornulier uses the meaning compositionality of the constituent terms to compute the semantics of these expressions. Let us look at it more closely. We can analyze the concessive SI as SI2 plus two extra meaning components. The first component concerns the argumentative force, regularly expressed by MÊME 'even'. Consider *Même Pierre est venu* 'Even Pierre came': the fact that Pierre came is presented as a strong argument for something. We call this semantic component an *overstatement*. The second component concerns the expectation expressed by both MÊME and BIEN QUE. With MÊME, it is the expectation of a simple fact, the expectation of a consequence with BIEN QUE. Compare *Même Pierre est venu*: one expects that Pierre did not come. *Marie n'est pas venu bien que Pierre soit venu* 'Marie did not come though Pierre came': one expects that the coming of Pierre has the coming of Marie as a consequence. So, we represent the semantic content of *même si* in the following way:

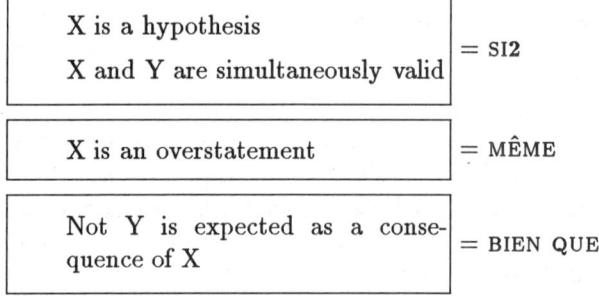

Then it is difficult to refer to the compositionality principle to account for the meaning of *même si*. *Même* in the context of SI must be partially interpreted as *bien que*.

It is even more difficult in the case of the causal SI. The *c'est que* marker introduces the expression of a reason or motive. Then, we must modify the analysis of SI1 given in Subsection 4.3.3. Here, Y is not a consequence but a reason for X. As for the subtractive SI, the compositional analysis proposed by De Cornulier makes it clear enough that the enterprise is particularly hazardous.[4]

We conclude that the compositional analysis of these structures can be defended only at the expense of a vagueness in the description of their constituent terms. This vagueness is not compatible with the requirements of a dictionary as the ECD. Although it is true that the meaning of constituent terms is related in some way to their meaning out of the context of this expression, deletions and semantic shifts in this context make it impossible for the global meaning of the expression to be computed. Even if we do not consider these expressions as semantically opaque set phrases, we think they should be described as independent entries, the same way phrasemes are.

Case II seems to be more problematic. The aspectual value of the example sentence in case 9, Subsection 4.3.1, is clearly supported by tenses and by the non-stative nature of verbs. In French, we could have the same iterative value with the Imperfect past tense form: *Si Pierre la regardait, elle rougissait* 'If Pierre was looking at her, she was blushing', but not with the Compound Past tense form: *Si Pierre l'a regardé, elle a rougi* 'If Pierre looked at her, she blushed'. Stative verbs do not allow the iterative interpretation: *Si Marie le connaît, elle ne l'aime guère* lit. 'If Marie knows him, she does not like him much' (i.e., 'Marie knows him, but she does not like him much). Besides this aspectual "coloration", the conjunction has no other meaning in the sentence in 9 than the semanteme SI2 mentioned above. Thus, it would not be founded to conceive a lexeme SIn that expresses iterativity since this meaning element exists by virtue of grammemes associated with the verb predicates.[3]

As for the restrictive SI, two factors contribute to this interpretation: the linear position of the conditional clause with respect to the main clause and the syntactic integration of the subordinate clause. SI has a restrictive value (necessary condition) when the conditional clause is both positioned after the main clause and non-dislocated.

A structure is considered to be dislocated if one of its terms is separated from the rest by a pause or melodic discontinuity for spoken text, or by a comma for written text. Dislocation generally causes a difference in the interpretation of sentences. Consider *Je travaille le soir* 'I work in the evening' vs. *Je travaille, le soir* 'I work, in the evening', which respectively mean *Le soir est le moment où je travaille* 'The evening is the moment when I work' and *Ce que je fais le soir, c'est travailler* 'What I am doing in the evening is to work'. However, we cannot use the information provided by dislocation to account for an extra restrictive value as we did with the aspectual information of verbal flexion to account for the iterative value. As a matter of fact, it is the non-dislocated structure, which takes this value. So, supposing we were able to account for the semantics of dislocation, whatever the structure implied, we should derive the interpretation of SI1 from that of the restrictive SI, not the other way. The restrictive value would not be an extra value but a basic one of SI. We will leave aside such an analysis. To discuss problems it would raise would require a development that goes beyond the scope of this paper. Then, we assume that the restrictive

---

[3] Can the conditional *vs.* counterfactual (Past, Future) distinction be treated in the same way? Such a hypothesis should be verified.

value is not independent from the meaning of the lexeme SI; it cannot be superimposed on any of the four semantemes mentioned above.

Let SI5 be the restrictive SI. Then, the structure $Y\ si_5\ X$ has the following characteristics:

(i) X and Y express a modal value;

(ii) the relation between X and Y indicates that Y has X as a necessary condition.

The difference in meaning between SI1 in (3a) and SI5 in (3b) is made explicit by the glosses:

(22) a. *S'il pleut, je resterai à la maison*
lit. 'If it rains, I will stay at home'.
'It might happen that it rains and, in that case, the consequence is that I will stay at home'.[5]
b. *Je resterai à la maison s'il pleut*
lit. 'I will stay at home if it rains'.
'It might happen that I stay at home and it is necessary that it rains for that to be so'.

Now we can state that there are several lexemes SI, more precisely, there are nine of them including complex expressions. So let us turn to the description of SI1 in the extended ECD.

In the following section, we will comment on L. Iordanskaja's study on the representation of conjunctions in MTT. Since the descriptive model she proposes constitutes an extension of the ECD, we call it *the extended ECD*. We will examine our temporary description and find out whether it is compatible with the extended model.

4.4 Description of SI1 in the extended ECD

4.4.1 Iordanskaja's Tests

L. Iordanskaja (1992) enriches descriptions of conjunctions with metalinguistic indications corresponding to a set of features that take into account the pragmatic and communicative dimension of lexemes. For a structure $P\ conj\ Q$, she identifies three kinds of parameters, referred to as *strictly semantic*, *pragmatico-communicative* and *syntactic parameters*.

(i) Strictly semantic parameters allow to characterize descriptive *vs.* rhetorical conjunctions, illocutionary *vs.* non-illocutionary conjunctions, and conjunctions that imply Speaker's commitment.[6]

(ii) Pragmatico-communicative parameters allow to characterize given *vs.* non-given character of information present in main and subordinate clauses, asserted *vs.* presupposed character of a subordinate clause, grammatical modality (declarative, injunctive, interrogative) of a main clause or coordinate clauses P and Q.

(iii) Syntactic parameters allow to characterize subordinating *vs.* coordinating conjunctions, syntactic types of Q (clause, coordinate syntagm, noun modifier, verb modifier), ability of the conjunction to introduce a separate sentence, and the linear position of Q with regard to P (before, within, after P).

Given the notion of hypothesis we have referred to for the above description of SI, we will focus on the distinction between descriptive and rhetorical conjunctions. L. Iordanskaja exemplifies this distinction by the following sentences: *J'ai mal à la tête parce que j'ai trop travaillé* lit. 'I have a headache because I worked too much' (cf. PARCE QUE1) expresses an "objective relation" between two facts. *Parce que* is a descriptive conjunction.[4] On the contrary, *J'ai mal à la tête car j'ai trop travaillé* 'I have a headache for I worked too much' expresses a speech act. Besides establishing a causal relation, the Speaker gives a hint about his intention of explaining. *Car* 'for' indicates that the causal relation established between P and Q aims at explaining (by giving the reason for) Q. Hence, the opposition descriptive *vs.* rhetorical parameter captures two groups of conjunctions. To identify, to which group a conjunction belongs, Iordanskaja suggests five tests. Conjunctions that can be negated, questioned, modified, extraposed, or that correspond to an interrogative pronoun are descriptive conjunctions. Let us consider how the expression *Si X, Y* reacts to these tests.

- **negation**:[5]

(23)   **Une configuration est interdite au décollage mais pas si elle comporte un réservoir au point central fuselage*
'A configuration is forbidden from taking off, but not if it contains a tank at the fuselage central point'.

(23) a. o*Une configuration de ce type est interdite au décollage mais pas si* ... (= *sauf si* ...)
'A configuration of this type is forbidden from taking off, but not if ... (= except if ...)'.

---

[4]To be more precise, both PARCE QUE1 (non-illocutionary) and PARCE QUE2 (illocutionary) are descriptive conjunctions.

[5]As usual, sentences marked with the sign '*' are not acceptable. Those marked with 'o' are acceptable, but realize a different SI sememe; see below.

b. ∘ *Une configuration est interdite au décollage non si ... (mais si ...)*
'A configuration is forbidden from taking off not if ... (but if ...)'.

- **interrogation:**

    (24) $^?$∘ *Est-ce si une configuration comporte ... qu'elle est interdite ...*
    'Is it if a configuration contains ... that it is forbidden ... '?

    (24) a. *Est-ce qu'une configuration est interdite ... , si elle comporte ...*
    'Is a configuration forbidden ... if it contains ... '?

- **modifiers:**

    (25)   *[*Probablement/surtout/seulement*] si une configuration comporte un réservoir ... , elle est interdite ...* [7]
    '[Probably/especially/only] if a configuration contains a tank ... , it is forbidden ... '.

    (25) a. ∘ *Une configuration est interdite au décollage [$^?$probablement/*∘*surtout/seulement] si elle comporte ...*
    'A configuration is forbidden from taking off [probably/especially/only] if it contains ... '.

- **corresponding interrogative pronoun:**

    – *si—dans quel cas* 'if—in which case'?

    Q: *Dans quel cas une configuration est-elle interdite au décollage*
    'In which case is a configuration forbidden from taking off'?

    (26)   **Si* une configuration comporte ... , elle est interdite ...*
    'If a configuration contains ... , it is forbidden ... '.

    (26) a. ∘ *Une configuration est interdite ... si elle comporte ...*
    'A configuration is forbidden ... if it contains ... '.

- **si—à quelle condition** 'if—under what condition'?

    Q: *A quelle condition une configuration est-elle interdite au décollage*
    'Under what condition is a configuration forbidden from taking off'?

    (27) ?**Si une configuration comporte ... , elle est interdite ...*
    'If a configuration contains ... , it is forbidden ... '.

    (27) a. o *Une configuration est interdite ... si elle comporte ...*
    'A configuration is forbidden ... if it contains ... '.

- **extraposition:**

    (28) o *C'est si une configuration comporte ... qu'elle est interdite au décollage*
    'It is if a configuration contains ... that it is forbidden from taking off'.

Sentence in (24a) seems correct. Sentences marked with the sign "o" seem also acceptable but they realize semanteme 'SI5'. The restrictive value they imply can be made explicit by glosses.[8] Sentences in (23), (25), (26), and (27) are unacceptable. They are ill-formed or do not, in the case of a question-answer exchange, constitute a coherent answer to the question. In fact, these tests are quite inconclusive. There are three reasons for that.

Firstly, it is hard to evaluate sentence acceptability. This is due to the modal nature of the tests themselves, such as interrogation, negation and some modifiers of the *probablement* 'probably'-type. The application to the conditional conjunction, a modal expression itself, causes the same difficulty in interpretability as a negation of negation. Particularly, it is difficult to see which meaning elements are under the scope of operators (i.e., expressions used as tests). It appears that in the case of SI1 it is the modal value expressed by the first argument of SI (i.e., X, the subordinate clause) which is not under the scope while in the case of SI5, it is the one expressed by the second argument (i.e., Y, the main clause) which is not. Compare:

    (24') a. *Est-ce qu'il aura des problèmes(,) si je viens*
    'Will there be any problem if I come'?:
    'I might come and, in that case, is the consequence that there will be problems?'

(24″) a. *Est-ce que si je viens il y aura des problèmes?*
'If I come, will there be any problem'?: cf. (24a′).

(24′) *Est-ce si je viens qu'il y aura des problèmes*
'Is it if I come that there will be problems'?:
'There will be problems, and is it necessary that I come for that to be so?'

Secondly, these tests do not take into account the linear position of the subordinate clause with respect to the main clause. Some of them impose a position different from that of the sentence to be tested; consider (23) and (28). We saw that the anteposition *vs.* postposition of the conditional clause had a strong influence on the interpretation of SI. Thus, most sentences we consider acceptable realize SI5. Their acceptability does not reveal anything about properties of SI1. With respect to this point, we notice a curious inversion of values of SI in the case of interrogation. SI1 is postpositioned to QUE (compare: *Est-ce* (...) *que*). SI5 is antepositioned to it. Actually, sentence (24) is hardly acceptable. It is mainly because of the genericity of the sentence, which is not very compatible with the presuppositional character of this construction (i.e., structure + linear position). Example (24′) shows that the anteposition of a conditional clause is possible in questions, with voice rising on SI. The interpretation of this sentence is close to: *Est-ce ma présence qui posera des problèmes* lit. 'Is it my presence that will cause problems'?

Thirdly, the test value of the interrogation, negation, and other operations, which are proposed by Iordanskaja, relies on the hypothesis that only the elements that can be under the scope of the operator are of a descriptive nature. As we saw before, this allows Iordanskaja to oppose PARCE QUE 'because' and CAR 'for' and two behaviors of BIEN QUE 'though'. In each case, only the subordinate clause is submitted to the test for it is the only clause constituent which contains the meaning elements attached to the conjunction. The case of SI is different. It is, in a way, a double conjunction. Consider *Si X, alors Y* 'If X, then Y'. The deletion test shows this difference:

(29) *Pierre viendra parce qu'il veut voir Marie*
lit.—2 'Pierre will come because he wants to see Marie'.

(30) *Pierre viendra bien que la date ne lui convienne pas*
lit. 'Pierre will come though the date does not suit him'.

(31) *Pierre viendra s'il n'a pas d'autre rendez-vous ce jour-là*
lit. 'Pierre will come if he does not have any other appointment that day'.

(31′) *S'il n'a pas d'autre rendez-vous ce jour-là, Pierre viendra* lit. 'If he does not have any other appointment that day, Pierre will come'.

Deletion of the subordinate clause in (29) and in (30) does not affect the interpretation of the main clause. It it not the case with (31) and (31′). Then, both the subordinate clause and the main clause must be submitted to the test so as to decide about the descriptive or rhetorical nature of the conjunction SI.

4.4.2 SI₁: *Speech Act and/or Descriptive Content*

The ineffectual character of the tests due to semantic shifts reveals the difficulty to grasp the issue of modality in the descriptive content *vs.* speech act opposition. Given the utterance *Il se peut que X* 'It might be possible that X', does the modal expression belong to the content of this utterance, or does it make explicit its illocutionary force (some kind of attenuated assertion), as performative expressions do (e.g., *J'affirme que X* 'I swear that X')? We notice that a different illocutionary force may be associated with a modal expression: *Se peut-il/Est-ce qu'il se peut que X* 'Might it be possible that X'? This reveals that the expression is independent from a specific illocutionary force. Then, it would belong to the descriptive content of the sentence.

However, we already saw that the expression *Il se peut que* cannot be under the scope of interrogation when given as rephrasing of SI1. It cannot be under the scope of negation as well. Indeed, the *mais* 'but'/*non* 'no' test does not apply to SI1; but we can test the descriptive nature of SI1 by insertion of the marker *Il est faux que* 'It is false that'. Consider *Il est faux que, si je viens, il y aura des problèmes* 'It is false that, if I come, there will be troubles'. This sentence does not mean: 'It is false that it might happen that I come and that, in that case, the consequence is that there will be troubles'. It means: 'It might happen that I come but, in that case, it is false that the consequence is that there will be troubles'. These observations lead us to the conclusion that the modal value, which is expressed by the first argument of SI1 must be treated as a rhetorical content. We will say that it expresses a speech act, i.e., a supposition.

According to Ducrot (1980), the description of *Si X, Y* should be given in two steps:

(i) The Speaker asks the Listener to imagine *X*,

(ii) once the dialogue is introduced in the frame of this imaginary situation, the Speaker asserts *Y*.

Then, SI1 would thus express a combination of speech acts. Yet, other illocutionary values may be associated with Y. Compare *S'il vient, viendras-tu?* 'If he comes will you come'? or *S'il vient, ne viens pas* 'If he comes, do not come'. So, we must restate (ii), so that the illocutionary force associated with the content Y remains undetermined. If we modify Ducrot's characterization in this direction and use it for defining SI1 in the extended ECD, it shows a combination of a speech act (supposition) and a content Y sequentially ordered. Hence the following description:

Y *si*1 X = *Le locuteur suppose que* X [*a/a eu/aura*] *lieu et, dans ce cas,* X *a pour conséquence que* Y [*a/a eu/aura*] *lieu*
'The Speaker supposes that X [happens/happened/will happen] and, in this case, the consequence of X is that Y [happens/happened/will happen]'.

However, what is the nature of the coordination in this definition? In fact, it is doubtful that coordination of a speech act and a descriptive content makes sense.

4.4.3 *Representation of Supposition in Terms of 'Asserted Content' and 'Presupposed Content'*

Considering the reaction of SI1 to tests of interrogation and falsity we notice that part of its content has the characteristics of presupposition. So, we will try to describe it as a presupposed content. We will restate the definition as follows:

Y *si*1 X = *Que* X [*ait/ait eu*] *lieu étant une supposition* (presupposed), X *a pour conséquence que* Y [*a/a eu/aura*] *lieu* 'That X [happens/happened/will happen] being a supposition, the consequence of X is that Y [happens/happened/will happen]' (asserted).

By doing so we also have problems. The definiens does not reflect in a proper way the properties of the definiendum; it expresses in terms of content what the conjunction accomplishes. Consider the difference between *S'il pleut, je resterai à la maison* lit. 'If it rains I will stay at home' and *Qu'il pleuve étant une supposition, la pluie aura pour conséquence que je resterai à la maison* lit. 'That it rains being a supposition, the consequence of the rain will be that I will stay at home'.

There is another reason for saying that the last definition is not sufficient. We implicitly admitted that the structures *Si* X, [*est-ce que?/il est faux que*] Y and [*Est-ce que?/Il est faux que*], *si X, Y* were equivalent. Nothing would prevent us then from considering the meaning elements 'cela a pour conséquence que Y' 'that has as consequence that Y' as the asserted part of the definition of si1. Partial interrogations forbid this analysis. With *Si je viens, que feras-tu* 'If I come what will you do'? it is impossible to apply the latter definition. Consider: *Que je vienne étant une supposition, la conséquence de ma venue sera-t-elle que* ... 'That I come being a supposition, the consequence of my coming will be that ... '? The interrogation does not concern the relation between antecedent and consequence as total interrogations, but the consequence itself. An approximate paraphrase would be: ' ... , quelle sera la conséquence en ce qui concerne ton comportement' ' ... the consequence is that you will do what'?/'what will be the consequence concerning your behavior'? In fact, the following restatement would be better: 'Qu'est-ce que tu feras en conséquence' ' ... what will you do as a consequence'? since the question does not concern the identification of the consequence as such. It rather concerns the fact itself which is given as consequence.

Taking into account partial interrogations leads us to redefine *Y si1 X* in the following way: *Que X [ait + ait eu] lieu étant une supposition* (presupposed), *Y [a/a eu/aura] lieu* (asserted), *le fait Y étant la conséquence du fait X* (presupposed) 'That X [happens/happened/will happen] being a supposition (presupposed), Y [has/has been/will] be (asserted), the fact Y being the consequence of X (presupposed)'. The asserted component of this definition of *Y si1 X* is reduced to *Y a lieu*. Compare the asserted part of *Si je viens, que feras-tu* 'If I come what will you do'? = *Que feras-tu* 'What will you do'? It seems that we have lost here the semantics proper of the conjunction we wanted to describe. In any case, the fact that the asserted part of partial interrogations is different from that of total interrogations clearly indicates that the asserted *vs.* presupposed distinction is not the solution for describing this entry.

4.4.4 Conclusion

Coming back to the initial issue, let us examine which kind of definition zone is to be attached to the sememe 'si1'. We saw how difficult it would be to associate to it a semantemic network. It is neither a real semantic primitive(cf. (ii.a) in Subsection 4.2) since our analysis of the conjunction showed notions of epistemic modality nor act of supposition and consequence. 'Si1' is not an indivisible seme: it is composed of simpler terms. It is therefore a (ii.b) primitive from Subsection 4.2, which amounts to admitting the limits of the descriptive model offered by the ECD.

5 Notions and the Notional Dictionary

Our discussion above has shown that lexemes such as SI cannot be described in terms of an explicitation of the predicate's semantic content. The meaning of the relation in this case is transferred to the arguments. We assume that the lexeme SI1 indicates a semantically empty relation between "typed" arguments. It does not express some identified semantic relation; it rather expresses a "relating" between semantically identified types of arguments. To be more precise, the relation that SI1 establishes between arguments has the effect of subcategorizing them respectively as supposition and consequence.

This kind of description is not compatible with the concept of a semanteme. By definition, a semanteme cannot represent a relation that is semantically empty. See case 1 in Subsection 4.2. Therefore, to describe the structure $Si1\ X,\ Y$, we will invoke another metalinguistic concept—the concept of *notion*. We will say that the notion $causalité(X,\ Y)$ 'causality(X, Y)' represents the meaning of $Si1\ X,\ Y$ as well as other realizations in the context of (1a) to (1d).

The notional description has the following two advantages over the semantemic description:

(i) it allows the description of functors that are deprived of content;

(ii) contrary to the concept of presupposition, the concept of an argument type is neutral with regards to the descriptive *vs.* rhetorical distinction.

Notional descriptions can be used as well to represent semantic relations as semantemic descriptions. Any type of relation can be represented as a relation between typed arguments. Consider conversives ACHETER1a '[to] buy' and VENDRE1b '[to] sell'. We state, as Fillmore (1977), that these two lexemes express a relation between a buyer, a seller, a merchandise and a tender. Using a functional notation, we create the notion $trans(X,\ Y,\ Z,\ W)$ that refers to $ACHETER1(X,\ Y,\ Z,\ W)$ and $VENDRE1(Z,\ Y,\ X,\ W)$. That way, it is the arguments that bear the whole meaning of the relation.

5.1 *Some Characteristics of Notions*

We will focus on the following three characteristics of notions:[6]

---

[6]We borrow the term of notion from Culioli (1990). However, what we mean here differs from the definition of notions given by Culioli as a set of physico-(pragmatico)-semantic properties.

(i) its functional notation;
(ii) its definition as semantic paradigm in a given linguistic context;
(iii) the non-explicitation of the semantic content of lexemes that notions refer to.

The functional notation we adopted is purely a writing convention and does not express in any case an orientation of the relation, *Deep Cases*, or distinct roles. The order in which arguments are presented is totally arbitrary. The only thing that matters is the identity relation between arguments of the notion and actants of functors which it refers to.

Most linguistic expressions have a double property. First, they have several distinct meanings depending on the context in which they appear. Second, in a given type of context, another expression can substitute them without seriously modifying the meaning of the sequence in which they are inserted. Consider ACHETER '[to] buy'. This expression does not have the same meaning in the following sentences: *Marie a acheté un tapis pour son salon* 'Marie bought a rag for her living room' and *Marie a acheté les témoins* 'Marie bought the witnesses' (cf. ACHETER1 and ACHETER2 in the ECD). In the second sentence, *acheter* can be replaced by *soudoyer* '[to] bribe', but not in the first one. In fact, it is precisely because substitutions are possible or impossible in a given case that an expression can be said to have different meanings depending on the context.

Notion is the name given to a semantic paradigm. It allows to gather, under the same label different lexemes, syntactic constructions, or grammatical elements that are related by a non-strict equivalence relation in a certain context. In other words, it constitutes an abstraction on lexemes which it refers to. This abstraction puts aside the discriminatory elements of lexemes, which can be specified as conditions on the use of the gathered linguistic expressions. Cf. the concept of paradigm in Saussure's work. A notion is thus a label that points to some linguistic realizations so as to represent their equivalence and to describe their differential values.

Notions do not represent a meaning as a decomposition of a semantic content, nor do they make such a meaning explicit or represent it as a semanteme does. For instance, the semanteme 'acheter1' is the name given to the semantic content of the form ACHETER in a certain context with the content made explicit by the definition. In contrast, the notion *trans* is the name of the semantic content common to n expressions in a certain context and cannot be made explicit as such without taking into account discriminatory elements which had been put aside. In essence, therefore, a notion is essentially non-explicitable; only the expressions which it refers to are. So, for our relation of causality, we will have the following description:

causalité(X, Y)

$Y\ si_1\ X$ → X is presented as a supposition;
$X\ entraîner_4\ Y$ → The relation X/Y is presented as the identification of a consequence;
$Y\ résulter_2\ X$ → The relation X/Y is presented as the identification of a cause;

$Y \xrightarrow{\text{II}} Z \xrightarrow{\text{ATTR}} X \xrightarrow{\text{I}} Z$ → X is presented as the distinctive property of Z.

5.2 *Theoretical Status of Notions*

The various characteristics mentioned above give the notion a particular theoretical status. Notions are metalinguistic entities. As such, they differ in nature from concepts. As considered by Cognitive Psychology, concepts are mental representations predetermined by culture. While we may think of concepts that do not have any designation in language, notions only reflect relations between lexical units of a given language or between some of these units and non-lexical realizations. A notional representation is then particularly dependent on the structuring of meaning that is specific to a particular language. It is not a concept as conceived in Artificial Intelligence; i.e., an object and a relation that is used to model a given domain. Conceptual representations in AI attempt to describe a 'reality' or some view on the world in a particular domain of activities. Their denotative nature makes them independent of a particular language, or even of language in general. *A fortiori* they are independent of the different ways of presenting a given content in a particular language. As for notions, the entities they manipulate are never referents nor representations of referents.

Furthermore, the metalinguistic nature of notions differs from that of semantemes and concepts as conceived in linguistics. As we already saw, notion is the name of a semantic paradigm. It is not associated with only one linguistic object. Thus, it does not constitute an abstraction of one linguistic expression at a given level of analysis as semantemes and (linguistic) concepts do.

As metalinguistic entities, semantemes and concepts allow to isolate some properties of lexical units. So, we may speak of the semantic or denotative content of a lexeme independently of its other properties (syntactic, morphological, etc.). Semantemes and concepts are based on a double principle of discrimination: for a given linguistic object, discrimination of properties belongs to different levels of analysis, and discrimination of objects on the basis of properties belongs to a given level. On the contrary, the concept of notion relies on a clustering principle.

Finally, notions do not constitute a level of analysis. It is not a given level of analysis where the properties, at that level, of a linguistic object are isolated (compare semanteme: semantic content of a lexeme; concept: denotative or representational content of a lexeme). If a notional description falls within the semantic level, it does not constitute a particular plane of existence of a linguistic object; it creates, as the archiphoneme does in phonology, a metalinguistic entity (i.e., a semantic kernel common to such lexemes) which has no linguistic realization.

5.3 *Advantages of the Notional Representation*

Evoking the relation between ACHETER1 and VENDRE1, we suggested that the usefulness of descriptive tools such as notions should not be restricted to the only description of SI1. Let us see more of the advantages of the notional representation.

1. Notions allow the representation of lexemes that are difficult to describe in semantemic terms. It is not only the case with SI1, but also with any conjunction (compare Iordanskaja's analysis). Insertion, in the definiens, of descriptive elements such as *Le locuteur justifie que* 'The speaker justifies that' (for rhetorical conjunctions) or *l'énoncé P* 'the utterance P' (i.e., the uttering of P, for illocutionary conjunctions) is problematic regarding the definitional form. It is quite obvious that it is no longer a matter of simple restatement (paraphrastic definition), but an explicitation of the discursive function that is realized by the conjunction, and thus a kind of comment whose metalinguistic nature is evidenced by the non-substitution of the definiens for the definiendum in the context of an utterance. Consider the definition of BIEN QUE1:

Personne n'est couché bien qu'il soit très tard ≠ [$^?$*Le locuteur* + *je*] *signale que le fait que personne n'est couché* ($^{??}$*a lieu*) *contredit le fait qu'il est très tard* ($^{??}$*a lieu*) 'Nobody slept, although it was very late* ≠ [The speaker + I] signals that the fact that nobody slept (happens) contradicts the fact that it is very late (happens)'

Even with non-illocutionary descriptive conjunctions as PARCE QUE1, the utterances produced by substitution are ill-formed or not equivalent: *La séance a été reportée parce que Pierre était absent* lit. 'The session has been postponed because Pierre was not there'/**Le fait que la séance a été reportée a été causé par le fait que Pierre était absent* 'The fact that the session has been postponed is caused by the fact that Pierre was not there'. Apart from the impossibility of making explicit the presupposed part of the definition (see 'qui a lieu' 'which happens' in the definition of PARCE QUE1), the restatement of the conjunction with the predicate *être causé par* '[to] be caused by' implies a temporalization of the causal relation itself, which is absent with the conjunction.[7] While with the conjunction the time reference of the utterance is expressed only by the temporal anchoring of the arguments, because of its verbal nature, the predicate *causer* '[to] cause' attributes a temporal dimension to the relating itself. From this point of view, the following utterance would be better: *Le report de la séance a été causé par le fait que Pierre était absent* lit. 'The postponing of the session has been caused by the fact that Pierre was absent'.

2. Notions allow for the direct representation of the equivalence between lexical and non-lexical realizations avoiding the need to postulate the presence of a semanteme where the corresponding lexeme is absent. In sentence (1a), the semantemic approach had forced us to postulate the presence of the semanteme 'si1', given as the meaning of the restrictive relative clause. Even though the lexeme SI1 was not in the sentence. The definition of the semanteme in terms of semantic content of a lexeme then became inappropriate and the status of this entity problematic.

3. Notions allow for the abstraction of semantic shifts which may be observed between non-strictly equivalent realizations. We already showed such shifts in (1a) to (1d). Each of these expressions presents a particular point of view from which the Speaker considers the relation (cf. supposition, consequence, cause, distinctive property) according to his communicative needs. In the case of these relations it seems that the denotative content and the Speaker's point of view overlap and therefore cannot be described separately.

4. Notions allow for the abstraction of different orientations between conversive lexemes (e.g., ACHETER1/VENDRE1). The orientation of a relation that expresses the point of view from which the Speaker considers this relation is an element of a communicative nature. Since it would seem reasonable to have a homogeneous treatment of both lexemes and utterances, we will assume that lexemes with the same denotative content and with

---

[7]It is not the matter of knowing whether the relation between a cause and a consequence may be perceived as a temporal relation of anteriority, but whether the relating is temporally situated with regard to the moment of enunciation.

different communicative components are equivalent. Yet, this equivalence cannot result from the semantemic definition of conversives. The definition reproduces the orientation of the definiendum. This cannot be any other way since all meaning elements of a semanteme must be reflected in its definition. The structure $X\ donner1\ Y\ à\ Z$ 'X give Y to Z' implies an agentive interpretation of X, which is absent from the structure $Z\ recevoir1\ Y\ de\ X$ 'Z receive Y from X'. Here again we can see that denotative content and communicative point of view are intricate. Therefore, it is only by giving up a description "of language by language" (semantemic description) that we will be able to draw a semantic kernel common to conversives and to specify the different points of view.

Whether we consider "meta-relations" (as the one of causality) or conversives,[8] we realize that the state of affairs virtually represented by the lexeme, i.e., by its denotation, is itself governed by the Speaker's point of view; more precisely by his way of presenting this state of affairs. Thus, there is an impact of the communicative element on the denotative element. Denotative and communicative elements are aggregated within the semantic content of lexemes. This also holds true of the so-called "subjective" terms (Kerbrat-Orecchioni, 1980). Subjective terms express, besides a property of the object they determine, an emotional commitment of the Speaker, whose presence they reveal in the utterance ("emotional words"), or which imply the existence of a norm internal to the Speaker and related to his systems of ethical, aesthetical evaluation ("evaluative terms"):

emotional:

poignant 'poignant', *drôle* 'funny', *pathétique* 'pathetic';

evaluative:

bon 'good', *beau* 'beautiful', *bien* 'well', *génie* 'genius', *catastrophe* 'disaster', *désespoir* 'despair', *haïr* '[to] hate', *se vanter* '[to] boast'.

The description of these terms in the ECD would integrate the subjective elements into the body of the definition. It is doubtful that one may invoke in this case the concepts of connotation or presupposition.

Thus, we may say that the problem raised by non-strict equivalence and interrelationship between the communicative and denotative elements of our realizations in (1a) to (1d) is not a marginal phenomenon, but crosses the whole lexicon. Thus, the realization of a notional dictionary is justified.

---

[8] As for meta-rules, consider also the relations consecutiveness/consequence and cause/goal.

5.4 Relations between a Notional Dictionary and the ECD

In the ECD, various lexemes of a given vocable are distinguished so that Lexical Functions may operate effectively. The distinction between lexemes of a vocable is supposed to account for the equivalence relation between these and other terms and since contextual neutralization is invoked in the case of such a relation.[9] So we may say that the distinguished semantemes of a word provide its "contextual meanings" (i.e., meanings that this word has in the context of sentences). Coming back to our realizations in (1a) to (1d), we see that there is still one problem we have not mentioned. Recall that the lexemes SI 'if', ENTRAÎNER '[to] entail' and RÉSULTER '[to] result' can be substituted for one another only when the aspectual value of the verbs allows a non-referential (out of context) interpretation of the sentences. Consider (1a) and (1b) vs. (1c) and (1d):

(1) a. *Si [une/la] configuration [comporte/comportait] un réservoir ... , elle [est/serait] interdite ...*
   lit. 'If [a/the] configuration [contains/contained] a tank ... , it [is/was] forbidden ... '.

   b. *La présence, dans [une/la] configuration, d'un réservoir ... [entraîne/entraînerait] son interdiction ...*
   lit. 'The presence in [a/the] configuration of a tank ... [entails/entailed] its forbidding ... '.

   c. *Si [une/la] configuration [*a comporté/comportait] un réservoir ... , elle a été interdite ...*
   lit. 'If [a/the] configuration [has contained/contained] a tank ... , it has been forbidden ... '.

   d. *La présence, dans [une/la] configuration, d'un réservoir ... a entraîné son interdiction ...*
   lit. 'The presence, in [a/the] configuration of a tank ... has entailed its forbidding ... '

This fact would certainly induce ECD lexicologists to create the entries SIj and ENTRAÎNERj, one referring to the other. These entries would be distinct from the entries SI1 (e.g., *S'il pleut, j'abandonnerai* lit. 'If it rains, I will give up') and ENTRAÎNER4 (e.g., *Sa faillite a entraîné la mienne* lit. 'His

---

[9]The purely syntactic differences do not play a role in identifying lexemes. In this case, different modes of a lexeme are invoked. See the entry *coûteux* 'costly' as Mod$_1$: *L'entretien de la voiture est coûteux* 'The maintenance of the car is costly' and as Mod$_2$: *La voiture est coûteuse d'entretien* 'The car is costly to maintain'.

bankruptcy led to mine'), between which there is no relation. However, according to our intuition, SIi and SIj have the same meaning, as ENTRAÎNERi and ENTRAÎNERj do. Then, there would be a conflict between the fact that two lexemes with different lexical zones should be distinguished and the fact that two lexemes have the same definitional zone.[10] Due to the existence of the established notion *causalité*(X, Y), whose purpose was to allow references, it is no longer necessary to distinguish SI1 and SIj. The notion would refer to the entry SI1 in the ECD and would specify a constraint on the aspectual value of the predicates.

The existence of a notional dictionary presupposes the existence of the ECD, i.e., a dictionary which discriminates the meaning of the words so as to allow effective references. In the framework of text generation, such a dictionary is a passage for accessing the lexemes.

5.5 *Notional Representation of the Meaning of Sentences*

The existence of a notional dictionary offers an advantage for a text generation system as well as for the notional representation of sentences it provides. From what has been said above about notions and semantemes, it appears that:

(i) The notional representation of meaning puts the paraphrasing power of LFs into the central position of the generation system. From this point of view, the fact that notions do not make explicit the semantic "invariant" of lexemes which they refer to is not a limitation. The "natural" paraphrases, which the MTT is able to produce are obtained by application of LFs and not by meaning decomposition which the semantemic representation allows. The somewhat metalinguistic touch of paraphrases obtained by decomposition is due to the difference between "expressed" meaning (the semanteme) and "represented" meaning (the definition). From *Pierre a promis de venir* 'Pierre promised to come', we get by the decomposition of PROMETTRE '[to] promise':

> *Pierre a communiqué [à Z] qu'il était certain qu'aurait lieu un événement (lié à) sa venue [qui concerne Z] (et Pierre communique qu'il promet de causer cet événement)*
> 'Pierre communicated [to Z] that he was certain there would be an event (linked to) his coming [which concerns Z] (and Pierre communicates that he promises to cause this event)'.

---

[10] SI with an iterative "coloration" would probably raise a similar problem.

For the same sentence, the application of the LF **Syn** would result in

Pierre [a annoncé/prédit/affirmé/assuré] qu'il viendrait
'Pierre [announced/predicted/asserted/granted] that he was coming'.

(ii) Only a notional representation of meaning allows to maintain the distinction between the SemS and the SemCommS. We saw that lexemes like SI and ENTRAÎNER, conversives, evaluative terms, and probably the whole lexicon integrated denotative and communicative elements. If we want to keep the hypothesis of a distinction between the representation of the semantic invariant and the representation of communicative elements, it is impossible to have a semantemic representation in the SemS.

(iii) From the processing point of view, when we consider the various lexicalizations of a semantic kernel, the notional representation allows to avoid the two-phase lexicalization imposed by the semantemic representation. In MTT, the SemR that is associated with the following paraphrastic sentences *Pierre a acheté une voiture de Jean* 'Pierre bought a car from Jean'/*Jean a vendu une voiture à Pierre* 'Jean sold a car to Pierre' forces to lexicalize first the predicate either as *acheter* '[to] buy' or *vendre* '[to] sell' and then to apply the LF **Conv**, which provides the resulting lexical form. The fact that the notion takes LFs into account allows the DSyntR of sentences that are to be produced from the semantic level to be obtained directly. That the Meaning-Text approach raises an optimization problem for implementation of the model is nothing compared to the fact that it supposes that one starts with the given meaning of one and only one utterance, represented exhaustively by the SemS, the SemCommS and the SemRhetS in the SemR. To generate a class of paraphrastic utterances, MTT has to start with a given utterance (Mel'čuk speaks in terms of an initial sentence) from which paraphrases are derived.

(iv) It is quite obvious that a text generation system does not have this type of knowledge. Only the enrichment of the conceptual representation with rhetorical and communicative specifications allows to produce an exhaustive representation (SemR) of the meaning of a given utterance. However, to take into account such specifications before the semantic level means to directly derive the SemR that is specific to each paraphrastic sentence from this enriched conceptual representation. Thus, the nature proper of the SemR in the MTT, i.e., the representation of all meaning elements in a sentence, forces the consideration of the relation between paraphrastic sentences as an equivalence relation between SemRs. Such a situation is problematic insofar as it suggests to consider all semantic paraphrases as proper semantic paraphrases for which the MTT has not been designed.

So, even in the case of an implementation of the standard MTT, the paraphrasing power of the model, which heavily relies on the application of LFs, is used before the level of semantic representation as an interface between concepts and semantemes, rhetorical-communicative specifications and syntactic structures. Then we can wonder about the role played by the MTT in a text generation system where linguistic choices are represented before the semantic level (properly linguistic level) of the system. The advantage of a notional representation of the meaning of utterances in a text generation system is that it allows to take into account linguistic choices available at the proper linguistic level.

Acknowledgements

We are greatly indebted to Igor Mel'čuk for the enlightening discussions we had on MTT and also to Antoine Culioli from whom we borrowed the term of *notion*. Although we propose a characterization different from the one he suggests in (Culioli, 1990), we think that we did not betray the spirit in which he conceived it.

Endnotes

[1] Any subject modifier in a generic context has a restrictive value unless it expresses a defining property of the object denoted by the noun:

(i) a. *Une femme intelligente ne réagit pas ainsi*
'An intelligent woman does not react this way'.
and
b. *Une femme qui est intelligente ne réagit pas ainsi*
'A woman who is intelligent does not react this way'.

Both sentences express a restriction which can be expressed by a conditional clause as well. Compare:

(i) c. *Une femme ne réagit pas ainsi si elle est intelligente*
'A woman does not react this way if she is intelligent'.

In

(i) d. *Les hommes qui sont mortels doivent craindre le jugement dernier*
'Men who are mortal must fear the Last Judgement'.

Être mortel '[to] be mortal' is a defining property of the object denoted by *homme* 'man'. The relative clause is not restrictive and cannot be substituted by a conditional clause.

[2] For the issue here is the correspondence between a semanteme (a given meaning) and a syntactic construction, we speak of meaning, not of meaning effect, of the structure. *Meaning effect* means an enrichment (an addition of meaning elements) of the "literal" meaning of an expression produced by the context of the utterance. Since, when associated with generic markers, the relative clause can always be paraphrased by a conditional clause—whatever the context of utterance or the Speaker's intentions—we conclude that it is its literal meaning in this linguistic context.

[3] De Cornulier strives to show that the pretended polysemy of the conjunction falls within pragmatics because it depends on the situational context and the world knowledge shared by the Speaker and Hearer. So, semantic nuances between the different uses of SI would be meaning effects, not senses. There are other analyses which refer to speech laws (cf. the *exhaustivity law* in Ducrot, 1972) to account for the distinction between the SI of sufficient condition (hypothetical SI) and the one of necessary condition (restrictive SI). We will leave them aside in the present article; they are not compatible with the approach pursued in the ECD and MTT.

[4] The argumentation developed by De Cornulier on this aspect uses as a premise the supposed equivalence of *C'est que P* 'It is that P'. Yet, the description of *C'est que (P)* would necessarily provide the expression with an explicative value which is absent in the simple clause. Compare *Je l'aime* 'I love him' and *C'est que je l'aime* 'The reason is I love him'.

[5] One could object that, even in the case of SI1, both arguments X and Y express a modal value. The deep meaning of the notion of consequence would also be modal. In that case, 'the consequence is that Y' would be equivalent to 'In that case, it might not happen that not Y', and thus to 'In that case, it is necessary that Y'. Yet, this objection is not relevant. On the one hand, it does not question the semantic opposition between SI1 and SI5. Compare *S'il pleut, je resterai à la maison* lit. 'If it rains, I will stay at home': 'It might happen that it rains and, in that case, it is necessary that I stay at home'/*Je resterai à la maison s'il pleut* 'I will stay at home if it rains': 'It might happen that I stay at home and it is necessary that it rains for that to be so'. On the other hand, it is a logician's approach to modality, which does not correspond to the linguistic intuition of Speakers. We think that the notion of consequence and hypothesis, contrary to that of condition, is not interpreted as modal by Speakers.

[6] The illocutionary vs. non-illocutionary parameter makes a distinction between conjunctions which denote a relation between two facts and those which denote a relation between a fact and the utterance of a fact. *J'ai mal à la tête parce que j'ai trop travaillé* 'I have a headache because I worked too much' illustrates a non-illocutionary use of the conjunction PARCE QUE1. In *Pierre doit être sympathique parce que mon frère l'aime beaucoup* 'Pierre must be nice because my brother likes him a lot', *parce que* is used illocutionary (PARCE QUE2). The fact that the Speaker commits himself to the truth of the fact expressed by the second argument of the conjunction allows to contrast the lexemes *puisque* 'since' and *car* 'for'.

[7] In fact, the structure *Surtout si X, Y* 'Especially if X, Y' is acceptable in a certain context, namely when Y has been previously asserted. So, the complete structure

is: '*Y. Surtout si X, Y*'. In this case, the expression *Surtout si* is related to the first occurrence of *Y* to which it is postpositioned. Consider *Pierre viendra. Surtout si tu lui demandes, il viendra* 'Pierre will come. Especially if you ask him, he will come'. Whatever the position of the subordinate clause, the restriction expressed by the conditional clause does not affect the meaning of the main clause, but rather the meaning of the expression *surtout* (i.e., *d'autant plus* 'all the more'). In the previous example, the Speaker asserts, without reservation, that Pierre will come.

[8] The semanteme 'si5' is realized in (23b), (24), and (28). These sentences can be glossed in the following way:

23b'. 'It might happen that a configuration is forbidden from taking off and it is false that it is necessary that it contains a tank ... for the configuration to be so (but it is necessary that ... for it to be so)'.

24'. 'It might happen that a configuration is forbidden from taking off ... and is it necessary that it contains a tank ... for it to be so'?

28'. 'It might happen that a configuration is forbidden from taking off and it is the fact that it contains a tank ... which is necessary for it to be so'.

Bibliography

Cornulier De, B. 1985. *Effets de sens*. Paris: Editions de Minuit.

Culioli, A. 1990. "Sur le concept de notion". *Pour une linguistique de l'énonciation—Opérations et représentations, T.I*. Paris: Ophrys.

Ducrot, O. 1972. *Dire et ne pas dire*. Paris: Hermann. 2e éd. augmentée, 1980.

Ducrot, O. 1980. "Analyses pragmatiques". *Communications*. 32.

Fillmore, C. 1977. "The Case for Case Reopened". *Grammatical Relations* (= *Syntax and Semantics, 8*) ed. by P. Cole & J. Sadock. 59–81. New York: Academic Press.

Iordanskaja, L. 1992. "Communicative Structure and Its Use during Text Generation". *International Forum on Information and Documentation*. 17.2:15–27.

Kerbrat-Orecchioni, C. 1980. *L'Enonciation—De la subjectivité dans le langage*. Paris: Armand Colin.

Martin, R. 1983. *Pour une logique du sens*. Paris: PUF.

Mel'čuk, I.A. 1988. *Dependency Syntax: Theory and Practice.* Albany: State University of New York Press.

Mel'čuk, I.A. 1996. "Lexical Functions: A Tool for the Description of Lexical Relations in a Lexicon". *Lexical Functions in Lexicography and Natural Language Processing* ed. by L. Wanner. 37–102. Amsterdam & Philadelphia: Benjamins Academic Publishers.

Mel'čuk, I., A. Clas & A. Polguère. 1995. *Introduction à la lexicologie explicative et combinatoire.* Louvain-la-Neuve: Duculot.

Verb Categorization and the Format of a Lexicographic Definition (Semantic Types of Causative Relations)

Elena V. Paducheva

1 Introduction

The verb [TO] CAUSE, which has no direct equivalent in Russian, is frequently used in lexicographic definitions formulated according to the principles of the *Meaning-Text Model* (MTM) (Mel'čuk, 1974; Apresjan, 1974; Mel'čuk & Žolkovskij, 1984) in terms of the artificial *kauzirovat'* '[to] cause'. For instance, *rasširit'* X '[to] make X broader' is defined as 'to cause X to become broader', *soobščit'* Y-u, čto X '[to] tell Y that X' as 'to cause Y to know about X'. In this paper, we show that there is a need for a more detailed and differentiated representation of causative relations in lexicographic definitions.

Causative relations became an object of a special analysis in (Wierzbicka, 1980), where it is shown that not only verbs like *nakormit'* '[to] feed' or *ubit'* '[to] kill' (secondary transitives according to J. Lyons), but also *myt'* '[to] wash' or *kopat'* '[to] dig' (primary transitives) and even non-transitive verbs like *vstat'* '[to] stand up' and *sest'* '[to] sit down' are, in their deep structure, causative. The difference between '[to] feed' and '[to] stand up' disappears if one takes into consideration the fact that '[to] stand up' has an Inner Object: *vstat'* = 'to cause one's own body to be in a certain position'. In a negative way, a causative relation is accounted for in lexicographic definitions of verbs that are not transitive altogether, e.g., of verbs denoting non-agentive processes. A process is something that happens without an internal causer, as if by itself (Gavrilova, 1990). For instance, *Dom razrušilsja* 'The house collapsed' = 'the house reached the state of collapse as if by itself' (the formula 'as if' is meant here to reflect the fact that it is not the real situation we speak about, but the way it is modelled in language). Indeed, we know that in the real world, the deterioration of a house is effected by the influence of "natural forces"; e.g., wind or water.

A. Wierzbicka establishes a relationship between causation and the basic taxonomic categories of verbs. She relates causation to such notions as action, process, event, happening, state, and other aspectual classes of Vendler (1967). In this paper, we attempt at a more detailed analysis of this relationship. We propose that verbs belonging to different taxonomic categories differ by the *format* (or *scheme*) of their lexicographic definition, whereas for verbs belonging to the same taxonomic category the format of the lexicographic definition is the same. We shall demonstrate that the difference between formats is determined first of all by the place occupied in a definition by the causative connector (and, of course, by the types of arguments of the causative relation).

We assume that arguments of a causative relation can only be situations (events, states of affairs) or facts: a person cannot be a Causer. Thus, if in the surface structure of a sentence the syntactic Subject of a causative verb of action is the name of a person, then "in the deep structure" the Causer will be this person's activity; e.g., according to Wierzbicka (1980):

(1) *John killed a fly* =
    'John's activity resulted in that the fly ceased to be alive'.

This definition may be reformulated as follows:

(1') 'John acted with a certain purpose' and 'John's activity resulted in that the fly ceased to be alive' and 'this result coincides with John's purpose' (i.e., 'by this activity John achieved his purpose'.)

In our model, each semantic component of a lexicographic definition must have some heading: the component is one of the values of the parameter named by the heading; thus, (1') =

I. Causer: John acted with a certain Purpose.

II. Causation (controlled): (I) resulted in (III).

III. Result coinciding with Purpose: the fly ceased to be alive.

Here (I) is the *categorial* component: it reveals the fact that the verb [*to*] *kill* belongs to the taxonomic category of actions. If the surface Subject of a causative verb is inanimate, i.e., if it denotes a physical object, then in the deep-structure of the sentence the Causer is some event, state or characteristics of that object—'something sayable about X' (the formula is from Wierzbicka, 1980), and such a verb does not denote any action, compare:

(2) Bant ukrasil plat'e
'The bow decorated the dress' =
'the bow made the contact with the dress <event> and because of that the dress began to look better'.

If so, then the difference between (3) and (4)

(3) Ivan napomnil mne, čto pora uxodit'
'Ivan reminded me that it was time to go'.

(4) Boj časov napomnil mne, čto pora uxodit'
'The chime of the clock reminded me that it was time to go'.

is not that in (4) the Causer is an event whereas in (3) the Causer is a person: in (3) the Causer is the person's action, i.e., also an event. What really matters is that in (3) the consequence is the EXPECTED RESULT of the activity Causer: the result desired by the Subject; whereas in (4) there is no potential Subject of volition. Hence, the scheme of definition for *napomnit'* '[to] remind' in (3) is:

I. Causer: The Subject acted with a certain Purpose.
II. Causation (controlled): (I) lead to (III).
III. Result coinciding with Purpose: in the active part of my consciousness an idea appeared: 'It's time for me to go'.

The scheme of definition for the verb *napomnit'* in (4), where it denotes non-controlled causation, is as follows:

I. Causer: event X took place.
II. Causation (non-controlled): (I) evoked (III).
III. Consequence: event Y took place: in the active part of my consciousness an idea appeared: 'It is time for me to go'.

Thus, the first semantic distinction in the class of causative relations is the opposition of *non-intentional* (non-controlled) causation, see Section 2, and *intentional* (controlled) causation, see Section 3. All oppositions discussed below are relevant only for intentional causation.

The opposition of *direct causation* (as in the definition of [*to*] *kill* we quoted) and *indirect causation* (unambiguously expressed in English by an analytical construction with the verb [*to*] *cause*) was analyzed in detail in (Wierzbicka, 1988) and will not be touched upon here. Note that in Russian, unlike in English, the difference between direct and indirect causation is not very well marked: the Russian sentence (5)

(5) *Ja sšila sebe jubku*

may be interpreted as expressing a direct as well as an indirect causation:

(5) a. 'I have sewn the skirt by myself'.
b. 'I have got a skirt sewn for myself by somebody'.

Another notion to be introduced in connection with causation is 'noncomplete control of the Subject over the situation'. Compare verbs like *zakryt'* '[to] cover', *postroit'* '[to] build', which denote actions with common controlled causation, and verbs like *rešit'* <*zadaču*> '[to] solve <a mathematical problem>', *ugovorit'* '[to] talk sb into doing sth', '[to] convince', *pojmat'* '[to] catch', whose meaning implies the idea of a good luck and, therefore, of noncomplete control. The opposition of complete and non-complete control is discussed in Section 4. On the other hand, common controlled causation contrasts with guaranteed causation (presupposing the impossibility of an unsuccessful attempt), which is exemplified by such verbs as *govorit'* '[to] say' and *obeščat'* '[to] promise'; see Section 5.

2 Non-intentional (Non-controlled) Causation

The distinction between controlled and non-controlled causation is determined, in the first place, by the nature of the first argument (Causer) of a causal relation: in the case of verbs of non-controlled causation, the Causer is an event or a state. For verbs of controlled causation, the first argument is the activity of the Subject. The second argument of the non-controlled causation is called "Consequence" (and not "Result coinciding with the Subject's Purpose", as with controlled causation). The following classes of verbs are to be distinguished:

(i) Verbs whose first argument denotes a situation, such as *udivit'* '[to] surprise', *ispugat'* '[to] frighten', *ogorčit'* '[to] upset', *napolnit'* '[to] fill', and *razbudit'* '[to] awake' (in one of its meanings):

(6) *Ego pojavlenie menja udivilo* 'His arrival surprised me'.

(7) *Menja razbudil zvonok v dver'*
'The bell (= the ringing of the bell) at the door woke me up'.

Verbs in examples (6) and (7) belong to the taxonomic category 'happening'; see (Wierzbicka, 1980:177). The meaning of verbs of non-controlled causation may be represented with the help of the verb *vyzvat'* '[to] evoke', whose arguments are events; compare the definition of *napomnit'* in sentence (4), Section 1.

(ii) Verbs with the first argument denoting a factor (force):

(8) *Veter zasypal moj stol lepestkami čerešni*
'The wind covered my desk with petals of a cherry-tree'.

(9) *Tvoja tabletka menja uspokoila*
'Your pill quieted me down'.

Verbs in (8) and (9) have Imperfective counterparts, so we must provide with definitions not only (8) and (9), but also (8') and (9'):

(8') *Veter zasypaet moj stol lepestkami čerešni*
'The wind is covering my desk with petals of a cherry-tree'.

(9') *Tvoja tabletka menja uspokaivaet*
'Your pill is quieting me down'.

Consider the semantic definition for (9'):

Exposition. Subject of the state is in a psychic state;

State is not normal.

I. Causer: The event took place; the factor is applied.
II. Causation: The factor caused and maintained the process in the Object; process has an inherent limit.
III. Limit of the process: Subject of the state is a psychic state: the state is normal.

(iii) Verbs with an animate Subject, which fall into three groups. Group 1 includes verbs of non-controlled causation such as *skončat'sja* '[to] die', *lišit'sja* '[to] loose', *pogibnut'* '[to] perish', *vspomnit'* '[to] recall <by chance>', and *najti* '[to] find <by chance>'. These verbs denote happenings: their Subject does not produce any action, being a passive participant of an event (a Patient of something that happens to him).

Group 2 contains verbs which imply some action or activity on the part of the Subject causing a consequence that was not intended by the Subject. As a rule, this consequence includes some non-intentional damage to the Subject or to somebody else.

Examples:
upast' '[to] fall', *ošibit'sja* '[to] make a mistake', *spotknut'sja* '[to] stumble', *uronit'* '[to] drop', *poskol'znut'sja* '[to] slip', *tolknut'* '[to] push', *promaxnut'sja* '[to] miss <a target>', *udarit'sja* '[to] strike against sth', *opozdat'* '[to] be late for', *poterjat'* '[to] loose', *svalit'sja* '[to] fall', *ušibit'sja* '[to] hurt oneself', *zadet'* '[to] touch <by chance>', *upustit'* '[to] loose/drop', *slomat'* '[to] break', *otdavit' nogu* '[to] tread on sb's foot', *nastupit' na nogu* '[to] step on sb's foot'.

The taxonomic category to which the verbs of this group belong is a happening with an acting Subject. The format of definition of these verbs also includes non-controlled causation, but it contains one additional component as compared with the format of definition of simple happenings: the component 'Subject acted with a certain purpose', which, as with actions, is not a Causer but occupies a separate zone of the format of definition called *Exposition*. The real Causer is not the Subject, but something that happened to the Subject. It is this anonymous Causer that brought about the consequence not coinciding with the purpose of the Subject's activity. Consider the definition of the verb *uronit'* '[to] drop':

First exposition: The Object had a support somehow connected with the Subject.

Second exposition: The Subject was acting with a certain Purpose

I. Causer: Sth happened to the Subject.

II. Causation (non-controlled): (I) caused (III).

III. Consequence: The Object lost its support and moved down.

III'. Subject is responsible for the damage caused.

The presence of the component 'damage' in definitions of verbs belonging to Group 2 is justified by the fact that two antonymous verbs, one of them signifying a non-intentional damage and the other a success, belong to different taxonomic categories: the former belongs to the category of happenings with an acting Subject, while the latter belongs to the category of result-oriented actions (Vendler's achievements); cf. pairs: *proigrat'* '[to] loose <a game>' [happening]–*vyigrat'* '[to] win <a game>' [achievement]; *promaxnut'sja* '[to] miss <a goal>' [happening]–*popast'* '[to] hit <a goal>' [achievement].

Group 3 contains verbs with an ambiguous meaning: they may denote, depending on the context, both actions and happenings. Here belong:

- verbs of destruction; e.g., *slomat'* '[to] break';
- verbs of deformation; e.g., *razbit'* '[to] shatter', *porvat'* '[to] tear', *porezat'* (*palec*) '[to] cut <a finger>', *razrezat'* '[to] cut <into pieces>', *razodrat'* '[to] tear', *raskolot'* '[to] crack', *razrubit'* '[to] chop <into pieces>', *otbit'* '[to] chop off', *otkolot'* '[to] chop off', *otorvat'* '[to] tear off', *probit'* '[to] break through', *prokolot'* '[to] pierce', *pognut'* '[to] bend', *sognut'* '[to] bend' (but not *razognut'* '[to] bend out'), *vyprjamit'* '[to] straighten';
- (– transitive verbs of movement; e.g., *prolit'* '[to] spill', *rassypat'* '[to] scatter', *vylit'* '[to] pour out', *vysypat'* '[to] scatter out';
- verbs denoting change of position; e.g., *oprokinut'* '[to] overturn', *perevernut'* '[to] upset', etc.

Compare controlled (10b) and non-controlled (10a) meanings of the verb *usypat'* '[to] scatter with sth' = 'to spread components of the object on the surface covering all the surface by dropping or scattering':

(10) a. *Ty usypal ves' pol kroškami*
lit. 'You have scattered all the floor with crumbs'.

b. *Ona usypala mogilu cvetami*
lit. 'She scattered the grave with flowers'.

In sentence (10c), it is not clear whether the action was intentional or what happened is an undesired or at least unneeded consequence of the Subject's activity; thus, it appears ambiguous or even strange:

(10) c. *Ya usypal pol v podvale opilkami*
lit. 'I scattered the floor in the basement with sundust'.

We interpret verbs in Group 3 as a case of regular ambiguity (in the sense of Apresjan, 1974). Meanwhile verbs of Group 2 have only one (non-controlled) meaning. Indeed, verbs of Group 2, such as *uronit'* '[to] drop', *slomat'* '[to] break', and *isportit'* '[to] damage' are used as verbs of action only on the condition of a categorial shift. Thus, in examples

(11) *Ty lomaeš' stul*
'You are breaking the chair' (from Apresjan, 1988) and

(12) *Ty portiš' mebel'* 'You are damaging the furniture',

with the verb in the Imperfective, the Speaker interprets the activity of the Subject as having a purpose which the Subject did not have in mind. Note that 'to cause' is used below in the meaning *vyzvat'* '[to] evoke', which is a momentary verb, and in the Imperfective it cannot have the meaning of the Progressive. The idea of "unfolding non-controlled causation" may be rendered by the verb *vozdejstvovat'* = 'cause and maintain a process in the Object'; it is employed in the definition of the verb *uspokaivat'* '[to] quiet down' in example (9′), Section 2.

3 Intentional (Controlled) Causation

Controlled causation takes part in the lexicographic definition of a verb that denotes an (intentional) action of a Subject capable of having a purpose (it must be a person or, sometimes, an animal); cf. *otkryt' okno* '[to] open a window' and *svit' gnezdo* '[to] make a nest'. Consider the lexicographic definition of [*to*] *kill* in Section 1. Lexicographic definitions in MTM do not make any distinction between controlled and non-controlled causation. For example, in (Apresjan, 1974:176-177), it is pointed out that controlled and non-controlled meanings of *porvat'* '[to] tear' exemplify speech ambiguity and are not lexicographically relevant. Indeed, distinctions like this one induce many inconveniences to a lexicographer, for regular ambiguity must be acknowledged for a large number of verbs (e.g., for all verbs of the Group 3 above). However, large scale regular ambiguity, if adequately represented, should not be an embarrassment for a lexicographer. On the other hand, if the distinction between actions and happenings is acknowledged we can make a number of useful generalizations concerning the combinability of lexemes and their surface behaviour. Some examples:

1. As a rule, an action verb in the Perfective Aspect (Pfv) has a corresponding Imperfective (Ipfv) with the meaning of the Progressive (Progr); compare *zakryt'* '[to] shut'—*zakryvat'* '[to] be shutting'. On the other hand, for verbs denoting happenings, such as *zametit'* '[to] notice', corresponding Ipfvs with the meaning of the Progr are excluded.

2. The acceptability of the so-called resultative interpretation of an Imperfective verb depends on whether it can denote an intentional action; see

(Paducheva, 1991). Thus, (13a) is acceptable in contrast to the anomalous (13b) where the context makes one interpret the verb as denoting a happening and not an intentional action:

(13) a. *Ja ostavljal čemodan v garderobe <poka my xodili v muzej>*
lit. 'I was leaving the suitcase in the cloak-room <while we went to the museum>'.
b. *Ja ostavljal čemodan v električke*
lit. 'I was leaving the suitcase in the train'.

3. As is known from Fillmore (1968), the argument Instrument is only possible for verbs denoting intentional <physical> actions. Thus, the notion of action is also relevant to complementation. Consider an example (after Bulygina, 1980):

(14) a. *Karenin zagorodil soboj Annu*
'Karenin hid Anna with his body'
(lit. 'Karenin blocked the access to Anna with himself')

b. ***Kamen' zagorodil soboj vxod*
lit. 'A (big) stone blocked the entrance with itself',

rather:

Kamen' zagorodil vxod
'A (big) stone blocked the entrance'.

In fact, if the situation denoted by the verb presupposes an Agent then the possessive pronoun in the Instrumental case is at place; if there is no Agent then there is no place for an Instrument.

These facts, as well as many others, demonstrate that a semantic dictionary should draw a distinction between actions and happenings, i.e., between controlled and non-controlled causation.

4 Partial Control

Let us now consider some semantic classes of verbs of action (i.e., of verbs with controlled causation). Actions may be classified on the basis of the opposition of *usual* vs. *non-complete* (= partial) control of the Subject over the situation. The lexical meaning of a verb may explicitly express the idea of non-complete control only: complete control of the Subject over the action is impossible—any action, e.g., the opening of a window, may result in failure; see (Zaliznjak, 1991). Momentary actions with guaranteed causation are an exception; see Section 5. The essence of non-complete control of the Subject over a situation consists of the idea that if the Subject has achieved the goal this means that he or she has been making attempts to achieve it and has, at last, succeeded. Thus the lexical definition for verbs denoting non-complete control should contain the element 'good luck'. Non-complete control is characteristic, for instance, of the group of verbs mentioned in (Apresjan, 1980:64), such as *rešiť* '[to] solve', *dobiť sja* '[to] get', *doždať sja* '[to] wait until the happy end', *dokazať* '[to] prove', *pojmať* '[to] catch', and the like. A peculiar feature of behaviour of these verbs is that the component 'the Subject was acting with a certain purpose' constitutes the presupposition in the meaning of a verb in the Pfv; e.g., *ne rešil* 'did not solve'–*rešal* 'had been solving, trying to solve'; *ne dobilsja* 'did not get'– *dobivalsja* 'had been trying to get'; *ne doždalsja* 'did not wait until'–*dožidalsja* 'had been waiting'; *ne pojmal* 'did not catch'–*lovil* 'had been catching, trying to catch'. This peculiarity of behaviour may be explained on semantic grounds if one acknowledges the semantic component 'X succeeded in P' as taking part in the lexical decomposition of these verbs. Indeed, 'X succeeded in P' implies:

(i) P is difficult to achieve;

(ii) X has been making attempts to achieve P (i.e., X has been acting).

Verbs of action that contain the semantic component 'attempt' are called *conatives*; see, e.g., (Tommola, 1986). The component 'success' opposes conatives to verbs denoting gradual accumulation of a property that are characterized by a component 'a certain process takes place in the object'. For a discussion of these two groups of verbs see (Maslov, 1948).

5 Guaranteed Causation

There exists a class of verbs in which the causative relation between the activity and its result is almost reduced to the identity of the action and its consequence. In such cases, we speak of *guaranteed causation*. We come across this type of causative connection, for instance, in verbs denoting speech acts. There are severe restrictions as to what can be caused by a speech act. The Speaker can:

(i) cause the Addressee to know the epistemic or volitive state (of the Speaker); for example, in stating something (cf. verb *utverždať* '[to] state'), the Speaker causes the Addressee to know the epistemic state of the Speaker (and, perhaps, is trying to change the epistemic state of the Addressee—to make him believe the Speaker's statement);

(ii) change the epistemic state of the Addressee; thus, *soobščit'* '[to] inform' = 'to cause to know' contains the component 'guaranteed causation'; hence the unacceptability of **soobščal, no ne soobščil* meaning 'informed but did not inform';

(iii) change the deontic state of the Addressee; thus, *razrešit'/zapretit'* '[to] allow/[to] forbid' = 'to cause to be able/not to be able'; here, the ability of the Subject to cause is based on a special relationship between the social or some other positions of the Speaker and the Addressee;

(iv) change the perceptive state of the Addressee; thus, the verb *pokazat'* '[to] show' may have a meaning of a momentary action causing a change of the perceptive state;

(v) to make an attempt to influence the volitive state of the Addressee; thus, *poprosit'* '[to] ask', *potrebovat'* '[to] require', etc. mean 'to make an attempt—with the help of words—to make do'.

As well, the Subject of a momentary action (not necessarily a speech act) has a number of ways to affect himself or herself:

(i) to change his own volitive state, e.g., *vybrat'* '[to] choose <lit. '[to] have chosen>), *rešit'* '[to] solve' (+ Infinitive), *predpočest'* '[to] prefer', *sčest'* '[to] consider <sb/sth to be sth>', and *peredumat'* '[to] change one's mind';

(ii) to change his own perceptual state, e.g., *predstavit' sebe* and *voobrazit'* '[to] imagine' (in contrast to *zametit'* '[to] notice', which seems to denote a happening, not an action);

(iii) to change his own epistemic state, e.g., *dogadat'sja* '[to] guess' and *uznat'* '[to] recognize', as in *Ja tebja srazu uznal* 'I recognized you immediately';

(iv) to change his own deontic state, e.g., *poobeščat'* '[to] promise' (according to Wierzbicka's analysis, causation here is based on the idea of damage expected by the Speaker if he does not fulfill his promise made in public).

Momentary acts, unlike result-oriented actions (including Vendler's achievements), do not imply any activity preceeding the transition to the resulting state.

6 Conclusion

We conclude by enumerating types of causation with paraphrases in a natural language (English, but it could also be Russian) where possible:

- intentional unfolding: 'activity of X is leading to the result Y' (as in *zakryvat' dver'* '[to] be shutting the door');
- intentional accomplished: 'activity of X has lead to the result Y' (as in *zakryvat' dver'* '[to] shut the door');
- intentional with non-complete control (as in [*to*] *solve* <*the problem*>);
- intentional guaranteed (as in [*to*] *promise*);
- non-intentional causation as a happening: 'event X evoked the consequence Y' (as in *ogorčit'* '[to] make sad');
- non-intentional unfolding: 'factor X caused and maintained a process in Y' (as in *Your pill is quieting me down*);
- non-intentional accomplished: 'factor X caused and maintained a process in Y that reached its inner limit' (as in *Your pill quieted me down*).

Bibliography

Apresjan, Ju.D. 1974. *Leksičeskaja semantika*. Moscow: Nauka. The English translation appeared as "*Lexical Semantics. User's Guide to Contemporary Russian Vocabulary*", Karoma, Ann Arbor, MI, 1992.

Apresjan, Ju.D. 1980. *Tipy informacii dlja poverxnostno-semantičeskogo komponenta modeli Smysl ⟺ Tekst* (= *Sonderband 1*). Vienna: Wiener Slawistischer Almanach.

Apresjan, Ju.D. 1988. "Glagoly momental'nogo dejstvija i performativy v russkom jazyke". *Russistika segodnja*.

Bulygina, T.V. 1980. "Grammatičeskie i semantičeskie kategorii i ix svjazi". *Aspekty semantičeskix issledovanij*. Moscow: Nauka.

Fillmore, C.J. 1968. "The Case for Case". *Universals in Linguistic Theory* ed. by E. Bach & R.T. Harms. New York: Holt, Rinehart & Wilson.

Gavrilova, V.J. 1990. *Kvazipassivnaja konstrukcija i sistem zalogovyx protivopostavlenij russkogo glagola*. Moscow: Voprosy Kibernetiki.

Maslov, Ju.S. 1948. "Vid i leksičeskoe znaženie glagola v russkom jazyke". *Izvestija Akademii nauk SSSR, Serija literatury i jazyka*. 7.4.

Mel'čuk, I.A. 1974. *Opyt teorii lingvističeskix modelej "Smysl—Tekst"*. Moscow: Nauka.

Mel'čuk, I.A. & A.K. Žolkovskij. 1984. *Explanatory Combinatorial Dictionary of Modern Russian*. Vienna: Wiener Slawistischer Almanach.

Paducheva, E.V. 1991. "K semantike nesoveršennogo vida v russkom jazyke: obščefaktičeskoe i akcional'noe značenie". *Voprosy jazykoznanija*. 6.

Tommola, H.H. 1986. "Aspektual'nost' v finskom i russkom jazykax". *Neuvostoliitto instituutin vuosikirja*. 28.

Vendler, Z. 1967. *Linguistics in Philosophy*. Ithaca: Cornell University Press.

Wierzbicka, A. 1980. *Lingua Mentalis*. Sydney etc.: Academic Press.

Wierzbicka, A. 1988. *The Semantics of Grammar* (= Studies in Language Companion Series *18*). Amsterdam & Philadelphia: Benjamins Academic Publishers.

Zaliznjak, Anna A. 1991. *Kontroliruemost' situacii v jazyke i v žizni*— *Logičeskij analiz jazyka: Modeli dejstvija*. Moscow: Nauka.

Semantic Communicative Structure of Verbal vs. Conjunctive Causative Expressions (TO KILL/TO CAUSE TO DIE vs. TO DIE BECAUSE P)

Jean St-Germain

1 Introduction

This paper considers some semantic-communicative differences in the following two pairs of expressions:

(i) between the verbal causative expression *X killed Y by P-ing Y* and the conjunctive causative expression *Y died because X P-ed Y*;

(ii) between the lexical verbal causative expression *X killed Y by P-ing Y* and its syntactic counterpart *X caused Y to die by P-ing Y*.

The majority of linguistic studies on causation deals with verbal causative expressions. Since it is impossible to comment on all the work done so far, we will just mention two studies that have singled out some criteria on which we base our discussion of lexical *vs.* syntactic verbal causative expressions: (Ruwet, 1972) and (Wierzbicka, 1975); see Section 3. Conjunctive causative expressions have been investigated to a lesser degree. See, for instance, (α 1, 1975) for the determination of the distribution of the Given/New elements in the Semantic Representation (SemR) of the French conjunction PARCE QUE 'because'.

Our discussion of sentences that include a causative expression will be valid only for English declarative sentences with such predicates as 'caus', 'die' and 'strangle', except for the discussion of *Theme* in Section 2.2, where content words such as 'Peter' and 'cat' will also be considered.

Before starting the discussion, we have to introduce the notions of *situation, situational meaning*, and *homosemy*.

A situation is a specific state of affairs perceived by a Speaker independently of how he wants to communicate it. For example, if a Speaker perceives the following situation: 'Mary causes the flat part of her hand to come violently into contact with Peter's face', he can express this situation by saying *Mary slapped Peter in the face*. For the same situation, another Speaker might say *Peter was slapped in the face by Mary*, *It was in the face that Mary slapped Peter*, etc.—depending on how he wants to express this situation. For all these different sentences the situation expressed remains the same.

The meaning that corresponds to a situation will be called *situational meaning* (see also Mel'čuk et al., 1992:11). Two sentences with the same situational meaning will be called *homosemous*, or said to be linked by a relation of *homosemy*. The term 'homosemous' is proposed instead of the term 'synonymous', which we consider distinct from the former. *X is synonymous to Y* means 'X is homosemous to Y and X has the same Semantic-Communicative Structure as Y'.

Let us now compare sentences (1a) and (1b):

(1) a. *Peter killed the cat by strangling it.*
     b. *The cat died because Peter strangled it.*

Sentence (1a) includes a verbal causative expression while sentence (1b) includes a conjunctive causative expression. Although syntactically different, these sentences are homosemous since they correspond to the same situational meaning: 'Peter strangled the cat $\xleftarrow{1}$ caus $\xrightarrow{2}$ the cat died'; see also Figure 1 in Section 2 below.

In spite of the fact that verbal causative expressions and conjunctive causative expressions can be homosemous, there are, to our knowledge, no linguistic studies on this homosemy. This seems to be partially due to two reasons:

(i) Most theories underlying studies of causative expressions are syntactically oriented (cf. the *Generative Grammar*). Within such a framework, only syntactically similar sentences are compared, independently of their semantic proximity.

(ii) Meaning is described using two-dimensional representations, such as phrase-structure trees (e.g., in *Generative Semantics* Fodor, 1977:77–81) or one-dimensional representations, either in terms of a restricted natural language like Wierzbicka (1980) or in terms of a "logical form" as in (Chomsky, 1981:34ff. and 101ff.) or in (Fodor, 1970). We think that these types of representation, by their very nature, make the comparison of homosemous but syntactically very different sentences difficult.

The present study discusses homosemy between sentences, regardless of their syntactic structure. That is why we use the terms *verbal causative expression* and *conjunctive causative expression* rather than *causative verbal expression* and *causative conjunctive expression*. In this way, their semantic similarities are highlighted rather than their syntactic differences. Thus, the expressions [to] *kill*, [to] *cause to die* and [to] *die because* will be treated equally since they are homosemous even if, from a syntactic viewpoint, the first two are quite different from the latter. In the first two expressions, the lexemes meaning (or those including the meaning) 'caus' can be syntactic heads of complete sentences (i.e., [to] *kill* and [to] *cause*), while in the last, the lexeme meaning 'caus', *because*, cannot (but [to] *die* can).

Two different semantemes are used in our work on causation: 'caus' and 'cause'. The first refers only to the relation of causation between two events while the second refers to a causing action. The expressions [to] *kill* and [to] *cause to die* include the semanteme 'cause' but not 'because'. Unlike the two first semantemes, 'because' does not refer to an event but to a relation of causation between two events. Since we want a uniform description of the meaning of [to] *kill*, [to] *cause to die* and *because*, the semanteme 'caus', which is common to all expressions, is used (see also Section 2.1).

We believe that a comparison between sentences which are homosemous but syntactically very different could make a substantial contribution to the research done on Communicative Structure, since it tackles problems of Semantic-Communicative Structure representation that a comparison made within only one syntactic type of sentences would miss. This paper gives an outline of these problems. More specifically, it describes, firstly, some communicative aspects that determine the Speaker's choice:

(i) between a verbal causative expression (e.g., [to] *kill*) and a conjunctive causative expression (e.g., [to] *die because*); and

(ii) between a lexical verbal causative expression (e.g., [to] *kill*) and its syntactic counterpart (e.g., [to] *cause to die*).

And secondly, this paper describes how these communicative aspects are distributed.

Our study of the Semantic-Communicative Structure requires an adequate semantic representation. This representation must:

(i) be able to describe the relations between semantemes independently of the relations between their corresponding lexemes,

(ii) be considered as the starting point for language generation, and

(iii) be composed of at least two structures: one describing situational meaning (the Semantic Structure) and one describing the organization of this meaning by the Speaker (the Semantic-Communicative Structure).[1] As all these characteristics appear in the *Meaning-Text Theory* (MTT), it was chosen as the framework of this study.

The two structures which make up the *Semantic Representation* (SemR) have been discussed at length in the literature on MTT; see, e.g., (Mel'čuk, 1981, 1988). Nevertheless, in order to avoid confusion, we shall characterize very briefly the concepts of *Semantic Structure* (SemS) and *Semantic-Communicative Structure* (SemCommS).

The SemS represents situational meaning. It is a network composed of semantemes (symbolized by labeled nodes) and of relations between these semantemes (symbolized by labeled arrows).

The SemCommS represents the organization of meaning by the Speaker. It is, so to speak, the itinerary followed by the Speaker across the SemS. SemCommS is composed of different substructures. Each substructure, in turn, consists of communicative elements that are opposed to one another according to given communicative aspects and divide the SemS into several parts. These communicative aspects are:

(i) specification (*Given/New/Parameter of interest*),

(ii) thematization (*Theme/Rheme*),

(iii) focalization (*Focalized/Non-focalized*), and

(iv) unitarization.

The first three aspects shall be characterized by a comparison of verbal causative expressions with conjunctional causative expressions. The last opposition, unitarization, shall be characterized by a comparison of lexical verbal causative expressions with their syntactic counterparts. Note that we seek only to determine a sufficient number of communicative aspects that enable us to distinguish between [*to*] *kill*, [*to*] *cause to die* and [*to*] *die because P*. Our SemCommSs could also include other communicative aspects like presupposition (Polguère, this volume).

---

[1]The third structure postulated by Meaning-Text Theory, the Rhetorical Structure, will not be discussed here; for further information, see (Me'čuk, 1988:59) and (Mel'čuk, 1997).

COMMUNICATIVE STRUCTURE OF CAUSATIVE EXPRESSIONS 79

2 Verbal vs. Conjunctive Causative Expressions: Specification, Thematization and Focalization

The communicative aspects that distinguish the verbal causative expressions from the conjunctive ones are: specification, thematization, and focalization. Our discussion will be based on the two homosemous sentences (1a) and (1b) from Section 1. (1a) includes a verbal causative expression and (1b) a conjunctive causative expression. For convenience, we repeat both sentences here:

(1) a. *Peter killed the cat by strangling it.*
     b. *The cat died because Peter strangled it.*

The SemS in Figure 1 corresponds to both (1a) and (1b).

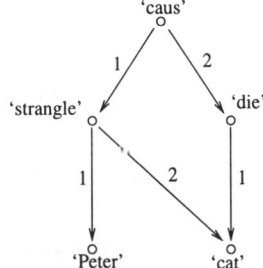

Figure 1: *SemS of the sentences (1a) and (1b)*

Specification and thematization have been studied at length in the literature on Communicative Structure; see (Sgall et al., 1986:175ff), (Mel'čuk, 1997), and (Sgall, this volume). Our discussion of these two communicative aspects is based mainly on (Halliday, 1968). The last opposition, focalization, has been discussed to a lesser extent; but, see, e.g., (Iordanskaja & Mel'čuk, 1995) and (McKeown, 1985:55–81).

2.1 Specification

In order to be able to analyze a sentence with respect to a specific communicative aspect, we must take the discourse context into account. We must determine which part of the sentence has been activated in the conversation (= new information) and which part has not (= given information) (see also Sgall, this volume on this topic). To make the opposition between *Given* and *New* clearer, let us look for questions to which the Speaker would produce either (1a) or (1b) as an answer.

Sentence (1a) answers either question (real or imaginary) (2) or (3):

(2) **Q.:** *What happened?*
(3) **Q.:** *How did Peter kill the cat?*

As an answer to question (2), sentence (1a) is entirely new to the Addressee. However, as an answer to question (3), the part of sentence (1a) which is new to the Addressee is only the complement of manner *by strangling it*. Therefore, the SemRs in Figures 2 and 3 both correspond to sentence (1a).

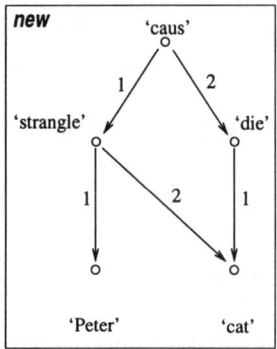

Figure 2: *SemR 1 of sentence (1a) answering question (2)*

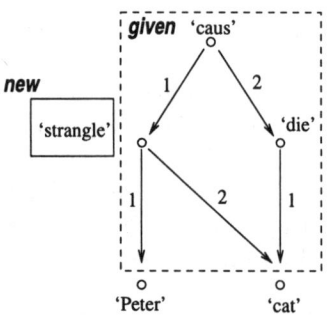

Figure 3: *SemR 2 of sentence (1a) answering question (3)*

Sentence (1b) answers either question (4) or question (5):

(4) **Q.:** *Why did the cat die?*
(5) **Q.:** *What can you say about the connection between Peter's strangling of the cat and the death of the cat?*

As an answer to question (4), the part of sentence (1b) that is new to the Addressee is the whole causal proposition *because Peter strangled it*. As an answer to (5), the situations 'the cat died' and 'Peter strangled the cat' are known to the Addressee. What is new, is the relation of cause to effect between these two situations (i.e., only the meaning that corresponds to the predicate 'caus'). Thus, if the Speaker stated that Peter strangled the cat, Mary struck it, John injected it with curare, and it died, he can produce sentence (1b) to specify that the cat's death was caused only by 'Peter's strangling of the cat'. Therefore, the SemRs of Figures 4 and 5 both correspond to sentence (1b).

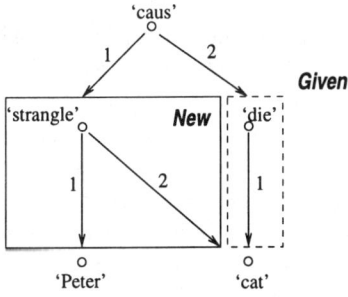

Figure 4: *SemR 1 of sentence (1b) answering question (4)*

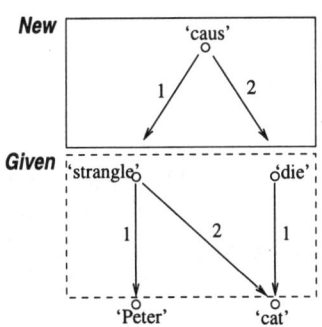

Figure 5: *SemR 2 of sentence (1b) answering question (5)*

The following characteristics of our SemRs call for some further comments: (i) the content words are not included in the Given or New areas, (ii) in Figure 3, the semanteme 'strangle' is not located in the same area as its node, and (iii) in Figure 4, the predicate 'caus' is included neither in the Given area nor in the New area.

(i) The inclusion of semantic nouns in the Given or New areas can create contradictions. For example, if in Figure 3 we include 'cat' in the specification areas, not only would this semanteme be part of the given information (*The cat died* ...), but it would also be part of the new information (... *because Peter strangled it*). The fact that a semanteme cannot be both Given and New makes us think that semantic nouns do not bear any communicative information by themselves, and that their integration into the SemCommS is fully dependent on the communicative information of their predicates.[1] For this reason, semantic nouns will always be excluded from Theme and Rheme areas. This comment is also valid for focalization.

(ii) In Figure 3, the semanteme 'strangle' is not included into the Given area but its node (the small circle near 'strangle') is. This notation reflects the fact that the verb [*to*] *kill* does not include the meaning 'strangle'; it includes, however, the 'causing' predicate. To explain this phenomenon better, it is necessary to make the nature of the predicate 'caus' more precise. The predicate 'caus' is a predicate that represents a relation between two events, a cause and an effect. More precisely, 'caus' is a predicate of a relation, such as 'and', 'or', 'if ... ', and therefore, it never denotes an event but a relation between events. Examining the meaning of the verb [*to*] *kill*, we notice that it denotes not only a relation from cause to effect ('caus') and a caused event ('die') but also a non-specified causing event ('do something'). Sentence (6) reflects this fact:

(6) *Peter kills the cat.*

Because obviously *Peter* does not denote an event, and because one cannot kill without doing something, we have no other choice than to consider [*to*] *kill* to possess the meaning 'X does something to Y $\xleftarrow{1}$ caus $\xrightarrow{2}$ Y dies' (see Vendler, 1967:165; Dowty, 1972; Wierzbicka, 1980:161–162; and Paducheva, this volume).

(iii) In Figure 4, 'caus' has not been included in either the Given or the New area for the following reason: before the Speaker produces sentence (1b), the Addressee might or might not know that there was a relationship of cause and effect between *the cat died* (which he already knew) and another event (unknown to him). However, he is likely to have asked the Speaker the question (4) repeated in (7) in order to ask him whether there is a relationship, presupposing, in a way, that there is one.

(7) *Why did the cat die?*

This kind of information, which is neither Given nor New, will be called, following (Iordanskaja, 1992), *the parameter of interest*. The parameter of interest can be characterized as being the aspect under which the given information is considered.

2.2 Thematization

The thematization substructure is composed of two communicative elements: Theme and Rheme. The term 'Theme' has various interpretations in the linguistic literature and has sometimes been presented as equivalent to Given. This is not the case in our work. We will make the distinction between Theme and Given, following Halliday:

> The difference between *theme* and *given* can be summarized by the observation that, while 'given' means 'what I/you was/were talking about', 'theme' means 'what I am talking about now'. (Halliday, 1968:212)

More precisely, we shall consider Theme as being that part of SemS the Speaker is talking about. Thematized meaning should not be confused with focalized meaning (see Subsection 2.3) or contrasting meaning.

A Speaker may either speak about a specific part of the situation or the whole situation. In the latter case, since the whole situation is new to the Addressee, there is no part of the corresponding SemS that can be considered as the Theme: one cannot talk about something the Addressee does not know yet. However, this does not mean, of course, that if there is no Theme in the SemS, there is no one on the conceptual level either (Iordanskaja, 1992:16). Since our study is semantically oriented, when we say that a sentence has no Theme, we mean only that there is no Theme at the semantic level.

At the syntactic level, the lexeme corresponding to a (neutral) Theme occupies the first position in a sentence. The choice of active or passive voice as well as the choice of the proper lexeme among a set of conversives depends on which semantic actant corresponds to the lexeme in the first position. When a SemR does not include a Theme, the active is used. As for the choice of a lexeme among conversives, the one which can be in the active voice shall be the one chosen by default if the corresponding SemR does not have any Theme. Let us consider sentences (8a) to (8e).

(8) a. *Mary gave a vase to Peter.*

b. *A vase was given to Peter by Mary.*
c. *Peter was given a vase by Mary.*
d. *Mary sent a vase to Peter.*
e. *Peter received a vase from Mary.*

In (8a) and (8d), there is either no Theme or the Theme is *Mary*; in (8b), the Theme is *vase*; and in (8c) and (8e), the Theme is *Peter*.

Let us now come back to the SemS represented in Figure 1. If the Speaker wants to talk about Peter, or if he does not want to talk about a specific entity but about the whole event, then he has to produce sentence (1a) (or another appropriate sentence). However, if the Speaker wants to talk about the caused event 'the cat died', he has to produce sentence (1b) (or another appropriate sentence). In the SemR of sentence (1b), the Theme is the whole effect, that is, 'the cat died'. Nevertheless, since sentence (1b) includes two propositions with a head in the active voice, each proposition can (but does not have to) have a sub-Theme which would be their respective Subject. To simplify the discussion, we shall ignore such cases.

In the linguistic literature, Theme is usually opposed to Rheme (especially in the Prague school's literature; cf. Sgall et al., 1986:175–176). We will define Rheme as what the Speaker says about the Theme. Unlike Theme, Rheme can never correspond to semantic nouns such as *Peter* and *cat*, but only to predicates. This is because when the Speaker says something about an entity, he always predicates an event, a characteristic, an existence, or a relation—never an entity. So, from thematization's point of view, the SemR in Figure 6 (with or without a Theme) will correspond to sentence (1a), and the SemR in Figure 7 will correspond to sentence (1b).

2.3 *Focalization*

To illustrate the notion of focalization, we will use the following two sentences:

(9) a. *Mary eats while watching television.*
 b. *Mary watches television while eating.*

The SemRs of sentences (9a) and (9b) have identical SemSs and can be communicatively identical from the viewpoint of specification and thematization. More precisely, for both sentences, the conveyed information can be entirely new, and the Theme is either *Mary* or there is no Theme. However, the SemCommSs of these two sentences show a difference in focalization. We will characterize focalization following (Iordanskaja & Mel'čuk, 1995):

COMMUNICATIVE STRUCTURE OF CAUSATIVE EXPRESSIONS 85

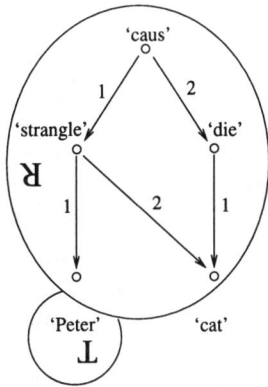

Figure 6: *SemR of sentence (1a)*

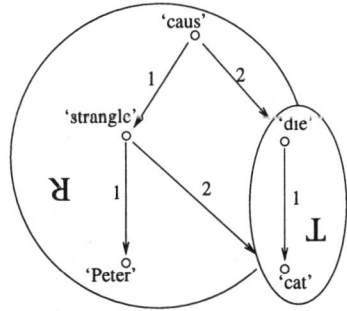

Figure 7: *SemR of sentence (1b)*

... focalization is MARKING OUT a part of the SemS as a specific target of the state of affairs [situation, in our terminology] being reported through this SemS—as if a spotlight were focused on an element of a painting in order to indicate that what is represented on the painting is, so to speak, "happening" to this element ...

Let us turn back to sentences (9a) and (9b). If the Speaker wants to talk about Mary's bad digestion, which could result from watching television, he will produce (9a) (or another appropriate sentence). 'Mary eats' is focalized because it is the specific target of the situation reported through Mary's *watching television*. However, if the Speaker wants to talk about the lack of attention paid to the television program, which could result from eating, he will produce (9b) (or another appropriate sentence). 'Mary's watching television' is focalized because it is the specific target of the situation reported through *Mary eats*. At the syntactic level, a focalized meaning is rendered by a main clause while a non-focalized meaning is rendered by a subordinate clause.

With respect to focalization, the sentences (1a) and (1b) differ in the following way. In the meaning of sentence (1a), the focalized meaning is '(Peter) did something $\xleftarrow{1}$ caus $\xrightarrow{2}$ (the cat) died' because it has been marked out as the specific target of 'the cat dies'. '(Peter) strangled (the cat)' is the non-focalized meaning because it is what has been reported about the focalized meaning. In the meaning of sentence (1b), however, the focalized meaning is 'the cat died' while the non focalized meaning is 'because (Peter) strangled (the cat)'. Therefore, the SemCommSs of (1a) and (1b) correspond respectively to Figures 8 and 9. In these figures, the big '**1**' means 'focalized' and the big '**2**' means 'non-focalized'.

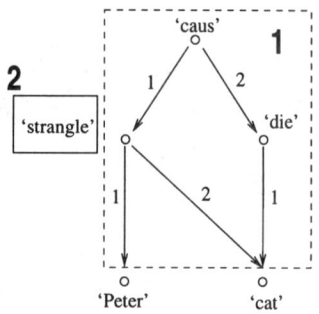

Figure 8: *SemR of sentence (1a)*

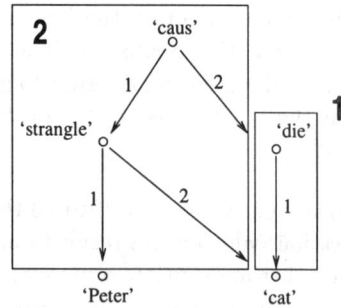

Figure 9: *SemR of sentence (1b)*

3 Lexical vs. Syntactic Verbal Causative Expressions: Unitarization

The communicative differences between lexical verbal causative expressions and their syntactic counterparts are minor compared to those between verbal causatives and the conjunctive causative expressions. In fact, the distribution of the communicative oppositions in sentence (1a) discussed so far would be also valid for sentence (16). Cf.:[2]

(1) a. *Peter killed the cat by strangling it.*

(16) *Peter caused the cat to die by strangling it.*

The Speaker's choice between (1a) and (16) depends on whether he considers the situation corresponding to 'Peter strangled the cat $\xleftarrow{1}$ caus $\xrightarrow{2}$ the cat died' as a whole or as composed of several parts. This meaning will be said to be *unitarized* in the first case and *non-unitarized* in the second case. Several factors determine the Speaker's choice between unitarized and non-unitarized meaning. They will not be discussed here in depth; for further discussion, see (Ruwet, 1972; Wierzbicka, 1975; St-Germain, 1988). Nevertheless, we will briefly explain two of these factors: unity of time and unity of place, in order to justify our claim that the difference between (1a) and (16) lies in the SemCommS rather than in the SemS.

Unity of time and unity of place can be roughly characterized as follows. A set of events possesses a unity of time and place if all events included in this set happen within a span of time and at a physical distance that is minimal for the set of events in question. As for (1a) and (16), it can be noticed that, generally, sentences including [*to*] *kill* express a greater unity of time and place than those that include [*to*] *cause to die*. Thus, in sentence (1a), there is a higher probability that 'Peter's strangling' and 'the death of the cat' occur practically at the same time and location than in sentence (16). Since unity of time and place is part of the perceived world, it should intuitively be denoted by situational meaning and therefore should be represented in the SemS. However, if we look at the differences between (1a) and (16), they seem to be radically different from those between (1a) and (17):

---

[2]These two sentences constitute a slightly modified version of the English sentences *Peter killed the cat in the attic* and *Peter caused the cat to die in the attic*, discussed by Wierzbicka (1975).

(17)   Mary killed the cat by strangling it.

Due to the fact that Peter and Mary are different persons, sentences (1a) and (17) can never denote the same situation. But sentences (1a) and (16) can. Of course, the stronger unity of time and place in the situation 'Peter strangled the cat $\xleftarrow{1}$ caus $\xrightarrow{2}$ the cat died', the higher the probability of sentence (1a) to be produced. But a situation that possesses a weak unity of time and place does not automatically correspond to a sentence which includes a syntactic verbal causative expression. The Speaker's choice of a sentence ultimately depends on the way he considers the situation. Thus, a sentence including [to] kill can be produced even if the event is far from having a real unity of time and place. For example, if a surgeon is to be blamed for the death of a patient because the operation was badly performed, this patient's mother could blame the surgeon by producing (18) even if the death occurred one week after the operation and in a hospital located a hundred miles from the one where the operation was performed.

(18)   You killed my son.

The psychological impact is such that the Speaker considers the whole event as one "block". As a matter of fact, if the Speaker wants to focus on the result rather than on the event itself, he will choose a lexical verbal expression instead of its syntactic counterpart, as if the event constitutes a block into which he cannot look. On the contrary, scientists studying the death of cats could say (19) even if their action and the death of the cat took place practically at the same time and place:

(19)   Today, we caused three cats to die.

The scientists' intention is not to get rid of the cats (= result) but to observe the phenomenon of their dying (= event). In fact, if the Speaker wants to focus on the event itself rather than on the result, he will choose a syntactic verbal expression. The syntactic verbal expressions tend to be used in less normal or less usual contexts where it is important to stress each part of the event.[2]

The fact that the choice of sentence (1a) or sentence (16) depends on the Speaker's intentions rather than on the situation leads us to consider the difference between (1a) and (16) as being a communicative one. In the SemS of sentence (1a), unitarization of '(do something) $\xleftarrow{1}$ caus $\xrightarrow{2}$ to die' shall be represented in the SemCommS, as shown in Figure 10),

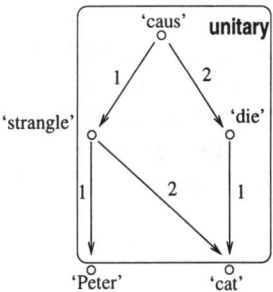

Figure 10: *SemR of sentence (1a)*

whereas there will not be any unitarization in the SemS of sentence (16); see Figure 1.

The notion of unitarization as a communicative element has not yet been discussed in the linguistic literature and is, thus, presented here for the first time.

4 Conclusion

Even though it is difficult to draw any valid conclusion from such a poor sample of SemRs as obtained from the oppositions discussed above, we can notice, however, that the unitarization block is indivisible. In other words, there is no frontier of any semantic communicative block that crosses the unitarization block. But this holds true (and must hold true!) only if we draw a clear distinction between non-specified and specified 'causing' predicates. There is no other predicate in our sample of representations that would also require this distinction.

The indivisibility of the unitarization block, along with the strong influence of situational meaning on the unitarization of a meaning, leads us to assign a special status to this communicative element.

Acknowledgements

Consecutive drafts of this paper have been read by and discussed with Igor Mel'čuk. I thank him from my heart for his suggestions and criticisms. I would also like to thank Sarah Anderson for having improved the English.

This paper is a part of my PhD Thesis (St-Germain, 1995) on the semantic representation of causative expressions in French, which has been made possible in part by scholarships from the *Social Sciences and Humanities Research Council of Canada* [no. 752-91-0207] and *The Association of Universities and Colleges of Canada* [no. 06.05U URSS]. I have replaced the French examples with the English equivalents since there seem to be no significant differences at the communicative level between the English expressions [*to*] *kill*/[*to*] *die because* and their French equivalents.

Endnotes

[1] The possible double communicative dependency of semantic nouns could be compared with the possible double morphological dependency of French adjectives, which can be controlled by several nouns of different genders (masculine and feminine) like in *Cette banane* [f.s.], *cette pomme* [f.s.] *et ce concombre* [m.s.] *sont verts* [m.p]. 'This banana, this apple and this cucumber are green'. Although the adjective *vert* 'green' agrees with several nouns of different genders, one cannot say that *vert* is both masculine and feminine. Like French adjectives, which do not bear any gender but just agree, semantic nouns do not bear any communicative information, they just "agree".

[2] The fact that syntactic verbal expressions tend to be used in less normal contexts than lexical verbal expressions is reflected by their lower frequency. From a corpus of French newspapers (*La Presse*) at the University of Montreal, only seventeen occurrences of *faire mourir* 'cause [to] die' were found against 1498 occurrences of *tuer* '[to] kill'.

Bibliography

α 1, Group. 1975. "Car, parce que, puisque". *Revue Romane*. 2.10:248–280.

Chomsky, N. 1981. *Lectures on Government and Binding*. Dordrecht: Foris.

Dowty, D.R. 1972. "On the Syntax and Semantics of the Atomic Predicate CAUSE". *Proceedings of the Chicago Linguistic Society, Volume 8* ed. by P.M. Peranteau, J.N. Levi & G.C. Phares. Chicago: Chicago University Press.

Fodor, J.D. 1970. "Three Reasons for not Deriving "kill" from "cause to die" ". *Linguistic Inquiry*. 1.4:429–438.

Fodor, J.D. 1977. *Semantics: Theories of Meaning in Generative Grammar*. Cambridge: Harvard University Press.

Halliday, M.A.K. 1968. "Notes on Transitivity and Theme in English— Part 2". *Journal of Linguistics*. 3.2:199–244.

Iordanskaja, L. 1992. "Communicative Structure and its Use during Text Generation". *International Forum on Information and Documentation.* 17.2:15-27.

Iordanskaja, L. & I. Mel'čuk. 1995. "Glaza Mashi golubye em vs. Glaza u Mashi golubye: Choosing between two Russian Constructions in the Domain of Body Parts". *The Language and Verse in Russia* ed. by H. Birnbaum & M.S. Flier. 147-171. Moscow: Vostočnaya Literature Publishers.

McKeown, K.R. 1985. *Text Generation: Using Discourse Strategies and Focus Constraints to Generate Natural Language Text.* Cambridge, England: Cambridge University Press.

Mel'čuk, I.A. 1981. "Meaning-Text Models: A Recent Trend in Soviet Linguistics". *Annual Review of Anthropology.* 10:27-62.

Mel'čuk, I.A. 1988. *Dependency Syntax: Theory and Practice.* Albany: State University of New York Press.

Mel'čuk, I.A. 1997. *The Communicative Structure in Language.* Technical report: Département de Linguistique et de Traduction, Université de Montréal.

Mel'čuk, I.A. (with N. Arbatchewsky-Jumarie, L. Iordanskaja & S. Mantha). 1992. *Dictionnaire explicatif et combinatoire du français contemporain, Volume III.* Montréal, Canada: Presses de l'Université de Montréal.

Ruwet, N. 1972. *Théorie syntaxique et syntaxe du français.* Paris: Éditions du Seuil.

Sgall, P., E. Hajičová & J. Panevová. 1986. *The Meaning of the Sentence in Its Semantic and Pragmatic Aspects.* Dordrecht: Reidel Publishing Company.

St-Germain, J. 1988. *Etude sémantico-syntaxique des expressions verbales causatives en français contemporain.* Master's thesis. Montréal: Département de linguistique, Université de Montréal.

St-Germain, J. 1995. *Incidence de la structure sémantique et communicative sur la structure syntaxique profonde des énoncés causatifs du français contemporain.* PhD thesis. Montréal: Département de linguistique, Université de Montréal.

Vendler, Z. 1967. *Linguistics in Philosophy.* Ithaca: Cornell University Press.

Wierzbicka, A. 1975. "Why "kill" Does not Mean "cause to die" ". *Foundations of Language*. 13.4:491–528.

Wierzbicka, A. 1980. *Lingua Mentalis*. Sydney etc.: Academic Press.

Theme, Rheme, and Communicative Structure in Lushootseed and Bella Coola

David Beck

1 Introduction

The Salishan family of languages—which encompasses some twenty-three languages spoken over a broad geographic area extending from the Pacific Ocean across Southern British Columbia, Washington State and Idaho as far east as the Rocky Mountains of Montana—constitutes the largest of the language families of the Pacific Northwest, with a time-depth estimated at between two and five thousand years (Kroeber, 1991). Because of their unique and rather unusual grammars, individual languages of the family have received widely varied and often idiosyncratic treatment in the literature (cf. Davis & Saunders, 1978; Kinkade, 1983; Jelinek & Demers, 1994), yet they are readily identifiable as group by a wide range of morphological and lexical features that they have in common, and it is worth asking if there might not be some common principles at work in the syntax as well. An examination of two of the most distantly related Salishan languages, Bella Coola and Lushootseed (a.k.a. Puget Salish), reveals deep-seated similarities in the organizing principles used to build sentences, which revolve not so much around issues of lexical category as around "thematic" (Halliday, 1970) or "communicative" (Mel'čuk, 1997) structure—in particular, the organization of the utterance into Theme and Rheme. This is especially true of so-called "verbless" sentences, or sentences with non-verbal predicates. In these structures, the syntactic predicate corresponds to the Rheme (referred to in some traditional grammars as the "semantic predicate" Sandmann, 1979), while the syntactic Subject is thematic and almost invariably a discourse topic. This pattern is also reflected in the syntax of Wh-questions in both languages, which are realized as verbless sentences whose syntactic predicate is the Wh-element itself, thereby eliciting replies in which the new, requested information is predicate and the thematic information contained in the question is realized syntactically as a complex clausal Subject. In addition, Lushootseed forms "existential" negatives (verbless sentences whose predicate is a negative adverb), which are used to negate a thematic element, most likely an assumption or presupposition held in discourse up until the point of utterance. Overall, what seems to be at work in these languages is a pattern whereby the communicative structure is the primary organizing principle of the syntax, the division of the sentence into Theme and Rheme being the determining factor in the choice of syntactic predicate; from a typological point of view, these languages present a fascinating contrast with the more familiar patterns found in Indo-European languages, a contrast which is captured nicely by analysis of the data from a Meaning-Text perspective.

2 Subject and Predicate

One of the most striking features of languages of the Salishan family—including Bella Coola and Lushootseed—is the tremendous flexibility that they show vis-à-vis the syntactic roles open to members of various lexical categories, something which has led a number of researchers (e.g., Kuipers, 1968; Kinkade, 1983; Jelinek & Demers, 1994) to propose that these languages lack an underlying distinction between nouns and verbs. While this position has been argued against elsewhere (van Eijk & Hess, 1986; Davis & Matthewson, 1995; Beck, 1995a), it is true that lexical category is not a reliable indicator of potential syntactic roles and, most significantly here, that members of almost any lexical category may act as syntactic predicates, creating a wide variety of "verbless" sentences. While these sentences might appear exotic to speakers of English, they are, in fact, not unique cross-linguistically: verbless sentences, even those with nominal predicates and complex clausal Subjects, are attested in a number of languages and language families other than Salish, although this fact seems to have been overlooked both by Salishanists and by syntacticians, among whom there has been a serious lack of attention to the theoretical treatment of such structures. Following a brief grammatical outline of the canonical clause in Lushootseed and Bella Coola in Section 2.1, I will turn my attention in Section 2.2 to precisely this issue, the syntactic organization of the verbless sentence, in order to set the stage for the discussion of its communicative structure and its semantics in Section 3 below.

2.1 The Canonical Clause

The structure of the canonical clause in Bella Coola and Lushootseed is well-described in grammatical terms in the principal sources on both languages (for Lushootseed: Hess, 1976, 1993; Bates et al., 1994; for Bella Coola: Davis & Saunders, 1978, 1980, 1984; Nater, 1984), although the terminology used in these sources is not always the terminology that will be used in this paper. As are other Salishan languages, Lushootseed and Bella Coola are usually predicate-initial, the unmarked sentence consisting of a finite verb followed immediately by its syntactic actants. Consider the data in (1):[1]

(1) a. Lushootseed

   ʔu+ʔəy̓+dxʷ   čəd tsi čačas
   [pnt]+find+[l.o.c.] 1s Df child
   'I found the girl'
                                          (Hess, 1993:24)

   b. Bella Coola

   k̓x+is   ti / ʔimlk+tx ci+xnus+cx
   see+3s-3s D+man+D D+woman+D
   'the man sees the woman'
                                  (Davis & Saunders, 1978:38)

As shown in (1a), the unmarked word-order in Lushootseed is predicate-pronominal-NP; in matrix clauses, Lushootseed verbs show no agreement for either Subject or Object, whereas Bella Coola verbs show both Subject and Object agreement using a set of portmanteau Object-Subject suffixes, as in (1b). Bella Coola adheres closely to a VSO word-order, which is used to mark the syntactic roles of third-person actants—the first of two NPs following the verb representing the syntactic Subject. While Lushootseed shows essentially the same order of syntactic elements, matters are complicated by some additional factors. Adverbial particles (adverbs that are not serving as predicates) are realized in sentence-initial position, as in (2):

(2) a. hikʷ čəxʷ ʔu   x̌u+x̌əɬ+qid
        big   2s   [int] [hab]+sick+head
        'do you generally get severe headaches?'
                                          (Hess, 1993:115)

---

[1] The abbreviations used here are listed at the end of this paper; predicates will be underlined in examples throughout for purposes of exposition.

b. ɬu+hikʷ čəd stubš ɬu+luʔx̌+il+əd
   [irr]+big 1s man [irr]+old+[trm]+1s-subordinate
   'I'm going to be a big man when I grow up'
   (Hess, 1976:191)

Both sentences here begin with the adverb *hikʷ* 'big', while their predicates—the verb *x̌əɬqid* 'have a headache' in (2a) and the noun *stubš* 'man' in (2b)—appear later in the clause, following the Subject pronominals (*čəxʷ* and *čəd*) and other particles such as the interrogative *ʔu*, which as a group are obligatorily sentence-second. The second, and more pervasive, factor affecting Lushootseed word-order is a constraint against the expression of two third-person NP actants unless one of these is realized as a prepositional phrase, as in middle forms (3a) or passives (3b):[1]

(3) a. ʔu+gʷəč+əb   ti luʔx̌ ʔə ti sqəlalitut
       [pnt]+look·for+[md] D old P D guardian·spirit
       'the old man quested for a guardian spirit'
    b. ʔu+gʷəč+t+əb   ʔə ti čačas tsi čačas
       [pnt]+look·for+[caus]+[md] P D child Df child
       'the boy looked for the girl'
       (lit. 'the girl was looked for by the boy')
                                          (Hess, 1993:43–44)

Outside of such constructions, one of the third-person actants is obligatorily elided (that is, removed by the surface-syntactic component), most likely a result of the absence of case-marking or rigid word-order requirements to differentiate the roles of NPs in a clause. This results in sentences such as that in (4) with two fully recoverable semantic arguments but only one overt NP actant:

(4) ʔu+šuu+c   tiʔiɬ sqʷəlaɬəd
    [pnt]+see+[appl] D berry
    '[he] looked at the berry'
                                          (Hess, 1993:193)

Which actant is elided (or surfaces as a PP) is determined by the verbalizing suffix on the stem: agent-orienting suffixes (such as -*m* "[middle]" in (3a)) create intransitive verbs in which the agentive actant will be realized, whereas patient-orienting suffixes (such as -*c* "[applicative]") transitivize the stem and force the elision of the Subject in favour of the Direct Object (unless the Subject is a first- or second-person pronominal, as in (1a)). In such sentences, the identity of the elided Subject NP is unambiguous and fully recoverable from discourse by dint of the fact that in Lushootseed, as in all Salishan languages, Subjects are almost inevitably equated with discourse topics (Kinkade, 1990).[2]

While Bella Coola does not have the same type of constraint against overt realization of actants that Lushootseed does, it is true that no Bella Coola clause admits more than two third-person NPs—that is, Subject and Direct Object, the "direct" actants:

(5) <u>tx+is</u>   ti+ƛ̓msta+tx ti+qlsxʷ +tx x+ti+tq̓ɬa+tx
    cut+3s-3s D+person+D D+rope+D P+D+knife+D
    'the person cut the rope with the knife'
    (Davis & Saunders, 1984:212)

In (5), the actant introduced by the prepositional clitic x- is considered to be "peripheral" in the sense that it is construed to be a less salient feature of the event as it is being described by the Speaker than are the Subject and Object (Davis & Saunders, 1984).[3] Thus, the relative saliency of event participants can be manipulated by changes in voice, as in (6):

(6) a. <u>tx+im</u>   ti+qslsxʷ +tx x+ti+ƛ̓msta+tx
       cut+3s-[pass] D+rope+D P+D+person+D
       x+ti+tq̓ɬa+tx
       P+D+knife+D
       'the rope was cut with the knife by the person'
    b. <u>tx+a+ø</u>   ti+ƛ̓msta+tx x+ti+qslsxʷ +tx
       cut+[ap]+3s D+person+D P+D+rope+D
       x+ti+tq̓ɬa+tx
       P+D+knife+D
       'the person cut through the rope with the knife'
    c. <u>tx+amk+is</u>   ti+ƛ̓msta+tx ti+tq̓ɬa+tx
       cut+[op]+3s-3s D+person+D D+knife+D
       ʔuɬ+ti+qslsxʷ +tx
       P+D+rope+D
       'the person used a knife to cut the rope'
       (Davis & Saunders, 1984:213–214)

---

[2]The properties of these actants that identify them as Subjects are discussed in detail in Beck (1996).

[3]The term "peripheral" is borrowed from Davis and Saunders (1984), where it has much the same meaning as it has here, although the distinction for these writers is a semantic rather than a syntactic one.

In each of the above examples, the same event is described from a different perspective, underscoring the role of certain actants and de-emphasizing the role of others. Similar principles hold in Lushootseed, and in both languages the issue of construal and peripherality of clausal participants is closely bound to issues such as rhematicity and discourse structure, although a detailed exploration of these aspects of the grammar will have to be left for future investigation.

2.2 *Verbless Sentences*

The verbless sentence is a sentence with a syntactic predicate that is a member of any major lexical category other than a verb. One of the more common types of these is the sentence with a nominal predicate, as in (7):

(7) a. Lushootseed

s?uladx^w ti?ł
salmon D
'that [is] a salmon'

(Hess & Hilbert, 1976:I,7)

b. Bella Coola

mna+ł
child+1p
'we [are] children'[4]

(Nater, 1984:36)

Both languages also have a set of emphatic pronouns that are inherently rhematic and act as syntactic predicates, thereby conforming to the pattern described by Jelinek (in press):

(8) a. Lushootseed

?əca k^{w}i łu+k^{w}əda+t+əb
1s D [irr]+take+[caus]+[md]
'the one who will be taken [is] me'

(Bates et al., 1994:10)

---

[4]In Bella Coola, the intransitive person-suffixes have collapsed into a single paradigm with the possessives; the same phrase headed by a deictic—*wa+mna+ł*—would be glossed as 'our children'.

b. Bella Coola

?inu ci+xnas+c
2s   D+wife+1po
'YOU [are] my wife'
(Nater, 1984:112)

Sentences with adjectival predicates are also well-attested:

(9) a. Lushootseed

ləʔ+q̓əd   čəd
[prog]+slow 1s
'I [am going] slow'
(Bates et al., 1994:183)

b. Bella Coola

ƛk̓ʷ+ø+tu   ta+smɬk ta+k̓x+ic
big+3s+indeed D+fish   D+see+3s-1s
?ala?awa
across-the-street
'the fish that I saw across the street [was] indeed big'
(Davis & Saunders, 1984:222)

With the exception of a class of transitive roots in Bella Coola, verbs in these languages are derived morphologically from adjectival radicals (Beck 1996), many of which are semantically equivalent to English verbs and form verbless, predicate-adjective sentences such as those in (10):

(10) a. Lushootseed

?u+pus   čəd
[pnt]+be·hit·by·flying·object 1s
'I [was] struck (by a flying object)'
(Hess & Hilbert, 1976:II,136)

b. Bella Coola

plikm+ap
capsized+2p
'you folks [are] capsized'
(Nater, 1984:36)

Verbless sentences may also have adverbs (11) and numerals (12) as syntactic predicates:

(11) a. Lushootseed

    tudiʔ   tə dukʷibəɬ
    way·over·there D Changer
    'Changer [is] way over there'

                                                        (Hess, 1993:103)

b. Bella Coola

    x̌iliwa+ø s+ʔmt+s
    quick+3s np+get·up+3s
    'he [was] quick as he got up'

                                                        (Nater, 1984:37)

(12) a. Lushootseed

    saliʔ tiʔəʔ sqʷigʷac
    two   D   deer
    'the deer [are] two'

                                                        (Hess, 1993:103)

b. Bella Coola

    smaw+liƛ+ø ti+nup+c
    one+skin+3s D+shirt+1s
    'my shirt [is] one'

                                                      (Nater, 1984:119)

Finally, in Lushootseed, prepositional phrases can also be predicates, as in (13):

(13)   *dxʷʔal* tə hud   tə s+xʷiƛ+il   ʔə tə biac
       P   D burning D np+fall+[trm] P D meat
       'the meat fell into the fire'
       (lit. 'the falling of the meat [is/was] into the fire')

                                                        (Kroeber, 1991:224)

In Bella Coola, however, it appears that only temporal PPs can play this role in the sentence (Kroeber, 1991)—with a few possible exceptions (Beck 1995a). One remarkable feature of the verbless sentence in Lushootseed and Bella Coola, however, is the way in which what is generally thought of as "verbal" morphology such as agreement features or pronominal clitics appears associated with a non-verbal predicate. This is quite obvious in Bella Coola, where all predicates bear intransitive Subject agreement (as in (7b) and (10b)), and also occurs in some Lushootseed subordinate clauses, which use a special series of Subject-clitics, as in the following example:

(14) ha?ɬ ti sq̓ədᶻu? ʔə ti sɬəɬq̓ʷi?
good D hair   P D bufflehead-drake
gʷə+sq̓əq̓dᶻu?+əs
[subj]+hair+3s-subordinate
'the drake bufflehead's hair [is] pretty, if it is hair'
(Hess, 1993:95)

This pattern is unusual, but it is not unique, being attested in languages such as Buriat:

(15) ferme daagša bi+b
farm manager 1+1s
'the farm-manager [is] me'
(Bertagaev & Tsydendambaev, 1962:58)

and Beja (a Cushitic language of Sudan), where a pronominal clitic agreeing in gender and number with the syntactic Subject is added to the nominal predicate:[5]

(16) a. ti+kʷ aa+t+oo+'k=t+u
D+sister+f+[gen]+2s=f+3s
'she [is] your sister'
(Hudson, 1974:126)

b. wí+ʔaandà gʷ a?+ee+n+è   búun=u
[rel]+men drink+[part]+3p+[rel] coffee=3s
'what men drink [is] coffee'
(Hudson, 1974:117)

The second example in (16), a verbless copular construction with a clausal (in this case, participial) Subject, is of particular interest to us here as a sentence-type. Such sentences are found in a wide variety of other languages such as Mongolian (Poppe 1970), Kalmyk, Even, Nanay, Ul'ch, Udeg, Aleut, Nivkh, and Ket (Skorik, 1968) and are also well-attested in Salish languages—including Lushootseed and Bella Coola. Compare (16b) with (17a,b) for Lushootseed and with (18a,b) for Bella Coola.

---

[5] The equals sign is used in these examples to mark the morphological boundaries of the pronominal clitic. Hudson analyzes these clitics as copular verbs, although beyond their use in this type of construction there seems to be nothing inherently verbal about them.

(17) a. _wiw̓su_ ti ʔu+čalad   tiʔəʔ sqʷəbayʔ
children D [pnt]+chase D   dog
'those chasing the dog [are] children'
(Hess, 1993:127)

b. _sʔuladxʷ_ tiʔəʔ _s_+u+ʔəɬəd   ʔə tiʔiɬ pišpiš
salmon D   np+[pnt]+eat P D   cat
'what the cat eats [is] a salmon'[6]
(Hess, 1993:133)

(18) a. _ti+sx̌ax̌t+kʷ_
D+caribou+[qt]
ti+nu+yaxʷ+im+kʷ+alu+č
D+[agt]+call·to·do+3s-[pass]+[qt]+[att]+[perf]
aɬ+tx̌ʷ
P+then
'the one they tried to call to do it then [was] the caribou'
(Davis & Saunders, 1980:90, line 33)

b. _p̓wi_   ti+_s_+pux̌+aylayx+aw
halibut D+np+(to)fish+[l.o.c.]+3p
'what they caught [is] a halibut'
(Nater, 1984:102)

In (17a) and (18a), the syntactic predicate corresponds to a direct actant—either Subject or Direct Object—of the clausal syntactic Subject, which takes the form of a relative clause headed by a pronominal deictic element (Beck 1995a); I will refer to such forms as "syntactic nominalizations" (a nominal created by the syntax from a clause). However, in (17b) and (18b), the predicative nominal corresponds to a peripheral actant (oblique Object) of the Subject clause, and so this clause is nominalized morphologically with the prefix _s-_ (underlined).[2] By using the strategies of syntactic and morphological nominalization, it is possible for Bella Coola and Lushootseed to create complex clausal Subjects and put almost any element of an utterance into predicate position, with little or no regard for its lexical category—thus creating a wide variety of verbless sentences and, as we will see below, allowing sentences to be built on communicative, rather than purely syntactic, principles of organization.

---

[6]The verb _ʔəɬəd_ 'to eat', like the Bella Coola _pux̌aylayx_ 'to fish' in (18b), is intransitive, the English Direct Object being realized as an oblique or peripheral actant in the Salish sentences.

3 Theme, Rheme, and Syntactic Structure

This remarkable potential for almost anything in Lushootseed and Bella Coola to serve as syntactic predicate raises an important question: if it is not lexical category that conditions the syntactic role of a given word in the sentence, then what is it that determines which element will surface as the syntactic predicate? For Bella Coola, Davis and Saunders (1978) claim that choice of predicate is dependent on the communicative structure of the sentence—in particular, what information is rhematic (or, in their terms, 'Comment') and what is thematic ('Topic'). These authors find this pattern so pervasive in the language that in their early work they attempt to substitute 'Topic' and 'Comment' for standard syntactic categories in the construction of tree-diagrams; although they seem to have abandoned this practice in later writings, the original insight remains: simply put, any element that is strongly rhematic in Bella Coola is inevitably realized as a syntactic predicate. Consider the question-and-answer frames in (19):

(19) a. *ʔalacix^w +ø+ʔiks   ci+xnas+cx*
do·what+3s+[int] D+woman+D
'what is the woman doing?'
sp̓+is   ci+xnas+cx   ti+ʔimlk+tx
hit+3s-3s D+woman+D D+man+D
'the woman is hitting the man'

b. *wa+ø+ks   ti+sp̓+is   ci+xnas+cx*
who+3s+[int] D+hit+3s-3s D+woman+D
'who did the woman hit?'
(lit. 'the one the woman hit [was] who?')
ti+ʔimlk+tx ti+sp̓+is   ci+xnas+cx
D+man+D D+hit+3s-3s D+woman+D
'the one the woman hit [is] the man'
(Davis & Saunders, 1978:39)[7]

Here the question in (19a) elicits a 'narratively focused' sentence (that is, a sentence typical of a narrative sequence focused on the flow of events rather than on the introduction of a new participant). On the other hand, the question in (19b) asks for the identity of a particular participant in an

---

[7]Both of these frames are presented in (Davis & Saunders, 1978); however, no Bella Coola version of the question "what is the woman doing?" is offered (English is used in the text). Sentence (19a) is based on the question *ʔalacix^w iks* 'what is he doing?' given in (Nater, 1984:116).

event and elicits a response in which that participant serves as the syntactic predicate, the 'residue' or thematic information presented in the question appearing as the syntactic Subject. The same pattern also holds for Lushootseed and concords very nicely with the more general requirement in both languages that the Subject correspond to a discourse topic, topics being elements which are thematic or directly related to Themes over a given stretch of discourse. The key to the verbless sentence, then, would appear to be its communicative structure, which has a direct expression in its syntax. This alignment of communicative and syntactic organization becomes most apparent in the structure of Wh-questions and, in Lushootseed, the construction of a particular class of negative expression, patterns to be discussed in more detail in the sections below.

3.1 *Wh-Questions*

The Rheme-Theme pattern in Lushootseed and Bella Coola is not only evidenced by the use of verbless sentences in frames such as that in (19), but also surfaces in the structure of Wh-questions, which are themselves verbless sentences. Consider (20):

(20) a. <u>Lushootseed</u>
 $g^w at\ k^w i\ ?u+?əy+du+b$ $?ə\ ti\ sq^wəbay?$
 who D [pnt]+find+[l.o.c.]+[md] P D dog
 'who did the dog find?'
 (lit. 'the one found by the dog [was] who'?)
 (Hess, 1993:128)

 b. <u>Bella Coola</u>
 $stam+ø+ks$ $wa+?anayk+m+ix^w$
 what+3s+[int] D+want+[md]+3s-2s
 $s+ka+qaax̌lam+ix^w$
 np+[irr]+drink+3s-2s
 'what do you want to drink?'
 (lit. 'that which you desire [so that] you may drink it [is] what'?)
 (Nater, 1984:103)

These examples, which ask for the identity of a direct actant of the Subject clause (in (20a), the Subject, in (b) the Direct Object), show the same pattern as the verbless sentences illustrated in Section 2.2, where a non-verbal element acts as predicate and the residue surfaces as a syntactically nominalized, thematic Subject. Lushootseed extends this pattern to those questions asking for the identity of a peripheral actant—although, predictably, in these sentences the Subject-clause bears a morphological marker of nominalization, as in (21b):

(21) a. ʔu+huy+yi+t+əb   ʔə t(i) ad+bad
       [pnt]+make+[ben]+[caus]+[md] P D   2po+father
       tiʔiɬ čačas
       D   child
       'your father made [it] for that boy'
       (lit. 'that boy was made·for by your father')
                                    (my sentence, based on (b))
    b. <u>stab</u> kʷi <u>s</u>+u+huy+yi+t+əb+s   ʔə
       what D   np+[pnt]+make+[ben]+[caus]+[md]+3po P
       t(i) ad+bad   tiʔɬ čačas
       D   2po+father D   child
       'what is your father making for that boy'?
                                    (Hess, 1993:137)

This replicates the pattern illustrated in (17b) and (18b), where the Subject appears as a morphological nominalization. In Lushootseed, gʷat 'who' and stab 'what' may be the predicates both of questions like (20) and of those like (21); other Wh-words by nature ask about peripheral roles in the sentence and so follow the second pattern, as in (22):

(22) <u>ʔəs+čal+əxʷ</u>   kʷi ɬu+<u>s</u>+huy+s
     [stat]+how+now D   [irr]+np+manage+3po
     'how will he manage'?
                                    (Hess, 1993:136)

In functional terms, the effect of such question forms is to place the Wh-word in predicate position, thereby making it rhematic, and to condition a response in which the new, requested information is also predicative and rhematic, the given information provided in the question remaining in thematic (Subject) position (hence, frames as in (19b)).

Bella Coola deals with questions formed on peripheral actants in a different manner altogether: instead of a clausal Subject, interrogatives take sentential complements, forming a kind of cleft with a zero third-person Subject and a nominalized clausal complement as in:

(23) a. maaskanmaakʔi+ø+ks <u>s</u>+ka+sčusmuc+iɬ
        at·what·time+3s+[int] np+[irr]+eat·dinner+1p
        'what time shall we have dinner?'
        (lit. 'it [is] at what time that we shall eat dinner'?)

b. <u>maaskuɬʔi+ø+ks</u>   <u>s+ʔaɬkult+c</u>   ʔaɬ+ʔinu
   how·much+3s+[int] <u>np</u>+be·in·debt+1s P+2s
   'how much do I owe you?'
   (lit. 'it [is] how much that I am indebted to you'?)
   (Nater, 1984:103)

Sentences such as these are, like the questions in (21) above, predicated on a Wh-element, but the Subject appears to be null, perhaps an expletive like the English *it* in *it is raining*, or an elision of some notion (such as "the time" in (23a)) which might be complementary to the meaning of the predicate. Such sentences in both languages have the effect of placing rhematic information in predicate position in the matrix clause and condensing the thematic residue into the complement; to the extent that this complement can be equated to or considered coreferent with the Subject, these sentences can be taken as conforming to the same principles of Subject-Theme-Topic alignment as the other types of questions and verbless sentences given in the examples above.

3.2 *The Lushootseed Existential Negative*

Lushootseed makes further use of verbless sentences in the construction of 'existential' negatives, negatives that deny the existence of an entity or the truth of a statement in its entirety. These sentences are formed by the use of the negative adverb $x^w i\ʔ$ as the syntactic predicate of the sentence, in contrast to the more mundane pattern of adverbial negation, which serves to negate the identification of the predicate with the Subject and involves placement of a negative adverb in sentence-initial position, as in (24):

(24) a. $x^w i\ʔ$ <u>lə+pišpiš</u> tiʔiɬ
          [neg] [clitic]+cat D
          'that [is] not a cat'
                                                    (Hess, 1993:121)

      b. $x^w i\ʔ$ čəd <u>lə+ʔaciɬtalbix^w</u>
          [neg] 1s [clitic]+Indian
          'I [am] not an Indian'
                                                    (Kroeber, 1991:79)

Note, however, that in spite of its being the first element in the sentence, the negative $x^w i\ʔ$ in (24a) and (b) is not the sentence predicate. Its adverbial nature is shown by the distribution of overt Subjects: in (a) the Subject, *tiʔiɬ*, is an NP (or, more strictly speaking, a DP) and so directly follows the predicate (cf. *$x^w i\ʔ$ *tiʔiɬ ləpišiš*), but in (b) the Subject pronominal precedes the predicate in the presence of an adverb, following the pattern illustrated in (2) above. This structure also requires the affixation of the proclitic lə to the predicate or to any adverb following the negative, although the function of this clitic is as of yet undetermined. The overall effect is one of negating the predicate in much the same way as a negative does in more familiar languages.

Like the adverbial negative, existential negation makes use of sentence-initial $x^w i\mathrm{?}$, but in these cases the negative adverb does serve as the syntactic predicate; the residue then surfaces as a morphological nominalization and appears with the remote/unreal deictic $k^w i$ and subjunctive prefix g^w-, as in (25b):

(25) a. ʔu+ʔəɬəd čəxʷ
         [pnt]+eat 2s
         'you ate'
                                        (my sentence, based on (b))
      b. xʷiʔ kʷi gʷ+ad+s+u+ʔəɬəd
         [neg] D [subj]+2po+np+[pnt]+eat
         'you did not eat'
         (lit. 'your eating [is] not')
                                                    (Hess, 1993:125)

This structure can be used to deny the existence of something or to negate possession:

(26) a. xʷiʔ kʷi gʷə+pišpiš
         [neg] D [subj]+cat
         'there are no cats'
                                                    (Hess, 1993:123)

      b. xʷiʔ kʷi gʷə+d+pišpiš
         [neg] D [subj]+1po+cat
         'I don't have a cat'[8]
         (lit. 'my cat [is] not')
                                                    (Hess, 1993:123)

The nominalization of the declarative sentence to form the clausal Subject ensures that it is the negation itself which is rhematic in the sentence, while the statement that is negated is relegated to the role of Theme— which, particularly in Lushootseed, is a role closely associated with given

---

[8] Cf. Russian possessive expressions of the form *u menja* (*net*) lit. ... 'there is (not) by me ... '.

event participants and propositions that are known or assumed to be true in discourse. This seems to coincide very well with a proposal made by Givón (1979) to the effect that the discourse function of a negative speech act is to deny an assumption (in Givón's terms, a 'discourse-presupposition') that has either been made by the Listener or that has been held in discourse up until the point of utterance. If the affirmative statement is indeed presupposed knowledge—and therefore thematic in nature—then the fact that the negative adverb (the only new or rhematic portion of the sentence) is the sentence predicate falls out from the same basic principles of rhematic organization that govern the formation of all other types of verbless sentence: it is the negation that carries the greater part of the communicative load, and so it is the negative adverb that becomes the sentence predicate, resulting in the familiar alignment of syntactic and communicative structure observed in the examples throughout this paper.

4 The Communicative Structure of the Verbless Sentence

Because of their highly unusual nature, the descriptive facts set out in the preceding section represent an interesting challenge for the linguist intent on developing a rigorous and generalizable model of natural language, particularly given the failure of many current theoretical frameworks to deal with the myriad issues revolving around the communicative structure of language. In the context of a formal treatment of this structure within *Meaning-Text Theory* (MTT), detailed information about communicative organization is first encoded in what is referred to as the *Semantic-Communicative Structure* (SemCommS), a portion of the *Semantic Representation* (SemR) of an utterance that contains the specifications of various parts of the Semantic Structure (SemS) for nine 'communicative oppositions'—*Communicative Dominance, Thematicity, Givenness, Foregrounding, Backgrounding, Emphasis, Presupposedness, Unitariness*, and *Locutionality* (for definitions and discussion of all of these, the reader is referred to Mel'čuk, 1997). Of greatest concern to us here are communicative dominance (versus communicative dependency), which plays a major role in "lexicalization" (the translation of semantic subnetworks into lexical items that can serve to label nodes in syntactic trees), and thematicity, which specifies the bipartition of an utterance into *Semantic Theme* and *Semantic Rheme*. In Bella Coola and Lushootseed, the SemCommS plays a significant role in mediating the process of "syntacticization", the translation of the diffuse, unordered semantic networks of the SemR into the hierarchical dependency trees of the *Deep-Syntactic Representation* (DSyntR). As we shall see below, the effects of these two communicative oppositions on the syntacticization process can be made to account for the syntactic structure of all of the verbless-sentence types enumerated in Sections 1 and 2 above. To this end, Section 4 will begin with an exploration of some of the subsidiary issues of syntactic representations in Salishan syntax, in particular the issue of deixis and how deictic elements are best dealt with in terms of both the Deep-Syntactic and Semantic Structures in which they appear (4.1). Following that, in Subsection 4.2, the effects of the Sem-CommS on the process of syntacticization will be examined in an effort to clarify the relation between the SemR and the DSyntR of the Bella Coola and Lushootseed sentence; in addition, the procedural rules for the selection of the "entry node"—that is, the node of the SemS that will surface as DSynt predicate—will be examined and contrasted with those at work in more ordinary languages such as English, with an eye towards showing how profound differences in surface forms can be the result of slight variations in fundamentally similar principles of communicative organization.

4.1 *The Syntactic and Semantic Representation of Deixis*

One of the more notable characteristics of the syntax of Lushootseed and Bella Coola is the extensive use both languages make of deixis in NPs. Deictics typically have two forms, one unmarked for gender and another (formed by the insertion of the infix -*s*- after the initial consonant of the morpheme) indicating that the referent is of natural feminine gender;[3] in both languages this is often the only method of distinguishing nouns referring to men from those referring to women. The Lushootseed deictic elements, adapted from (Hess, 1993), are given in Table 1.

Table 1: *Lushootseed deictics*

	distal	proximal	unique	non-contrastive	remote/unreal
non-fem	tiʔiɬ	tiʔəʔ	ti	tə	$k^w i$
fem	tsiʔiɬ	tsiʔəʔ	tsi	tsə	$k^w si$

The distal and proximal forms may be used on their own as pronominals, and only these have reduplicated plural forms, *tiʔiʔiɬ* and *tiʔiʔəʔ*, although these are not obligatorily used in plural contexts. Number is not marked at all in the remainder of the paradigm. The remote/unreal (or, in Hess's terms, 'remote/hypothetical') deictic $k^w i$ is used for any element that is invisible to the Speaker by virtue of distance and is thus, by extension, used for hypothetical, unidentified, or unrealized participants in discourse, as in the questions in (21a) and (22) and the negatives in (26). Deictics are used with all nouns, including participles and proper nouns, with the apparent exception of place-names; deixis is also omitted from the names of people in informal speech.

The deictic system of Bella Coola is even more involved. In addition to the 'proximal indefinite' forms ti-/ci-, which resemble the Lushootseed unique-reference deictics, Bella Coola has a large set of deictics consisting of proclitic-enclitic pairs. The paradigm for these elements distinguishes gender/number, distance, and demonstrative/non-demonstrative, and is given in Table 2.

Table 2: *Bella Coola deictic clitics*

	proximal		middle		distal	
	dem.	non-dem.	dem.	non-dem.	dem.	non-dem.
non-fem	ti-ɬayx	ti-tx	ta-ɬax̌	ta-ɬ	ta-tix	ta-tx̌
fem	ci-ɬayx	ci-cx	ʔiɬ-ʔiɬayɬ	ʔiɬ-ɬ	ʔiɬ-cix	ʔiɬ-ʔiɬ
plural	wa-ʔac	wa-c	ta-ɬax̌^{w}	ta-ɬ	ta-tax̌	ta-tx̌^{w}

(Davis & Saunders, 1980:254)

As the table shows, the enclitic makes the demonstrative/non-demonstrative distinction and the proclitic distinguishes proximal, middle, and distal; nouns that bear only the proclitic have an indefinite or non-referential reading. Abstract nouns appear with the proximal-plural proclitic wa-. Note that Davis and Saunders's term 'middle' is approximately equivalent to Hess's 'distal' in Lushootseed, the Lushootseed 'remote/unreal' corresponding to 'distal' in Table 2. Unlike Lushootseed, Bella Coola does not equate unreality/hypotheticality with remoteness.

An important issue with respect to deictics, not only in Bella Coola and Lushootseed, but in Salish in general, has to do with their status in syntactic representations—specifically, whether they are heads or complements of the nouns with which they appear. Determiners (which is the class that subsumes the deictics of Lushootseed and Bella Coola) have traditionally been considered as subordinate in some way to the nouns they are associated with—either as specifiers in phrase-structure grammars (Radford, 1988) or as dependents in dependency grammars (Mel'čuk, 1988). Some recent work, however, has centred on the proposal that determiners may in fact be the heads of the noun phrases in which they occur (Abney, 1987; Hudson, 1990; for a critical appraisal of these proposals with respect to English, see van Langendonck, 1994), and a number of quite common phenomena in Salish languages have given rise to specific proposals for Determiner Phrases (DPs) in Straits Salish (Jelinek & Demers, 1994) and Sƛ'aƛ'imcets (Lillooet)

(Davis & Matthewson, 1996). Perhaps the most obvious intuitive evidence for a DP analysis in Bella Coola and Lushootseed is the phenomenon of syntactic nominalization, the formation of nominals from finite clauses with no morphological marking—amply illustrated in the examples throughout this paper (for example, (17a) and (18a)), and in the Lushootseed sentence in (27):

(27)   put   x̌u+bə+ʔitut   tiʔił   ʔəs+dxʷ +pakʷ +ah+əb
       only [hab]+[add]+sleep D   [stat]+[dp]+lie+ass+[md]
       'this He-Lies-With-His-Ass-In-The-Air would only sleep'
                                        (Hess, 1993:183, line 57)

Structures such as these suggest that it is the appearance of the deictic that marks the status of the clause as a nominal—in effect, licensing its appearance in a specific syntactic role, a property generally attributed to the phrasal head in constituency-based grammars.

In dependency theory, however, the properties of a head are not automatically conferred upon the head-dependent complex and so the apparent "licensing" of one element in a given syntactic environment by its association with another is not necessarily proof of the direction of the dependent-head relation (although it may well be an indication thereof). In MTT, syntactic dependency is established on the basis of the distribution or "passive valency" of wordforms (as opposed to the "active valency", which is the set of syntactic units that a wordform subcategorizes for). For a given syntactic unit U of a language, the passive surface-syntactic valency of U is defined as "the list of surface syntactic roles in which U can appear either as a dependent ... or as an absolute head (i.e., an element that is dependent on nothing)" (Mel'čuk, 1988:112). When considering the relation of two wordforms, w_1 and w_2, at the surface-syntactic (SS) level, the direction of the dependency (that is, which of the two is the head and which is the dependent) can be established by one of two criteria, the relevant one for our purposes here being Criterion B.I., which states that the surface-syntactic head of a "phrase w_1—w_2 is the wordform that determines the passive SS-valency of the phrase to a greater degree than the other wordform" (Mel'čuk, 1988:132).[9] In order to express this criterion in more rigorous terms, it is necessary to speak of the passive surface-syntactic valency of a lexeme L containing a wordform w, or $VAL^{SS}_{pass}(L(w))$; the direction of the dependency w_1—w_2 is then decided by comparing $VAL^{SS}_{pass}(L(w_1))$, $VAL^{SS}_{pass}(L(w_2))$, and $VAL^{SS}_{pass}(L(w_1))$—$L(w_2))$ according to the formulation of Criterion B.I. given in (28):

---
[9]The notation w_1—w_2 indicates a dependency whose direction has yet to be determined.

(28) Criterion B.I. (imposition of passive SS-valencies)

IFF $\{\text{VAL}^{SS}_{\text{pass}}(L(w_1)\text{—}L(w_2)) = \text{VAL}^{SS}_{\text{pass}}(L(w_2))$
OR $\text{VAL}^{SS}_{\text{pass}}(L(w_1)\text{—}L(w_2)) \cap \text{VAL}^{SS}_{\text{pass}}(L(w_2)) >$
$\text{VAL}^{SS}_{\text{pass}}(L(w_1)\text{—}L(w_2)) \cap \text{VAL}^{SS}_{\text{pass}}(L(w_1))\}$
AND $\text{VAL}^{SS}_{\text{pass}}(L(w_1)\text{-}L(w_2)) \neq \text{VAL}^{SS}_{\text{pass}}(L(w_1))$
THEN wordform w_2 is the SS-governor of w_1—that is,
$w_2 \longrightarrow w_1$

(Mel'čuk, 1988:133)

In plain language, this rule states that w_1 is a dependent of w_2 if the environments in which w_2 appears are a) the same environments in which the syntagm w_1—w_2 appears, or b) those environments in which the distribution of w_2 and w_1—w_2 coincide are numerically greater than those in which w_1 and w_1—w_2 coincide (as long as w_1 does not meet the first condition, in which case it is the surface-syntactic governor).

One of the clearest applications of this criterion comes in the case where one of the wordforms, w_2, occurs only in the context of the relation w_1—w_2, as is the case, for example, with prepositions in many languages, which occur only in association with NPs. The passive valency of a PP differs from that of an NP, meeting the second condition of B.I., while the fact that prepositions may occur only in the context of a PP means that the passive valency of the preposition is precisely that of the prepositional phrase. The same argument holds for most deictics in Bella Coola and Lushootseed. The Lushootseed deictics and the Bella Coola proclitic-enclitic pairs, like prepositions, appear only in the context of a nominal, making $\text{VAL}^{SS}_{\text{pass}}(D)$ equal to $\text{VAL}^{SS}_{\text{pass}}(D+\text{nominal})$. By the same token, $\text{VAL}^{SS}_{\text{pass}}(\text{nominal}) \neq \text{VAL}^{SS}_{\text{pass}}(D+\text{nominal})$, as there are two environments in which nominals regularly appear without a deictic marker. The first of these is as the predicate of a verbless sentence, although the fact that deictics may appear on some predicate nominals makes this a weak indicator of a difference in passive valency. The second environment where nominals appear without a determiner in the surface syntax is when they modify other nouns. This is clearest in Lushootseed:

(29) a. *tiʔəʔ kiyuuqʷs stətudəq*
    D   seagull   slaves
    'these seagull slaves'

(Hess, 1993:117)

b. **tiʔəʔ tiʔəʔ kiyuuqʷs stətudəq*
    D   D   seagull   slaves

c. *tiʔəʔ kiyuuqʷs tiʔəʔ stətudəq
   D   seagull D   slaves

In Bella Coola, however, the deictic proclitics do appear on nominal modifiers, as in (30):

(30) k̕x+ic   ti+staltmx ti+ʔimlk+tx
      see+3s-1p D+chief   D+man+D
      'I see the man [who is] chief'
                                    (Davis & Saunders, 1978:41)

Note, however, that they appear on other modifiers of nouns as well:

(31) a. k̕x+ic   ti+ya   ti+ʔimlk+tx
        see+3s-1s D+good   D+man+D
        'I see the good man'
     b. k̕x+ic   ti+ʔimlk ti+ya+tx
        see+3s-1s D+man   D+good+D
        'I see the good man'
                                    (Davis & Saunders, 1978:40)

Here, as in all phrases consisting of a noun and modifiers, the proclitic is applied to the modifying element(s) as well as to the noun, although the enclitic appears only phrase-finally. I have argued elsewhere that the iteration of the proclitic throughout the NP is best treated in terms of a rule of deictic spreading (Beck, 1995b), which is applied in the surface-syntactic component—meaning that in the DSynt and SSyntRs, the passive valency of the deictic-nominal string does not include the role of modifier of a noun and, therefore, the deictic can be treated as the surface-syntactic governor under Criterion B.I.

There is, however, a set of deictics in both languages that, in addition to their use as the heads of DPs, also appear independently as pronominals: these are the Bella Coola enclitics and the Lushootseed *tiʔiɬ* and *tiʔəʔ* (and their feminine and plural counterparts). This is illustrated in the Lushootseed sentence in (7a) and the Bella Coola example here in (32):

(32) ƛap+aw+tu+c̕   ac
      go+3p+[cnf]+[perf] D
      'they went again'
                                    (Davis & Saunders, 1980:148, line 198)

Because these appear on their own as pronominals, they are not covered by the first part of Criterion B.I. (the passive-valency of the D not being the equivalent of the valency of the DP).[10] Thus, it becomes necessary to enumerate more precisely the passive SS-valencies of the syntactic units we are comparing in order to determine if, in all of their uses, these elements meet the second half of the criterion. This is done in Table 3.

Table 3: *Comparative* VAL^{SS}_{pass} *of pronominal deictics, DPs, and bare nominals*

$VAL^{SS}_{pass}(D_{pro})$	$VAL^{SS}_{pass}(D+\text{nominal})$	$VAL^{SS}_{pass}(\text{nominal})$
actant of verb	actant of verb	—
object of preposition	object of preposition	—
predicate (Lush only)	predicate	predicate
—	adverbial	adverbial
—	—	nominal modifier

From the table we can see that the intersection of the set of syntactic environments in which pronominally-used deictics occur ($VAL^{SS}_{pass}(D_{pro})$) and the set of environments where DPs occur ($VAL^{SS}_{pass}(D+\text{nominal})$)—the double-outlined box—is greater than the intersection the valencies of DPs and bare nominals ($VAL^{SS}_{pass}(\text{nominal})$) outlined in bold. This pattern conforms to the second condition of Criterion B.I. given in (28). Once again, this is clearer in Lushootseed, where deictics can serve as sentence predicates, as in

(33) tiʔəʔ tə čx̌a
 D   D   stone
 'the stone [is] this [one]'

(Hess, 1993:103)

Such a structure is not possible in Bella Coola, which employs a special set of elements for sentences of this type, meaning that in Bella Coola $VAL^{SS}_{pass}(D_{pro})$ is (numerically) equal to $VAL^{SS}_{pass}(\text{nominal})$. Nonetheless, pending further investigation of the issue, it is still desirable to decide the tie in favour of the deictic enclitic as syntactic head: not applying the DP analysis to the deictic enclitics that do appear as independent pronominals

---

[10]The fact that these deictics are pronominals is in itself, however, a point in favour of the DP-analysis, and this argument has been applied to English and related languages (R. Hudson, personal communication).

would create a discrepancy between these, which thus would be the dependents of the nominals with which they appear, and the proclitic members of the same paradigm, which we have already shown to be the heads of their phrases.[4]

If deictics are phrasal heads in the DSyntR, the question arises as to what type of syntactic relation holds between the deictic and its dependent, or, more specifically, if the nominal (or other) dependent of the deictic element should be taken as its actant or as an attributive. One approach to this problem stems from an observation made by Kinkade (1983). Lawrence Nicodemus, a native speaker of Coeur D'Alene (an Interior Salish language) with some linguistic training, regularly glosses DPs as relative clauses, as in

(34)   x̌es+iɬčəʔ x^w e čiʔ
       good+flesh D   deer
       'they are good to eat those which are deer'
                         (Nicodemus, 1975 cited in Kinkade, 1983:34)

Treating the deictic as a pronominal element (and, as we have seen above, many do serve that role), an even more literal gloss might be 'the ones who are deer [are] good meat', the determiner x^w e serving as the pronominal head of a relative clause formed from the sentence 'they are deer'. Although it is difficult to know how seriously to take such considerations, Kinkade's interpretation of Nicodemus (that all overt NP-complements, which are obligatorily headed by determiners, are full clauses) has had a certain intuitive appeal among some Salishanists and has come to play a crucial role in some of the more recent theoretical work on these languages (e.g., Jelinek & Demers, 1994). While it seems unlikely that such an analysis will bear out in the long run-requiring as it does that nouns such as čiʔ 'deer' be treated syntactically as predicates—the fact remains that there is a high degree of similarity between the syntax of the DP and that of the relative clause and other nominal-modifier constructions.[11] Because the relation between noun and modifier, like that between a relative clause and its head, is an attributive one, establishing an equivalency between this relation and that which holds within the DP would mean that deictics too govern attributive, rather than actantial, dependents in the DSyntR.

One advantage of treating the D⟶N DSyntRel as an attributive one is that it gives us a clue to the proper treatment of deictics in the SemR.

---

[11]This point is argued in more detail in (Beck, 1995b), which sets out formal criteria by which the SSyntRel between deictic and dependent can be analyzed as a modificative one.

In most languages—the status of the deictic element as syntactic governor aside—the ordinary treatment of a deictic or a determiner in the SemR would be that of a functor which links its argument to a specific location in space *vis-à-vis* the Speaker and the speech act. The nature of the deictic in Lushootseed and Bella Coola, however, is somewhat different from the norm in that deictic elements serve not only to locate entities in space but in some circumstances seem themselves to serve as entities and event participants, both in pronominal expressions such as that in (7a) and as heads of relative clauses as in (17a) and (18a). In these environments, deictics act very much like pronouns and show agreement for number and gender features with antecedent event participants, as in the Lushootseed sentence in (35), where a feminine deictic heads a morphological nominalization (the Salishan equivalent of an oblique-centred relative clause) describing an action performed by a woman:

(35) ʔəs+šuu+c   tsiʔəʔ sɬadəyʔ ʔal tsi
      [stat]+see+[appl] Df woman P Df
      s+u+ɬukʷ +txʷ +s   tiʔəʔ čačas
      np+[pnt]+go·home+[caus]+3po D   child
      'I see the woman taking the boy home'
      (lit. 'I look at the woman, at she who is the one taking the boy home')

                                         (Hess, personal communication)

Similarly, Lushootseed (and to a lesser extent Bella Coola) makes use of nominal expressions such as those in (36), which consist of nothing but a deictic and an adjectival radical in which the gender-marking of the deictic plays a crucial role in determining meaning:

(36) a. *ti čačas*   *tsi čačas*
         D young   Df young
         'boy'   'girl'
      b. *ti luxʼ*   *tsi luxʼ*
         D old   Df old
         'old man'   'old woman'

This being the case, it seems inevitable that the semantic makeup of deictics in these environments contain the notion of that element as an individuable entity or 'thing' (in the sense of Langacker, 1991), which I will represent in the SemRs given below as the semanteme 'object'. This seems to give us a contrast between the lexical subnetwork for an ordinary deictic heading an NP, shown in Figure 1a for *tsi?ə?sqʷbay?* 'this (female) dog', and one used pronominally, as in Figure 1b for *tsi?ə?luƛ* 'this old woman', which represents a deictic acting as the argument of a functor corresponding to an adjectival radical such as that in the Lushootseed examples in (36).

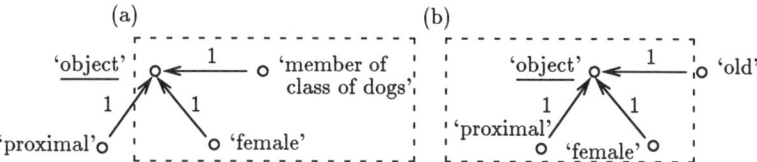

Figure 1: *SemSs of ordinary and pronominal proximal deictics*

This apparent distinction between the two deictics, which would require treatment as separate lexemes, has to do with the lexicalization patterns, indicated by the dashed boxes in the diagrams in Figure 1. In the first example, representing the more cross-linguistically usual deictic pattern, the semantemes 'object' and 'feminine' are lexicalized with the functor 'member of class of dogs'—which serves here as shorthand for the sum of the properties attributed to an object by its inclusion in the class of dogs—to form the noun *dog*. Being an inflectional feature, 'feminine' would appear as a subscript on *dog* in the DSyntR and would be realized as the feminine form of the proximal deictic in the morphology. In Figure 1b, on the other hand, lexicalization groups 'object' and 'feminine' together with the functor node 'proximal', giving us a pronominal reading of the proximal deictic.

Interestingly enough, this analysis also offers an account of why it is that pronominal deictics surface as syntactic heads in an attributive relation to their dependents. According to Mel'čuk (1997), a SemR-configuration of the form $\sigma_1 \circ \longrightarrow \circ \sigma_2$—that is, a predicate-argument relation—in which the argument node, σ_2, is the Comm-Dominant node will result in the DSynt-configuration $L(\sigma_1) \circ \xrightarrow{\text{ATTR}} \circ L(\sigma_2)$. In the case of semantic networks such as that illustrated in Figure 1b, the relation between the functor node 'old' and the argument node 'object' is such that the subordinate argument node is communicatively dominant—the Comm-Dominant node of a subnetwork representing the generic meaning of that subnetwork (Mel'čuk, 1997, observation attributed to A. Polguère), and the generic meaning of *old woman* corresponding (at its most generic) to 'object' rather than to 'old'. This property of Comm-Dominance thus predicts the fact that the lexicalization of the deictic area of the network is realized as a syntactic head and that the part of the network corresponding to the semantic predicate should be its attributive dependent.

This, of course, raises the question of why it is that non-pronominal deictics also surface as syntactic governors. One possibility is that in SemSs such as in Figure 1a, the semanteme 'object' is lexicalized not only as a part of 'dog' but appears in the lexical entry of *ti?ə?* as well: this would, in effect, erase the distinction between the two deictics in Figure 1 posited earlier and reduce the differences between the situations in (a) and (b) to a difference in the distribution of the 'object' node. In (a) the semanteme figures in the lexicalization of two functors ('proximal' and 'member of class of dogs'), and in (b) it appears in only one of them. Taking this approach not only allows us to treat all deictics as inherently pronominal, lending some intuitive weight to the proposal for an attributive relation between head and dependent in a DP, but it also allows us to extend the linkage of Comm-Dominance to the selection of syntactic head to these cases as well: if, for the purposes of syntacticization, the semanteme 'proximal'—or the configuration 'proximal' ⟶ 'object'—in some way "inherits" the Comm-Dominance of the 'object' node itself, then the syntacticization process can be allowed to select the lexicalization of the Comm-Dominant subnetwork as a syntactic head. While this raises a number of technical issues which are not germane to our discussion, it does seem to highlight an important point about the communicative organization of languages such as Bella Coola and Lushootseed versus languages like English. According to the definition of Comm-Dominance—that the Comm-Dominant node of a subnetwork $\sum$ represents the generic meaning of $\sum$—it seems that 'dog' (or, more accurately, 'member of class of dogs' ⟶ 'object') is a better candidate for Comm-Dominance than 'proximal' (that is, 'proximal' → 'object'). Certainly, in a lexicographic sense, 'dog' is the more generic meaning of *this dog* and in English this is reflected in the relative Comm-Dominance of nodes in the SemR. In Bella Coola and Lushootseed, however, there is a strong tendency to organize discourse in terms of the relative location of objects in space and to identify event participants in terms of these locations; in other words, to present the identify of objects as classes to which items at specified location belong.[5] Thus, where the English phrase *this dog* breaks down into 'dog at this location', the Lushootseed equivalent, *ti?ə? sq*^{w}*əbay?*, breaks down as 'object at this location which is a member of the class of dogs', highlighting once again another important difference in the communicative organization of these two types of language.

4.2 Sem-Theme, Sem-Rheme, and the DSyntR

Having established some of the basics of Bella Coola and Lushootseed syntax, it now remains to be shown how these, coupled with the principles of syntacticization and communicative structure, can be made to account for the syntactic patterns illustrated throughout the preceding sections. In particular, we are looking for an account of the verbless sentence, a sentence with a non-verbal predicate whose syntactic structure is headed by an element from the Sem-Rheme. In the simplest case, such constructions consist of a nominal acting as syntactic predicate with a pronominal deictic as its syntactic subject. This is illustrated by the Lushootseed sentence in (7a), whose SemR and DSyntR are given in Figure 2.[12]

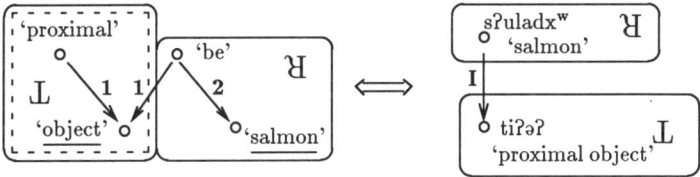

Figure 2: *Syntacticization of* sʔuladx^w tiʔəʔ *'this [is] a salmon'*

The sentence here, a proper response to the question "What is that?", is quite straightforward in propositional terms, its SemS consisting of a functor node, 'be', indicating an identification of a particular entity pointed to by the speaker—Semantic Argument (SemA) 1—as a member of a designated class of entities (SemA 2). In languages with copular verbs, the semanteme 'be' would be realized as the language-specific equivalent of the English lexeme *be*: in Lushootseed and Bella Coola, however, there is no copula and, hence, no lexical equivalent of 'be' to appear in the DSyntR. Instead, SemA 2 of 'be', 'salmon', becomes DSynt-predicate, taking SemA 1 as its syntactic Subject, the 'be' itself disappearing, perhaps finding its expression in the actantial relation between *sʔuladx^w* 'salmon' and its Subject. An alternative analysis would be that the meaning of 'be' may be subsumed in the lexicalization of 'salmon' in the same way that the notion of 'object' is subsumed in the lexicalizations of pronominal deictics in Figure 1—in effect, creating a zero-derived verb, which seems a highly plausible strategic alternative to the more familiar process of inserting copula in predicate-nominal environments.

In terms of its communicative structure, the sentence in Figure 2 can be compared with the sentence in Figure 3, taken from (32) above, which would be the answer to a question such as "Which stone is it?". Here, as

---

[12]In this section I will draw almost exclusively on data from Lushootseed, principally because the rich morphology of Bella Coola tends to obscure the underlying syntactic structures. Unless stated otherwise, generalizations drawn from the Lushootseed data are intended to apply to both languages.

in Figure 2, we have the SemS of a sentence whose DSynt-predicate corresponds to a SemA rather than to the semantic predicate, once again the bivalent functor 'be'.[13] Unlike in Figure 2, however, the DSyntR in Figure 3 takes as syntactic predicate SemA 1 rather than SemA 2 of 'be'—in other words, the entity whose identity is established by the predication becomes the DSynt-predicate, rather than the identity attributed to it as in Figure 2. The source of this difference lies in the SemCommS. In Figure 2, SemA 1 (the entity being identified) belongs to the Sem-Theme (L) and SemA 2 (the identity attributed to it) lies within the Sem-Rheme (Я), whereas in Figure 3, SemA 1 is rhematic and SemA 2 is the Sem-Theme. The fact that Lushootseed and Bella Coola require that the syntactic predicate belong to the Sem-Rheme of the sentence results in SemA 2 surfacing as syntactic predicate in Figure 2, and SemA 1 becoming predicate in Figure 3—the communicative structure of the sentence, rather than its propositional content, determining the deep-syntactic structure.

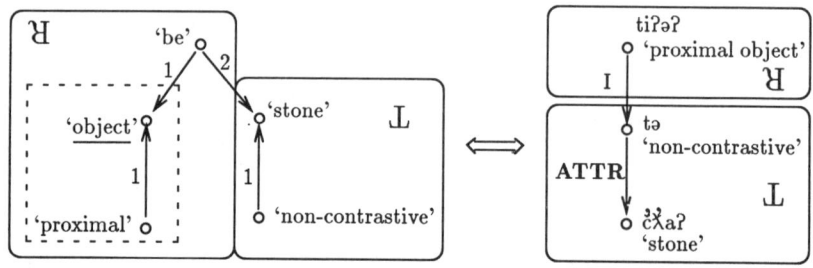

Figure 3: *Syntacticization of* tiʔəʔ tə čXaʔ *'the stone [is] this one'*

Another important effect of the SemCommS on the elaboration of the DSyntS has to do with the process of lexicalization, which seems to require that the top of a D-tree be filled by a lexical word rather than a clitic. This gives us a contrast between sentences whose predicates are emphatic pronouns such as that in (37a)—the response to the question "Who will be taken?"—and its narratively-focused counterpart, which would be realized by the pronominal Subject clitic čəd 'I', as in (37b):

(37) a. ʔəca kʷi ɬu+kʷəda+t+əb
     1s   D [irr]+take+[caus]+[md]
     'the one who will be taken [is] me'
                           (Bates *et al.*, 1994:10)

---

[13]Technically, of course, the two 'be's have slightly different meanings: that in Figure 2 serves to establish class membership while that in Figure 3 serves to establish identity—although it might be argued that identity is in fact membership in a class having only one member.

b. *ɬu+kʷəda+t+əb*   *čəd*
[irr]+take+[caus]+[md] 1s
'[he/she] will take me'
(lit. 'I will be taken')

Here we have alternative lexicalizations of the first-person participant in the event, choice of which depends on the sentence's SemCommS rather than on its propositional content. This implies that there are words in Lushootseed (and Bella Coola, which expresses (37a) and (b) in exactly parallel fashion) whose lexical entry specifies them as being inherently rhematic. Included in this class of words are the members of the emphatic pronominal paradigm to which the Lushootseed *ʔəca* and the Bella Coola *ʔinu* (from (8b) above) belong, Wh-question words (as shown in Section 3.1), certain demonstrative predicates, and a number of quantifiers. Such items are realized in sentences only in contexts where the semantic subnetworks corresponding to their lexical entries appear as the Comm-Dominant node in the Sem-Rheme; as a result, they become deep-syntactic predicates during syntacticization, as in Figure 4.[14]

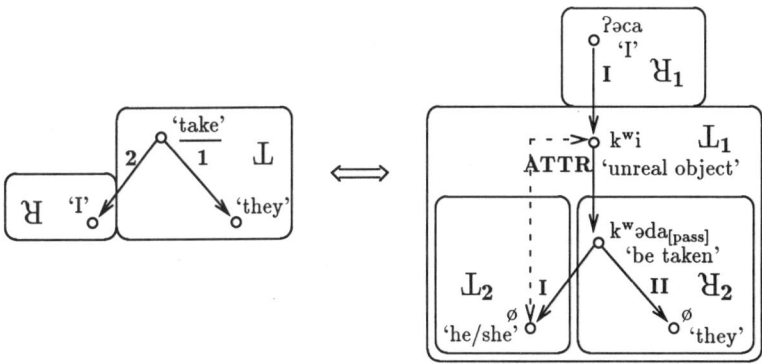

Figure 4: *Syntacticization of* ʔəca kʷi ɬukʷədatəb *'the one who will be taken [is] me'*

Note that the embedded Subject-clause in this sentence is syntactically a passive. The passive conversion operation (not shown in the diagram) is triggered, as it often is in English, by the requirement that Subject *cum* first Deep-Syntactic Actant (DSyntA) be thematic. In this particular case,

---

[14]The zero pronominals present in the DSyntS are required in Lushootseed to account for agreement facts in slightly different but structurally comparable environments, as they are in all clauses in Bella Coola.

the Subject of the embedded clause is required to appear in a 'secondary thematization' (Mel'čuk, 1997)—that is, a Theme/Rheme partition contained within the bounds of a higher-order thematic partition (the orders of the partitions are indicated by the subscripts provided in the diagram). In other words, the embedded clause itself has a Theme/Rheme division, and it is within this partition that its Subject is required to be thematic—thereby triggering the use of the passive. The structures in Figure 4 can be contrasted with those in Figure 5, which represent the syntacticization of the narratively-focused sentence in (37b).

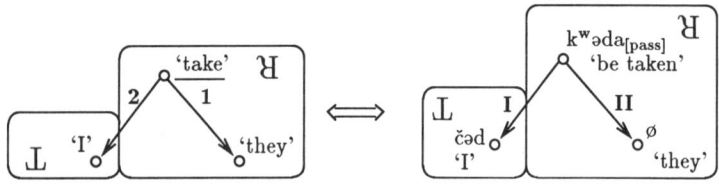

Figure 5: *Syntacticization of ɬuk^wədatəb čəd '[he/she] will take me'*

A legitimate answer to a question such as "How will you get there?", the sentence here has a SemCommS which is the thematic inverse of that illustrated in Figure 4. The Sem-Rheme consists of a functor and a single argument and during syntacticization the functor is realized as the DSynt-predicate and the argument becomes its DSyntA, precisely as in languages such as English. The fundamental differences between the principles of syntacticization in English and Salish, however, can be seen in syntacticization of a nominal-predicate construction with a SemS similar to that in Figure 5 but with the opposite SemCommS. Consider Figure 6, which illustrates the Lushootseed example in (17a) above, the answer to the question "Who chased the dog?".

Unlike in the previous examples, in Figure 6 we actually have an eligible functor in the SemS which might legitimately serve as predicate in the DSyntR of an English sentence—the semanteme 'chase', which surfaces as a syntactic predicate in narratively-focused Lushootseed sentences such as *ʔučalad tiʔəʔ sq^wəbayʔ* '[they] chased the dog'. In Figure 6, however, the semanteme 'chase' is part of the Theme rather than the Rheme, and so is not eligible to be a syntactic (matrix) predicate (or, more specifically, an entry node for the DSyntR—see Section 4.2 below): instead, 'children' becomes DSynt-predicate and the remainder of the sentence, the Sem-Theme, is realized as a syntactically nominalized clausal Subject.

An unresolved issue surrounding the syntacticization of sentences with complex clausal Subjects is the origin of deictic elements such as *ti* 'unique

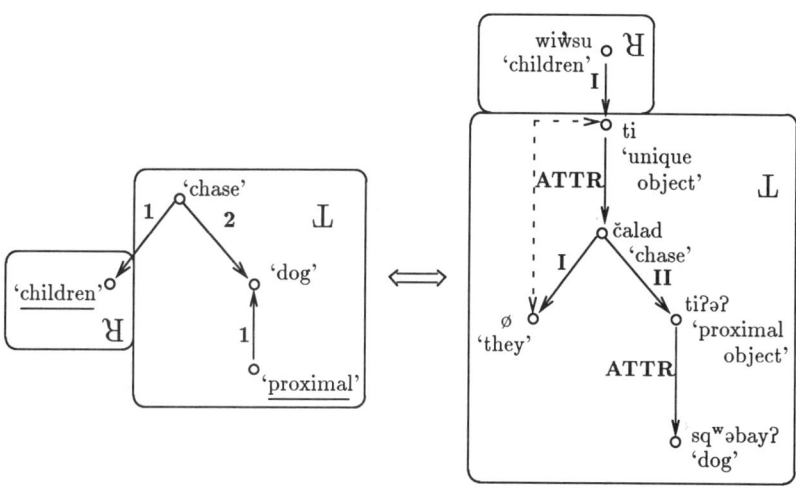

Figure 6: *Syntacticization of* wiẃsu ti ʔučalad tiʔəʔ sqʷəbayʔ *'the ones who chased the dog [are] children'*

object' shown as the syntactic head of the Subject-clause of the DSyntS in Figure 6. Given that these elements seem essentially to be pronominals referring to the entity named by the syntactic predicate, a logical supposition would be that they have their origin in the SemR as functor nodes associated with that entity, the syntacticization process stripping away the functor from a nominal predicate and realizing it as a syntactic head of the clause from which the nominal was "extracted".[15] This possibility, however, seems to be ruled out by sentences such as (38), where there is an overt deictic element, *tiʔəʔ* 'proximal', associated with *sqʷəbayʔ* 'dog', which is different from the pronominal deictic head of the Subject clause, *ti* 'unique Object':

(38) *tiʔəʔ sqʷəbayʔ ti ʔu+čala+t+əb*
 D   dog   D [pnt]+chase+[caus]+[md]
 ʔə tiʔił wiẃsu
 P D   children 'the one the children chased [is] this dog'
 (lit. 'the one chased by the children [is] this dog')
 (Hess, 1993:128)

This sentence would correspond to the structures shown in Figure 7.

---

[15]Number is not obligatorily marked in Lushootseed, and so the deictic *ti* in Figure 6 can be coreferential with either a singular or a plural noun. In Bella Coola, the deictic would be the proximal plural *wa*.

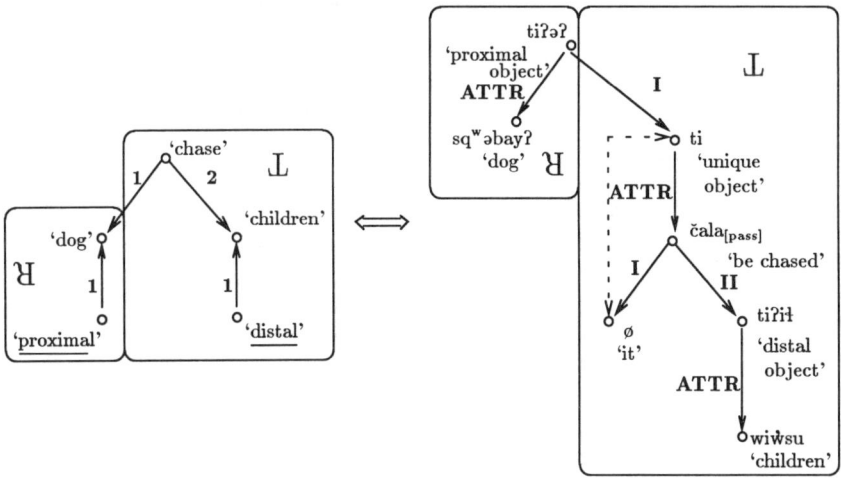

Figure 7: *Syntacticization of* tiʔəʔ sqʷəbayʔ ti ʔučalatəb ʔə tiʔiɬ wiw̓su *'the one the children chased [is] this dog'*

It should be noted that, while the deictic in the DSynt-Rheme does not have to be identical to the deictic heading the DSynt-Theme, it seems likely that the two must agree in features such as gender and number.[16] For Bella Coola, Davis and Saunders (1975) point out that deictic "mismatches" between event participants indicate a past time context for an event—for example, a sentence such as that in (19a), *spis cixnascx tiʔimlktx* 'the [proximal] woman hit the [proximal] man' may have an indefinite temporal reading (past or present), whereas a sentence such as *spis ɬaxnasʔiɬaʔiɬ tiʔimlktx* 'the [middle-distance] woman hit the [proximal] man' will generally have a recent-past reading, the difference in the spatial locations of the participants indicating that enough time has elapsed since the event that the two are no longer at the same location. Whether or not similar principles are at work in the selection of deictic heads of Subject clauses such as those in Figures 6 and 7 is at present not entirely clear, although it seems likely that this is indeed the case, the perceived location of the event in discourse space (and, hence, the location of the event-participant/deictic antecedent) being the source of the deictic that appears as the head of the relative clause. One indication of this is the appearance of the remote/unreal deic-

---

[16]Or, more accurately for Lushootseed, they must not disagree for marked values: even when possible, plural-marking is always optional and gender-marking of clauses headed by deictics is often considered redundant. In Bella Coola, the rules for agreement for both person and number seem to be strictly adhered to.

tic in sentences referring to future events such as the Lushootseed sentence first cited in (8a):

(39) ʔəca kʷi ɬu+kʷəda+t+əb
    1s D [irr]+take+[caus]+[md]
    'the one who will be taken [is] me'
                                        (Bates et al., 1994:10)

Typically, the deictic element $k^w i$ is used to refer to Objects which, because of their spatial location, are out of sight of the Speaker or which, by analogy, are considered to be unreal and/or hypothetical (and, hence, invisible to the speaker). Clearly, however, in (39) the syntactic predicate of the sentence, the deictic centre of the speech act, can not be either hypothetical or remote in and of itself—the irreality marked by $k^w i$ in this case being clearly a property of the event and, by extension, of the non-real participant affected by this event, whose identity with the speaker is being asserted. The issue of how this is best handled in terms of semantic representation, however, awaits further investigation.

Another environment in which the 'remote/unreal' deictic $k^w i$ appears in the DSyntR is in the formation of Wh-questions such as the Lushootseed sentence given in (20), although in such cases the semantic origins of a 'remote/unreal' deictic referring to an unknown and potentially non-existent entity are not terribly mysterious. Leaving aside the development of a formal apparatus for the insertion of this deictic (which would likely fall out from the semantic decomposition of the semanteme 'who'), we can represent the correspondence between the SemR and the DSyntR of (20) as in Figure 8.

The structures shown here are precisely analogous to those shown for other verbless sentences above, in all of these cases the Sem-Rheme being realized as DSynt-predicate.

The same pattern holds for the formation of existential negatives such as that in (26a), illustrated by Figure 8, which shows the predicative use of $x^w iʔ$ '[neg]' to express the negation of a semantic functor 'exist', which—like 'be' in Figures 2 and 3—has no lexical form and seems to be incorporated into the meaning of 'not' during lexicalization; see Figure 9.

The example in Figure 9 contrasts with the syntacticization of sentences involving adverbial negation such as (24a) shown in Figure 10.

In these cases, the negative lexeme $x^w iʔ$ is not a syntactic predicate but instead is realized as an adverbial dependent of the nominal, pišpiš 'cat', which seems to be lexicalized with the meaning of 'be', precisely as 'salmon' is in Figure 2.

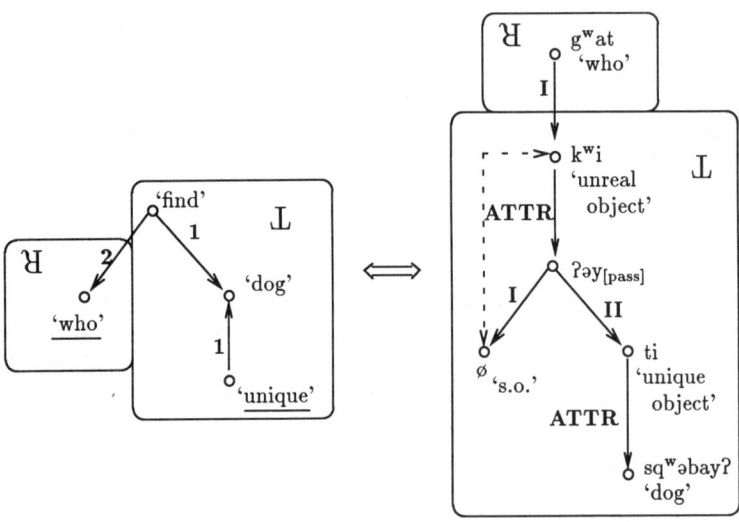

Figure 8: *Syntacticization of* gʷat kʷi ʔuʔəy̌dub ʔə ti sqʷəbay? *'who did the dog find'?*

In technical terms, the syntacticization of the two negative sentences in the Figures 9 and 10 differs in choice of the "entry node" in the SemR—that is, the selection of which node in the semantic network will be realized in the syntax as the top of the deep-syntactic tree. For more familiar languages, selection of the entry node is governed by a few simple procedural rules, originally set out by Iordanskaja and Polguère (Iordanskaja & Polguère, 1988; Iordanskaja, 1990)—both cited in (Mel'čuk, 1997), paraphrased in (40):

(40) Rule$_{\text{Synt}}$ 1
A semantic node 'σ' in a SemS is its entry node IFF it is a functor and a Comm-Dominant node.

Rule$_{\text{Synt}}$ 2

(a) If one candidate for entry node has a natural verbal expression while the other does not, prefer the first one.

(b) If both candidates have (or lack) a natural verbal expression, prefer the candidate from the Sem-Rheme.

As a result of these rules, the choice of lexical entry node is in first place a verb (which is the natural lexicalization of a functor) and is only secondarily rhematic. As the rules are formulated here, the issue of lexical

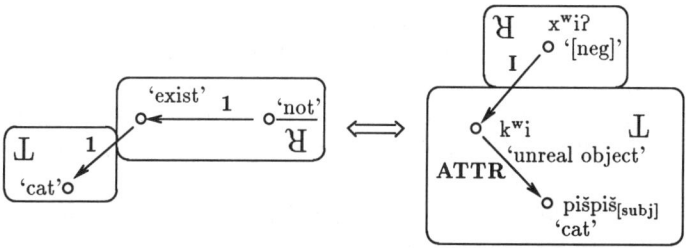

Figure 9: *Syntacticization of* xʷiʔ kʷi gʷəpišpiš *'there are no cats'*

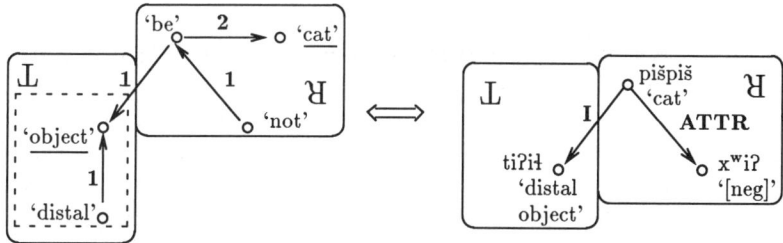

Figure 10: *Syntacticization of* xʷiʔ ləpišpiš tiʔiɬ *'that [is] not a cat'*

category takes precedence over thematicity, languages that follow the rules as laid out in (40) preferring the use of non-rhematic verbal elements (or the creation of dummy copular predicates) to the use of a non-verbal element as the top of a DSynt-tree. The situation in Lushootseed and Bella Coola, however, is quite different. In these languages, because whatever is Sem-Rheme must be realized as syntactic predicate, thematicity takes precedence over both lexical category and functor status in the SemR. This is seen clearly in examples such as the Lushootseed sentence, *wiwsu ti ʔučalad tiʔəʔ sqʷəbayʔ* 'the ones who chased the dog [are] children', in Figure 6 above. The choice of entry node (syntactic predicate) being restricted to elements from the Sem-Rheme, *wiwsu* 'children' becomes the DSynt-predicate whereas the verb *čalad* 'chase' surfaces in syntactically nominalized form in the Subject clause. On the other hand, in narratively-focused sentences such as that in (37b), where the event is rhematic, we get structures like Figure 4, in which it is the verb that is realized as DSynt-predicate. It is in these narratively-focused sentences, which have a Comm-Dominant functor (CDF) in the Sem-Rheme, that we find syntactic structures most closely parallel to those familiar to us from English.

An important point to make note of here is that in the SemR in Figure 4, there are two nodes contained within the Sem-Rheme—the functor 'take' and its first semantic argument, 'they'. The fact that in such sentences it is the verb that is realized as the top of the D-tree, rather than its co-rhematic nominal actant, is reminiscent of the rules for selection of the entry node in (40), and this observation is significant in that it gives us a clue as to how we might want to reformulate these rules for languages like Lushootseed and Bella Coola. Clearly, while there are profound differences in the conditioning of syntacticization by the SemCommS, the same types of process do seem to be at work. In the discussion of the structures in Figure 4, for instance, we saw the kind of preference for a verb as the entry node for a DSynt-structure expressed in $Rule_{Synt}$ 2(a), whereas in Figure 5 we have a structure in which the top node of the DSynt-tree is filled by a deictic—that is, by a Comm-Dominant node—as predicted by $Rule_{Synt}$ 1. Even the major difference between Lushootseed and Bella Coola and languages like English—the requirement that predicates be Sem-Rhemes—is captured by (or is at least latent in) $Rule_{Synt}$ 2(b), which states that an entry node from the Sem-Rheme will be preferred over one from the Sem-Theme. What really seems to make Salishan languages distinctive is not so much the rules for selection of the entry node as it is the relative weight these rules are given. Borrowing a page from Optimality Theory (McCarthy & Prince, 1993), we can re-write the rules in (40) as the constraints in (41):

(41) <u>Comm-Dominant Functor</u> (CDF ≈ $Rule_{Synt}$ 1)
The entry node is a functor and a Comm-Dominant node.
<u>Select Verb</u> (SV ≈ $Rule_{Synt}$ 2(a))
The entry node is a verb.
<u>Rhematic Entry Node</u> (REN ≈ $Rule_{Synt}$ 2(b))
The entry node is from the Sem-Rheme.

These constraints, then, would show relative rankings for English and Salish as in (42):

(42) <u>English</u>
CDF >> SV >> REN
<u>Salish</u>
REN >> CDF, SV

According to (42), when selecting the entry node in an English-type language the first consideration is that the entry node be a semantic functor, after which considerations of lexical category and then thematicity come into play. In Bella Coola and Lushootseed, on the other hand, thematicity is the first concern, and issues of lexical category and functor-status in the SemR become secondary.[17] The nice thing about this analysis is that it permits all of the same constraints to be operative in all the languages discussed here, but allows for different outcomes in that when these constraints come into conflict, the two types of language make different choices about which constraint will be violated in favour of another. For instance, the SemR in Figure 6, the answer to the question "Who chased the dog?", gives rise to a nominal predicate in Lushootseed because a violation of SV and CDF is preferred over a violation of REN,[18] whereas the same SemR in English would give us the sentence *The children chased the dog*, which obeys CDF and SV, but violates REN in that the syntactic predicate has been selected from the Sem-Theme rather than the Sem-Rheme. Comparisons of this type are an important first step in the treatment of cross-linguistic variation in the patterns of communicative organization, and highlight the advantages of frameworks such as the MTT that allow for a thorough and rigorous treatment of the details of communicative structure.

5 Conclusion: Towards a Communicative Typology of Language

The principal goal of this paper has been to elucidate some of the basic syntactic patterns of Bella Coola and Lushootseed and to illustrate the effects the Semantic-Communicative Structure of a sentence has on the syntax of these languages. As we have seen, the Theme/Rheme division is absolutely essential in determining the most basic characteristics of the DSyntS of a sentence in that it is this communicative opposition that determines which element in the sentence will be realized as the syntactic predicate. As a result, words belonging to any lexical category can take on this role, as long as these elements belong to the Sem-Rheme. This presents an interesting contrast with the patterns found in more familiar languages, where considerations such as whether or not a given candidate for entry node is a semantic functor or whether it is lexicalizable as a verb seem to take precedence over issues of thematicity. Seen in this light, we might characterize the syntacticization process of Lushootseed and Bella Coola as being communicatively, or thematically, driven, whereas syntacticization

---

[17]At this point, there is little evidence for a relative ranking of CDF and SV, the environments necessary for establishing this kind of ranking not having been found in the data.
[18]Although if we take the nominal predicate as a zero-derived verb, SV is not violated, avoidance of an SV-violation being the trigger for the incorporation of the semanteme 'be' in the lexicalization of 'children'.

in languages such as English seems to be more lexically-driven, the major restriction on the identity of the syntactic predicate being that of lexical category. By the same token, analogous differences at other levels of representation might yield further material for cross-linguistic comparison—as, for instance, between languages like English—which ranks constraints on word-order highly—and languages like Russian, which encode such things as thematicity and foregrounding using permutations of linear order where English is forced to use alternations in voice and other conversion operations; see Mel'čuk 1997:126ff) for further discussion. Clearly, we have here the beginnings of a new kind of typology of human language, one based on the implementation of communicative structure, the varying strategies used to encode communicative oppositions, and the representational levels at which these oppositions find expression. The importance of such a typology for the understanding of natural language can not be emphasized enough, and represents a new and exciting avenue for research within Meaning-Text Theory.

Notes

[1] Hess (personal communication) does not accept the term "passive", particularly in third person, as in

(i) $\text{?}u+\text{?}əy+dx^w$ $ti\ sq^wəbay\text{?}$
[pnt]+find+[l.o.c.] D dog
'[he/she] found the dog'

(ii) $\text{?}u+\text{?}əy+du+b$ $\text{?}ə\ ti\ čačas\ ti\ sq^wəbay\text{?}$
[pnt]+find+[l.o.c.]+[md] P D child D dog
'the boy found the dog'

(Hess, 1993:29)

Here, the unrealized Agent in (i) surfaces in the oblique position in (ii), but according to Hess the overt NP undergoes no change in syntactic role. Under my own analysis, the finder (whose identity would be understood from discourse) in (i) is in fact present in the SyntR and acts as syntactic Subject, but is unrealized in the surface form of the utterance. Thus, the unrealized Subject in (i) does undergo demotion to Oblique Object in (ii), just as the Direct Object of (i) undergoes promotion to Subject, although this promotion receives no overt morphosyntactic marking beyond the change in verbal morphology (specifically, the occurrence of a causative with a middle-suffix) which marks any non-oblique NP as the clausal Subject. For further justification of the term 'passive', see (Beck, 1996). Note also that, as Hess quite correctly points out, the pragmatic uses of the Lushootseed passive differs from those of its English counterpart (hence the active glosses); in discourse terms, this voice may fall into the functional category of "inverse". Jacobs (1994) offers such an analysis for the cognate voice in another Salish language, Squamish, based on statistical studies of topicality; it remains to be seen what the results of applying this method to Lushootseed would be.

[2] In Lushootseed, morphological nominalizations can be treated as participles or gerunds, the Subject surfacing as a possessor (marked in (17b) by the preposition ʔə) as it does in such constructions in numerous languages. In Bella Coola, the nominalized clause is indistinguishable from a finite clause except for the addition of the s-prefix, and so is best treated as a "sentential nominalization", the semantic equivalent of English *that*-constructions, e.g., [*That she snores at night*] *bothers me no end*.

[3] Nater (1984) claims that gender in Bella Coola is grammatical and posits three classes—female, non-female, and neutral. The neutral class, however, has no forms of its own but instead alternates between feminine and non-feminine forms; furthermore, all of Nater's examples of this alternation seem to indicate that it is, in fact, a reflection of natural gender, as in *ti+skma* 'bull moose'/*ci+skma* 'cow moose'. As Nater himself points out, membership in a given gender class is predictable on a semantic basis: the only example he gives of what might be purely grammatical gender is *ci+waac* 'wristwatch'. Thus, it seems preferable to follow Davis and Saunders and treat Bella Coola gender as a natural, feminine/non-feminine distinction. Hess (personal communication) notes that in Lushootseed the feminine deictic *tsi* is used occasionally with genderless objects (for example by men referring to their hunting canoes) and small animals. Note also that while the Lushootseed feminine deictic is pronounced [ci], it will be presented here in standard Lushootseed orthographic form <tsi>, which makes explicit the presence of the feminine infix.

[4] An alternative to this would be to treat the two uses of the deictics as two separate lexemes, one of which appears as an enclitic in NPs and the other which serves as a pronoun. In this case, the distribution of the pronominal form would not have any bearing on our analysis of the head-dependent status of the proclitic-enclitic pairs, which would be heads based on the first part of Criterion B.I. alone.

[5] Donna Gerdts (personal communication) reports that videotapes of Speakers of Halkomelem (a language closely related to Lushootseed) reveal storytellers using body language to establish locations associated with particular event participants, which they then manipulate to maintain and shift topics (bringing topical participants "closer" to the Speaker by gesture, using established points to identify referents of pronominals or agentless clauses, etc.) in a way reminiscent of techniques used by speakers of American Sign Language.

List of Abbreviations

1	first person	md	middle
2	second person	neg	negative
3	third person	NP	noun phrase
add	additive	np	nominalizing prefix
agt	agent	op	object-permutative
ap	antipassive	P	preposition
appl	applicative	p	plural
att	attemptive	part	participle
ben	benefactive	pass	passive

caus	causative	perf	perfective
cnf	confirmative	pnt	punctual
D	deictic	po	possessive
dp	derivational prefix	prog	progressive
f	feminine	qtv	quotative
gen	genitive	rel	relative-marker
hab	habitual	s	singular
int	interrogative	stat	stative
irr	irrealis	subj	subjunctive
l.o.c.	lack of control	trm	transmutative

Acknowledgements

The author would like to acknowledge the helpful advice provided on this paper by Elaine Gold, Keren Rice, and Leslie Saxon, and—as ever—the detailed and insightful criticisms of Igor Mel'čuk. Of course, none of the aforementioned are to be held responsible for the shortcomings that remain.

Bibliography

Abney, S. 1987. *The English Noun Phrase in Its Sentential Aspect*. PhD thesis. Cambridge, MA: Massachusetts Institute of Technology.

Bates, D., T. Hess & V. Hilbert. 1994. *Lushootseed Dictionary*. Seattle: University of Washington Press.

Beck, D. 1995a. "Conceptual Approach to Lexical Categories in Bella Coola and Lushootseed". *Proceedings of the 30th International Conference on Salish and Neighbouring Languages*. 1–31. Victoria, B.C.: University of Victoria.

Beck, D. J. 1995b. *A Comparative Conceptual Grammar of Bella Coola and Lushootseed*. Master's thesis. Victoria, B.C.: University of Victoria.

Beck, D. 1996. "Transitivity and Causation in Lushootseed Morphology". *Proceedings of the 11th Northwest Linguistics Conference*. Victoria, B.C.: Linguistics Circle of the University of Victoria.

Bertagaev, T. A. & T. B. Tsydendambaev. 1962. *Grammatika burjatskogo jazyka. (A grammar of Buriat.)*. Moscow: Vostočnaja Literatura.

Davis, H. & L. Matthewson. 1995. "Yet more on Category-Neutrality in Salish". *Paper presented to the III UVic Salish Morphosyntax Workshop.* Victoria, B.C.: University of Victoria.

Davis, H. & L. Matthewson. 1996. "The Structure of DP in Statimcets (Lillooet Salish)". *Proceedings of the 30th International Conference on Salish and Neighbouring Languages.* 55–68. Victoria, B.C.: University of Victoria.

Davis, P. & R. Saunders. 1975. "Bella Coola Nominal Deixis". *Language.* 51:845–858.

Davis, P. & R. Saunders. 1978. "Bella Coola Syntax". *Linguistic Studies of Native Canada* ed. by E. Cook & J. Kaye. 37–65. Vancouver: University of British Columbia Press.

Davis, P. & R. Saunders. 1980. *Bella Coola Texts.* Victoria: British Columbia Provincial Museum.

Davis, P. & R. Saunders. 1984. "Propositional Organization: The "s-" and "si-" Prefixes in Bella Coola". *International Journal of American Linguistics.* 50:208–231.

Givón, T. 1979. *On Understanding Grammar.* New York: Academic Press.

Halliday, M.A.K. 1970. "Language Structure and Language Function". *New Horizons in Linguistics* ed. by J. Lyons. 140–165. Aylesbury: Penguin.

Hess, T. 1976. *Dictionary of Puget Salish.* Seattle: University of Washington Press.

Hess, T. 1993. *Lushootseed Reader with Introductory Grammar: Volume I—Four Stories from Edward Sam (revised edition).* Victoria: Tulalip.

Hess, T. & V. Hilbert. 1976. *Lushootseed: An Introduction, Books 1 and 2.* University of Washington: American Indian Studies.

Hudson, R. 1974. "Structural Sketch of Beja". *African Language Studies.* XV:111–142.

Hudson, R. 1990. *English Word Grammar.* Basil Blackwell: Oxford.

Iordanskaja, L.N. 1990. "Ot semantičeskoj seti k glubinno-sintaksičeskomu derevu: pravila naxoždenija veršiny dereva". *Metody formalne w opisie języków słowiańskich [= Festschrift Jurij Apresjan]* ed. by Z. Saloni. 33–46. Białystok: Uniwersytet Warszawski.

Iordanskaja, I.A. & A. Polguère. 1988. "Semantic Processing for Text Generation". *Proceedings of the International Computer Science Conference '88.* 310–318. Hong Kong.

Jacobs, P. 1994. "The Inverse in Squamish". *Voice and inversion* ed. by T. Givón. 121–145. Amsterdam & Philadelphia: Benjamins Academic Publishers.

Jelinek, E. in press. "Pronoun Classes and Focus". *Workshop on Focus.* Amherst, MA: University of Massachusetts at Amherst.

Jelinek, E. & R. Demers. 1994. "Predicates and Pronominal Arguments in Straits Salish". *Language.* 70:697–736.

Kinkade, M. D. 1983. "Salishan Evidence against the Universality of 'noun' and 'verb' ". *Lingua.* 60:25–40.

Kinkade, M. D. 1990. "Sorting out Third Persons in Salish Discourse". *International Journal of American Linguistics.* 56:341–360.

Kroeber, P. 1991. *Comparative Syntax of Subordination in Salish.* PhD thesis. Chicago, IL: University of Chicago.

Kuipers, A. 1968. "The Categories of Verb-Noun and Transitive-Intransitive in English and Squamish". *Lingua.* 21:610–626.

Langacker, R. 1991. *Foundations of Cognitive Grammar, Volume 2: Descriptive Application.* Stanford: Stanford University Press.

McCarthy, J. & A. Prince. *Prosodic Morphology I: Constraint Interaction and Satisfaction.* 1993. University of Massachusetts and Brandeis University.

Mel'čuk, I.A. 1988. *Dependency Syntax: Theory and Practice.* Albany: State University of New York Press.

Mel'čuk, I.A. 1997. *The Communicative Structure in Language.* Technical report: Département de Linguistique et de Traduction, Université de Montréal.

Nater, H. 1984. *The Bella Coola Language.* Ottawa: National Museum of Man.

Nicodemus, L. 1975. *Snchitsu'umshtsn: The Coeur D'Alene Language: A Modern Course.* Plummer, ID: The Coeur D'Alene Tribe.

Radford, A. 1988. *Transformational Grammar*. Cambridge: Cambridge University Press.

Sandmann, M. 1979. *Subject and Predicate*. Heidelberg: Carl Winter.

Skorik, P. I. 1968. *Jazyki narodov S.S.S.R.: Tom V—Mongol'skie, tunguso-manžurskie i paleoaziatskie jazyki. (Languages of the peoples of the U.S.S.R.: Volume V—Mongolian, Tungus-Manchu and Paleo-asiatic languages.)*. St. Petersburg: Nauka.

van Eijk, J. & T. Hess. 1986. "Noun and Verb in Salishan". *Lingua*. 69:319–331.

van Langendonck, W. 1994. "Determiners as Heads?". *Cognitive Linguistics*. 5:243–259.

Scope of Generic Noun Phrases and Its Correlation with the Verb Meaning in Russian

Igor Boguslavsky

1 Introduction

The problem we are dealing with in this paper concerns the question of how the meanings of sentence elements combine with each other to form the meaning of the whole sentence. As it is well-known, the most common means of meaning combination is valency filling. Normally, a word L fills its valencies with a phrase consisting of one or several words. However, there are cases where only some part of the lexical meaning of a word or of a word combination fills a valency of L; that is, falls within the scope of L. In such situations we say that L has an *inner* scope. The most obvious example of a word with the inner scope is negation, since it affects only the assertive part of a word meaning and leaves the presupposition beyond its scope. Examples of the inner scope abound in (Mel'čuk & Žolkovskij, 1984). These examples show that some correlates of certain Lexical Functions, in particular **Magn**, not only can affect the meaning of the key word as a whole, but also are in the position to act upon some of its components. Only a very restricted class of words is capable of having an inner scope. In particular, quantifiers of the *every/some/any* type are devoid of this property. If a word falls within the scope of a quantifier, it falls there as a whole (Ioup, 1975; Saarinen, 1981). In this paper we argue that:

(i) the meaning of genericity that distinguishes generic noun phrases from non-generic ones is a meaning of the quantifier type;

(ii) as opposed to the quantifiers of the *every/some/any* type, the generic quantifier can have an inner scope, at least in Russian, and at least with respect to the predicates of a certain semantic class.

2 Predicates of Change and Conservation of State and the Problem of Coreferentiality

Let us consider a class of Russian predicates denoting the change or conservation of state (CCS) predicates. This class includes in particular such words as:
perestavat′ '[to] stop', *prekraščat′* '[to] cease', *končat′* '[to] finish', *utračivat′* '[to] lose', *brosat′* '[to] give up', ... ;

načinat′ '[to] begin', *vozobnovljat′* '[to] resume', ... ;

zainteresovat′sja '[to] take an interest (in)', *prodolžat′* '[to] continue', etc.;

eščë 'still', *uže* 'already', *uže ne* 'no more', *bol′še ne* 'no longer',
...

These words have a common property which is essential for the present discussion: their meaning contains two propositions describing the state of affairs at different times. For example, the meaning of a sentence containing *bol′še ne* 'no longer' can be (somewhat roughly) represented by the following semantic structure (we shall, for the sake of simplicity, represent semantic structures by ordinary English sentences; this will not have any significant impact on the outcome of our discussion):

(1)   *Ivan bol′še ne podražaet svoemu učitelju*
      'Ivan no longer imitates his teacher'.

(1′)   a. 'before a given moment Ivan imitated his teacher';
       b. 'after this moment Ivan does not imitate him'.

When speaking about semantic structures of such sentences, we shall, for the sake of brevity, refer to propositions of type (a), which denote a preceding state, as *initial propositions*, and to propositions of type (b), which denote a state that follows, as *final propositions*.

It is evident that certain sentential elements, primarily noun phrases, which occur only once in sentence (1) appear to be represented twice in its semantic structure (1′). Naturally, occurrences of a noun phrase which go back to the same noun phrase in the original sentence (1) should be coreferential in the semantic structure. Propositions (1′a) and (1′b), for example, refer to the same Ivan and the same teacher.

In a general case, coreferentiality of noun phrases that denote the same semantic entity in the real sentence is not so obvious as it may seem in the semantic structure. Consider sentence (2):

(2) *Učeniki bol'še ne podražajut svoemu učitelju*
'Students do not imitate their teacher any more'.

This sentence is open to two interpretations. On the one hand, the Speaker may have in mind some people who had imitated their teacher but later ceased to do so. In this case, the two occurrences of the noun phrase *učeniki* 'students' in the semantic structure are coreferential in exactly the same way as the two occurrences of *Ivan* in (1').

On the other hand, sentence (2) can be used in a situation where present students do not imitate their teacher, as opposed to the students he had in the past. Under this interpretation, the mentions of the noun phrase *učeniki* in the initial and in the final proposition do not necessarily denote the same people.

Many other CCS predicates behave in the same way. The sentences (3a) to (3f) contain two propositions corresponding to different periods of time. Each time, the persons mentioned in the initial and in the final proposition may be either identical or different.

(3) a. *Studenty načali <perestali> interesovat' sja politikoj*
'Students took <lost> interest in politics'.
b. *Matematiki poljubili <razljubili> lingvistiku*
'Mathematicians began <ceased> to like linguistics'.
c. *Molodjož uvleklas' <zainteresovalas'> biznesom*
'Young people became enthusiastic about <took an interest in> business'.
d. *Anglijskie koroli utratili pravo vvodit' novye nalogi*
'English kings lost the right to introduce new taxes'.
e. *Činovniki prodolžajut brat' vzjatki*
'Officials continue to accept bribes'.
f. *Staršeklassniki eščë <vse eščë/uže/uže ne/bol'še ne> kurjat*
'High school students still <still/already/already do not/no longer> smoke'.

In what follows, we will aim at disclosing the essence of this phenomenon. How do interpretations arise under which the objects mentioned in the initial and final propositions need not be identical? Should it mean that the CCS predicates may allow non-coreferential mentions of the same noun phrase in the semantic structure?

3 Coreferentiality of Generic Noun Phrases

It would be wrong to make the proposal suggested at the end of the last section that the CCS predicates may allow non-coreferential mentions of the same noun phrase in the semantic structure. Referential identity of referential noun phrases that go back to the same prototype in the real sentence is an obligatory property of CCS predicates. It is the character of this identity that can be different.

Note, first of all, that the discussed interpretation of a noun phrase is only possible when the latter is generic and denotes an open class of objects (i.e., has unlimited extension). The identity of open classes is not treated in natural language in the same way as the identity of closed classes (and, in particular, the identity of singular objects). If a class is closed, the initial and the final propositions of the CCS predicates strictly refer to the same objects. In the case of open classes, the coreferentiality takes on a slightly different appearance. When such a class is mentioned for the second time, it is not supposed to consist of exactly the same elements. A class may retain its identity even if all its elements have changed. For example, in (4)

(4) *Kogda-to v Sredizemnom more vodilis' kity, a teper' ix tam ne najti*
'In the old days, there were whales in the Mediterranean, and now they cannot be found there'

the personal pronoun *ix* 'they' does not refer to the same animals that used to live in the Mediterranean. What is conceived of as identical is the class of whales itself, and not its specific members. Although this class consists now of entirely different elements than earlier, we can still consider it to be the same class because the elements have the same definitional properties.

Naturally, when noun phrases denoting classes are coreferential, in a particular case, the elements of these classes may coincide. It is just this fact that makes a two-way interpretation for sentences (2) to (3) possible.

It is important now to agree on the terms. Let a noun phrase denoting an open class have coreferential occurrences in propositions P and P'. We shall call an interpretation of a sentence *generally coreferential*, if it does not require that the elements referred to in P and P' necessarily be identical. In contrast to this, we shall call an interpretation *distributively coreferential*, if P and P' must apply to the same objects.

The question arises whether there exist predicates that require distributive coreferentiality. First of all, one should mention the verb *brosat'* '[to] give up', which is quasisynonymous with *perestavat'* '[to] stop'. Sentences (5) and (6) can be used to refer to the same state of affairs:

(5) *V prošlom godu Meri perestala kurit'*
'Last year, Mary stopped smoking'.
(6) *V prošlom godu Meri brosila kurit'*
'Last year, Mary gave up smoking'.

The main difference between the situation *brosat'* '[to] give up' and *perestavat'* '[to] stop' consists in the fact that in the first case the subject decides to stop performing the action, while in the second case this is not necessarily so.

Let us compare these verbs in the sentences containing generic noun phrases:

(7) *Amerikanskie devuški perestali kurit'*
'American girls stopped smoking'.
(8) *Amerikanskie devuški brosili kurit'*
'American girls gave up smoking'.

One can easily see that sentences (7) and (8) have lost the parallelism that existed between their non-generic counterparts (5) and (6). In (7), the noun phrase *amerikanskie devuški* 'American girls' can have a generally coreferential interpretation: formerly, it was typical of American girls to smoke, and now it is no longer the case. It is not supposed that any concrete girl had smoked and later stopped smoking. Sentence (8) does not allow this interpretation. It can only refer to the people who made themselves a transition from smoking to non-smoking.

This difference between sentences (7) and (8) is clearly motivated by the difference in the lexical meaning of *perestavat'* '[to] stop' and *brosat'* '[to] give up', which we mentioned above. For *brosat'*, the interpretation 'the girls of earlier days smoked and the present ones do not smoke' is impossible—if only because the situation of giving up necessarily presupposes that the person who smokes should take the decision to stop smoking.

Another example of predicates requiring distributive coreferentiality is the group of verbs consisting of *vyrasti* '[to] grow', *uveličit' sja* '[to] increase', *umen'šit' sja* '[to] grow smaller', and some others. Sentences (9) and (10), which refer to singular objects, are very close to be synonymous:

(9) *Sosna stala nemnogo vyše*
'The pine tree became a little higher'.
(10) *Sosna nemnogo vyrosla*
'The pine tree grew a little'.

However, if the Subject is generic, sentences are no longer synonymous:

(11) *Sosny v našix lesax stali nemnogo vyše*
'Pine trees in our forests became a little higher'.

(12) *Sosny v našix lesax nemnogo vyrosli*
'Pine trees in our forests grew a little'.

Sentence (11) allows generalized coreferentiality and can be easily interpreted in the sense 'the pine trees of today are higher than the pine trees of former times'. Sentence (12) can normally refer to the same trees. Should one try to use the verb *vyrasti* '[to] grow' in context which requires generalized coreferentiality, the sentence will result in a metaphor:

(13) *Za poslednie trista let evropejcy vyrosli na poltora santimetra*
'For the last three centuries Europeans grew by one centimeter and a half'.

The property of the verb *vyrasti* '[to] grow' of having a distributionally coreferential interpretation, just as it was the case of the verb *brosit'*, also seems to be motivated by the lexical meaning: *vyrasti* means 'to become higher due to an inner process'. For this reason, in the context of (14), *stat' vyše* '[to] become higher' is appropriate while *vyrasti* '[to] grow' is not:

(14) *Ja narastil nožki stola, i on stal vyše <*vyros>*
'I extended the legs of the table and it became higher'.

Another example of the same type is the verb *zabyvat'* '[to] forget'. Sentences (15a) and (15b) are very close in meaning whereas (16a) and (16b) are clearly opposed. (16a) has only a distributively coreferential interpretation, and (16b) can be interpreted in both ways:

(15) a. *Ja zabyl, kak eë zovut*
'I have forgotten her name'.
b. *Ja uže ne pomnju, kak eë zovut*
'I no longer remember her name'.

(16) a. *Ja zabyl, kak zovut moix studentov*
'I have forgotten my students' names'.
b. *Ja uže ne pomnju, kak zovut moix studentov*
'I no longer remember my students' names'.

These examples show that the difference between generalized and distributive coreferentiality is linguistically (and lexicographically) relevant.

4 Scope of the Genericity Quantifier

Now I shall try to find out about the semantic source of the difference between generalized and distributive coreferentiality, which cannot be reduced to possible differences in lexical meanings.

To do this, I shall consider generic noun phrases against the background of other types of quantified noun phrases. I shall take two types of quantified noun phrases which, for the properties relevant to the present discussion, are radically opposed to each other: the noun phrases that contain quantifiers *vse* 'all', *nekotorye* 'some', and the like and the noun phrases that are only quantified by the grammatical number. I shall compare them with respect to two features—a formal and a semantic one.

From the formal point of view, the quantification meaning in the first case is expressed by an autonomous word. In the second case, the meaning 'one'/'more than one' is conveyed within the nominal wordform.

From the semantic viewpoint, quantifying adjectives *vse* 'all', *nekotorye* 'some', and the like, as is well-known, include in their scope not only the noun phrase, but also the verbal phrase. Sentence (17)

(17)   *Vse deti ljubjat moroženoe*
'All children like ice cream'.

means 'for every child it is true that he likes ice-cream'. The combination *vse deti* 'all children' cannot be interpreted in and of itself, unless a predicate is specified which is ascribed to every child.

The grammemes of number behave differently. They semantically affect only the noun phrase in which they are included. The plural of the wordform *mal'čiki* 'boys' only means that the number of boys exceeds one. For a semantic interpretation, the plural does not need to go beyond the limits of the noun phrase.

These properties of noun phrases that are quantified by quantifiers of *vse/nekotorye*-type or by grammatical number are not independent from each other. There exists an important correlation between them. This correlation can be formulated as follows: the scope of a predicate expressed within the wordform does not, as a rule, go beyond its limits. Let me illustrate this point.

As is well-known, negation can be expressed in Russian both by means of a separate word (particle *ne* 'not') and within a lexeme. It is instructive to take a pair of antonyms, such as *sobljudat'* (*pravila*) '[to] observe (the rules)'—*narušat'* (*pravila*) '[to] break (the rules)'. As *narušat'* differs from *sobljudat'* in intralexical negation, one can achieve synonymous expressions by adding the negative particle *ne* to *sobljudat'* (Apresjan, 1974):

(18) a. *On ne budet sobljudat' priličija*
'He will not observe the proprieties'.
b. *On budet narušat' priličija*
'He will break the proprieties'.

Sentences (18a) and (18b) are synonymous because in both the negation has identical scope. Now, let me introduce into (18a,b) an adverbial capable of entering within the scope of negation:

(19) a. *On ne budet sobljudat' priličija radi tebja*
'He will not observe the proprieties for your sake'.
b. *On budet narušat' priličija radi tebja*
'He will break the proprieties for your sake'.

The synonymy vanishes. Sentence (19a) can mean 'it will not be true that he will observe the proprieties for your sake'. Sentence (19b) does not allow this interpretation. The reason is obvious: the particle *ne* in (19a) can easily include the adverbial into its scope, while the intralexical negation in (19b) is devoid of this ability.

Let us return to generic noun phrases and compare them to the quantified phrases discussed above. From the viewpoint of formal autonomy, the meaning of genericity is similar to the meaning of number grammemes. It is also melted into the nominal wordform. From the semantic viewpoint, however, it rather tends towards the *vse* 'all' type. Sentences (17) and (20) are very close in meaning though not fully identical:

(17) *Vse deti ljubjat moroženoe*
'All children like ice cream'.

(20) *Deti ljubjat moroženoe*
'Children like ice cream'.

In particular, sentence (17) seems to be more outright than (20). However, the difference between noun phrases in (17) and (20) is now less important than their similarity: a generic noun phrase of the *deti* 'children' type contains a quantifying meaning (*quantifier of genericity*), which can be roughly rendered as 'for all typical X's it is true that ... '.

It follows that the generic meaning occupies an intermediate position between quantifiers of the *vse* 'all'/*nekotorye* 'some' type and grammatical meanings of the 'singular'/'plural' type, and therefore is an arena of struggle between the two poles.

Due to its non-autonomy, the generic meaning is similar to number grammemes, which makes one expect its scope to be confined to the noun phrase. Due to its meaning, it gravitates towards the universal quantifier *vse*, and therefore should be able to include a verbal phrase into its scope.

Our main point is that both of these alternatives take place in reality, and it is just the difference between them that accounts for the opposition of generalized and distributive coreferentiality.

Let us turn once again to sentences (7) and (8).

(7) *Amerikanskie devuški perestali kurit'*
'American girls stopped smoking'.

(8) *Amerikanskie devuški brosili kurit'*
'American girls gave up smoking'.

Our hypothesis claims that the generic quantifier has different scopes in these sentences. Sentences (7) and (8) differ as to what element of the sentence has the wider scope—the verb or the quantifier of genericity. In (8) it is the quantifier that has the wider scope. This means that in constructing the semantic structure of the sentence one should begin with making explicit the meaning of the quantifier:

(8') 'for any typical X from the class of American girls it is true: X gave up smoking'.

In (8') the generic quantifier is already eliminated while the meaning of the verb still remains intact. Now we can make use of the semantic definition of the verb:

(8") 'for any typical X from the class of American girls it is true:
(a) before some moment X smoked;
(b) after this moment X does not smoke'.

In sentence (7), on the contrary, it is the verb that has the wider scope. Therefore, the first step in the meaning explication should be the elimination of the verb:

(7′) a. 'before some moment American girls smoked';
b. 'after this moment American girls do not smoke'.

In both propositions of (7′), the noun phrase *American girls* is generic. As was noted at the beginning of the paper, all CCS predicates require that Subjects in the propositions (a) and (b) be coreferential. This requirement is met in both (8″) and (7′), but in slightly different ways. In (8″), it is realized as the coreferentiality of individuals (the girls who do not smoke now are identical to those who used to smoke before). In (7′), it is the classes that are coreferential, which, as we have seen above, does not imply the identity of their elements. The genericity receives independent interpretations in (7″a) and (7″b):

(7″) a. 'before some moment for any typical X from the class of American girls it was true: X smoked';
b. 'after this moment for any typical X from the class of American girls it is true: X does not smoke'.

Semantic structures (7″) and (8″) explicitly reflect the semantic difference between the interpretations under discussion.

On the one hand, this difference manifests itself as the statement vs. the non-statement of the identity of the people who smoked earlier and do not smoke now. On the other hand, this difference should be considered as a direct effect of the difference in scope correlation: in (8) the meaning of cessation falls within the scope of the generic quantifier, and in (7), on the contrary, the quantifier finds itself in the scope of the verb. This scope difference automatically explains why the introduction of *vse* 'all' produces different results in (7) and (8).

In (8), the quantifier of genericity, exactly like the universal quantifier, extends its scope over the verb. For this reason, sentence (21) only differs from (8) to the extent to which the generic meaning differs from the meaning 'all' (cf. (17) vs. (20) above):

(21) *Vse amerikanskie devuški brosili kuritʹ*
'All American girls gave up smoking'.

In (7) the verb does not fall within the scope of the quantifier. If one introduces *vse* into this sentence, this pronoun will necessarily include the verb in its scope and the meaning of the sentence will drastically change:

(22) *Vse amerikanskie devuški perestali kuritʹ*
'All American girls stopped smoking'.

The coreferentiality of classes becomes impossible. The meaning of sentence (22) is much closer to that of (21) than the meaning of (7) to that of (8). Sentence (22) cannot be interpreted as 'American girls of earlier days smoked and the present ones do not smoke'.

A similar opposition holds between the meanings of *vyrasti* '[to] grow' and *stat′ vyše* '[to] become higher' (see (11) and (12) above). As opposed to (11), sentence (12) obviously implies that both propositions of the semantic structure refer to the same pine trees. As shown by our previous analysis, it is accounted for by the fact that the quantifier of genericity in (12) includes the verb into its scope and therefore affects both propositions of the verb meaning.

It should be stressed that no differences in the lexical meaning of the verbs *perestat′/brosit′* or *stat′ vyše/vyrasti* can account for different results when the *vse* 'all' quantifier is introduced in sentences (7) and (8) or (11) and (12). This discrepancy cannot be explained away without reference to the scope differences of the genericity quantifier.

5 Conclusion: Lexicographic Implications

To conclude, I shall touch the question of lexicographic description. What is the actual difference between the verbs of the *perestat′* and *stat′ vyše*-type, on the one hand, and the verbs of the *brosit′* and *vyrasti* type, on the other hand?

It is well-known that referential characteristics of actants belong to lexicographically relevant parameters of verbs. In particular, verbs can be restricted in their co-occurrence with noun phrases of certain referential status. For example, the verbs *vodit′sja* '[to] live somewhere (about animals, etc.)' and *vymirat′* '[to] die out' require their Subject to be of generic type.

The differences between the verbs that have been discussed above also have a bearing on the referential status of actants. But this requirement is of a quite different nature. It is not a question of the ability of the verb to co-occur with generic noun phrases. All the verbs mentioned freely co-occur with them. The restriction concerns the correlation of the verbal meaning and the meaning of genericity.

This problem is far from being relevant for every verb. It only arises when the meaning of a verb comprises two or more propositions, and each of them contains a mention of one and the same generic actant. Verbs may differ as to whether all the propositions fall within the scope of the same quantifier of genericity, or whether each proposition contains its own quantifier. It would be very interesting to examine from this perspective the whole class of multi-propositional predicates, but this task goes far beyond the limits of this short article.

Acknowledgements

I would like to express my deep gratitude to the colleagues with whom I have had an opportunity to discuss the problems touched upon in this paper. I have much benefited from the comments made by Ju. Apresjan, A. Bogusławski, L. Iomdin, I. Mel'čuk, and A. Šmelev.

Bibliography

Apresjan, Ju.D. 1974. *Leksičeskaja semantika*. Moscow: Nauka. The English translation appeared as *"Lexical Semantics. User's Guide to Contemporary Russian Vocabulary"*, Karoma, Ann Arbor, MI, 1992.

Ioup, G. 1975. "Some Universals for Quantifier Scope". *Syntax and Semantics, Vol. 4* ed. by J. P. Kimball. New York: Academic Press.

Mel'čuk, I.A. & A.K. Žolkovskij. 1984. *Explanatory Combinatorial Dictionary of Modern Russian*. Vienna: Wiener Slawistischer Almanach.

Saarinen, E. 1981. "Quantifier Phrases Are (At Least) Five Ways Ambiguous in Intentional Contexts". *Ambiguities in Intentional Contexts* ed. by F. Heny. Dordrecht: Reidel Publishing Company.

Valency and Underlying Structure: An Alternative View on Dependency

Petr Sgall

1 Introduction

Unfortunately, the development of linguistic thinking has not been studied and taken into account to a sufficient degree in all schools of modern theoretical linguistics. Some schools have not been able to avoid certain fallacies that have already been recognized in other schools. One of the issues that illustrate this negligence is (immediate) constituent and phrase structure, which does not account for the functional aspects of language. The notion of constituency and phrase structure has been adopted by N. Chomsky and his followers from Bloomfield's descriptive linguistics, whose view on language Chomsky has found unsatisfactory probably in all other basic topics. It has also been taken up by those who develop new approaches taking otherwise Chomsky's theory as their starting point only with highly polemic attitudes. With the single exception of Fillmore's *Case Theory*, it has not been registered in the main-stream linguistics that European structural linguistics developed another view on syntax, a view that is based on *valency*, or *dependency*.

Similarly to I. Mel'čuk, Ju. Apresjan, R. Hudson, P. Hellwig, J. Kunze, S. Starosta, and many other linguists, we (in *The Prague Charles University Research Group on Theoretical and Computational Linguistics*) subscribe to the dependency-based approach and are convinced that it is adequate for a formal functional description of language, as well as for computational treatment. We also understand it as a condition of adequacy for a linguistic description to proceed from meaning to the outer shape of sentences. This has always been a feature common to the *Meaning-Text Theory* (MTT) and to the framework of *Functional Generative Description* (FGD) developed by the Prague group.[1]

One of the indications for the adequacy of dependency syntax is that its elements are present in theories overtly based on other approaches. Thus, e.g., Fillmore's account of *Deep Cases* has finally found a reflection in Chomsky's theory: *theta roles* and *theta grids* represent an ultimate intrusion of valency into the *Theory of Principles and Parameters*. Already at the preceding stages of Chomsky's approach, several notions derived from dependency were present. Thus, terms like *head* and *modifier* have always been employed—although with no firm basis in the formal framework of the approach. The use of such names as NP, AP, etc. for grammatical categories also discloses that phrases are understood to have heads or governors. Moreover, the *X-Bar Theory* can be directly compared with dependency syntax formalisms, be it the one known from Gaifman (1965) or those formulated by the authors quoted above.

2 Dependency Syntax and Underlying Structure

Thus we can state that dependency is combined with constituency not only in approaches that proclaim the fundamental importance of functions and relations, as *Lexical Functional Grammar* and *Relational Grammar*, but also in Chomsky's theory. We may then ask whether the theta roles can be understood as primitive notions, instead of being derived from constituent structure, i.e., whether a more economical description without constituency can be found.[2] This concerns not only the theta roles proper, i.e., arguments, or participants (inner complementations), but also the free (adverbial) complementations, or adjuncts. One might argue that the number of primitive notions would then grow too big. However, it should be recalled that most of the kinds of complementations are underlying counterparts of prepositions, subordinating conjunctions or similar morphemes, which most theories understand as primitives. They cannot be considered as purely lexical items since they clearly function as grammatical means: they cannot be freely syntactically expanded. Thus, we do not consider their underlying correlates to be lexical units, and we treat them as parts (indices) of complex labels of nodes of a syntactic tree, rather than as corresponding to specific nodes.

Due to such restrictions as projectivity of the dependency tree, the syntactic representations of sentences can be handled by limited means—although they possess more than two dimensions, and thus constitute networks in a sense more complex than planar graphs. Example (1) shows such a network in linearized form, as a string of complex symbols with two kinds of parentheses (one of which denotes dependency, the other coordination together with apposition). Each of the complex symbols consists of a lexical part and a combination of symbols (called *grammatemes*) for

VALENCY AND UNDERLYING STRUCTURE 151

values of grammatical categories (number, tense, modality, etc.) and the type of syntactic dependency, i.e., valency. The structure of the lexical part can only be described adequately if the achievements of V. Rozencvejg, I. Mel'čuk, Ju. Apresjan and their followers are taken into account. Valency can equivalently be denoted in terms of indices of arcs in a network or in terms of indices of parentheses. The possibility to use such a framework for the description of various combinations of the two kinds of relations (dependency and coordination) can be illustrated by our example, where (1b) is a simplified underlying representation of the sentence (1a), or, more precisely, the representation of one of its readings.

(1) a. *Martin's brother and Ann, who are a nice pair, moved from a town to a village.*
  b. ([[(*Martin*.Appurt) *brother*.Def.Sg.Actor *Ann*.Actor.Conj]
  ((**Rel**.Actor) *be*.Pres.Decl.Gener
  (*pair*.Specif.Sg.Obj (*nice*.Gener))))
  move.f.Pret.Decl
  (*town*.Specif.Sg.Dir-1) (*village*.Specif.Sg.Dir-2)

The symbols for Actor, Appurtenance, General Relationship, Objective, Directional-1 and Directional-2 as types of dependency are self-explanatory, and so are the symbols for conjunction as a kind of coordination (*vs.* disjunction, apposition, and other values) and definite, specifying, singular, present, declarative, etc., as values of morphological categories. 'Rel' denotes the (prototypical case of a) relative pronoun. The index 'f' indicates that the verb belongs to the Focus. The differences between the underlying and the surface word order positions of the noun *pair* and the adjective *nice* are due to the fact that in the scale of communicative dynamism (see Section 3), in the prototypical case, an adjective is more dynamic than its head noun.

The units of the syntactic and morphological layers of the underlying structure can be delimited on the basis of operational criteria, as has been discussed in detail in (Panevová, 1974; Hajičová, 1979, 1983; Hajičová & Panevová, 1984; and Sgall, 1980); for more recent presentation, see especially (Sgall *et al.*, 1986).[3] Let us briefly mention here just one of the crucial problems related to the underlying structure. If the complementations (modifications, valency slots, roles, or kinds of dependency) are classified into inner and free complementations (Arguments and Adjuncts, Participants and Circumstantials, etc.), it is often not taken into account that the character of individual complementations as such has to be distinguished from their relationships to their individual heads. Thus, in our approach,

Actor, Addressee, Objective, Origin, and Effect are understood as inner participants. Most of these roles are illustrated by (2). The main criterion applied here is that each of the roles can occur at most once with a head-verb token (if neither coordination nor apposition is present), be they obligatory or optional with a given verb.

(2) Mother changed Jane's hair from a braid into ...
     Actor   Objective   Origin   Effect

On the other hand, the so-called free complementations, i.e., adverbials or adjuncts, are in some cases obligatory in connection with individual head words. For instance, the complementation of Dir-1 with [to] *arrive*, of Manner with [to] *behave*, of Appurtenance with *brother*, and so on. Thus, it is necessary to work with four cases as illustrated in Figure 1. Three of the cases (marked with the sign "+") must be specified in individual lexical entries—for instance, by means of indices that are identical for small groups of words with the same distributional properties. The fourth case (that of optional free complementations, marked with "−") can be handled uniformly for a whole word class with a single index common to the lexical entries of the class.

relationship to the head:	oblig.	optional
inner participant:	+	+
"free" adjunct:	+	−

Figure 1: *The two classes of complementations, their possible relationships to their heads, and the necessity to include them (+) or not (−) into lexical entries*

It should be borne in mind that complementations that are present (or even obligatory) in underlying structure can be absent at the surface (if the Speaker assumes that the specific context makes them easily recoverable for the Hearer). A suitable operational criterion for deletion of complementations at the surface level is given in Panevová's (1974) 'dialogue test':

> If A says: *Jim has already arrived*, this includes an assumption that the hearer will know whether *here* or *there* has been deleted; however, if this assumption is not met and the hearer asks *Where*, then A cannot answer *I don't know*.[4]

This shows that such a complementation is obligatory, although deletable.

The following examples of valency frames (see Section 5 for their more complete description) illustrate our classification of complementations.

bring	V Act$_1^1$ Obj$_1^1$ Dir.2
change	V Act$_1^1$ Obj$_1^1$ Or$_1$ Eff$_1^1$
give	Act$_1^1$ Addr$_1^1$ Obj$_1^1$
rain	V
brother	N Appurt^1
glass	N Material
man	N
full	A Material$_1^1$
green	A

Obligatory complementations have a superscript '^{1}', and the inner participants have a subscript '$_1$'. The symbol of the word class allows for a generally available list of free modifications (Adverbials, Adjuncts) to be identified. We present a list of valency patterns for verbs, with many omissions, in Section 3.

Another set of problems related to the underlying structure concerns the delimitation between underlying structure (and valency arguments, slots, or types of dependency relations as its main syntactic units) and the domain of cognition (the cognitive or ontological content). Underlying structure, which can be understood as the level of linguistic meaning in the sense of F. de Saussure, L. Hjelmslev, E. Coseriu and their followers (from a certain viewpoint also in the sense of R. Jakobson's invariants), is one of the levels of the language system (of linguistic competence). The cognitive content itself is not directly patterned by language and is not directly accessible to human observation. We return to these issues in Section 4.

The dependency-based approach seems to be suitable to describe the language system not just as an abstract mechanism (enumerating sentences with their structural description), but also as a mechanism that is anchored in context, i.e., that functions in communication. The importance of the communicative conditioning of language has recently clearly been substantiated, especially by Schnelle (1991). In this connection, it can be well shown that the structure of a sentence seen with due regard to its position in the context should be described as including *Topic-Focus Articulation* (TFA), i.e., what the sentence is about and what is new in the sentence. The presence of TFA in the sentence structure reflects the impact of communication on the structure of natural language. Language has developed during hundreds of millennia as a means of human communication, and factors that are determined by the "Given–New" strategy have highly influenced its structure. In order to be easily understood when formulating a sentence, the Speaker usually selects certain entities that may be assumed to be readily accessible in the Hearer's memory. These entities are then set into (new) relationships with other entities (possibly new for the Hearer). As we illustrate in Section 3, TFA is expressed by grammatical means and is relevant semantically. Thus, TFA has to be understood as one of the dimensions that constitute the basis of the sentence structure. This is well possible within dependency syntax, whereas in phrase structure-based approaches the notions of Topic and Focus (either of which often has a shape other than a constituent of whichever level) have not yet found a systematic description.[1] However, even with respect to a formal description of sentences it has been found (especially by the authors quoted above) that dependency may be understood as a more adequate basis than constituency. We shall see in Section 4 that a dependency-based model of syntax is suitable for handling underlying structure as a linguistic pattern of content. This model also allows for a great deal of grammatical information to be included in lexical entries (see Section 5). And, finally, it is also suitable for a specification of the representation of a sentence by means of a very economical mechanism, based on a few general and natural principles (Section 6).

It would be highly useful and interesting to compare the view of underlying syntax presented here in a systematic and detailed way with the syntactic levels as described in the MTT-framework.

3 Topic-Focus Articulation

Topic-Focus Articulation, whose crucial importance for understanding language as anchored in communication has been pointed out above, can be systematically described if it is taken into account that the repertoires of types of complementation (Arguments and Adjuncts) display a certain ordering. What we have in mind here is an ordering that corresponds primarily to the scale of *Communicative Dynamism* (CD) as known from Firbas's (1957; 1975) analysis of TFA, i.e., to the scale that goes from *topic proper* (what the sentence "is about") to *focus proper* (the core of the "new information"). As discussed by Sgall *et al.* (1986, Chapter 3), the scale of CD (or the underlying word order) reflects this basic order of complementations within the Focus part of the sentence. The basic order is called *Systemic Ordering* (SO). Only if a complementation is *contextually bound* (CB) in a sentence,[2] can its position be shifted on the scale of CD more to the left than it is according to SO.[5] Such a shift is illustrated by example (3), as compared to (1a) above:

---

[1]The constituency-based approaches that work with some kind of Focus inheritance find it difficult to account, e.g., for cases in which the Focus consists of more than a single NP, but less than the whole VP.

[2]A complementation is considered to be contextually bound, if, roughly speaking, it belongs to the topic of a sentence, i.e., to the "given" or "known" information.

(3) *Martin and Ann moved to a village from a town.*

This sentence (pronounced with normal intonation, i.e., with the intonation center at the end) is less ambiguous than (1a), in that here the Dir-2 group (*to a village*) belongs to the Topic (is CB) in all readings, whereas the Dir group (*from* ...) belongs to the Topic in some of the readings of (1a), and to the Focus in others. The rightmost group, which bears the intonation center, always belongs to the Focus. In (3), this is Dir-1, which precedes Dir-2 according to SO. With other pairs of complementations a similar relationship can be found; consider the following examples:

(4) a. *They went by car to a river.*
     b. *They went to a river by car.*

(5) a. *Jim dug a ditch with a hoe.*
     b. *Jim dug a DITCH with a hoe.*

(6) a. *Ron cannot sleep quietly in a hotel.*
     b. *In a hotel, Ron cannot sleep quietly.*

(7) a. *Dutch companies published many books on linguistics.*
     b. *Many books on linguistics were published by Dutch companies.*

Here again, each of the (a) examples is ambiguous in that in some of its readings, the penultimate complementation belongs to the Focus, and in some to the Topic. The (b) examples are less ambiguous in that the correlate of the group just mentioned belongs to the Topic (is CB) in all readings (with the given intonation pattern, where the capitals denote its secondary placement). Let us add that the "free" word order, which is also present in English (see especially the examples (3) and (4)), is not really free, but is determined by TFA, or more precisely, by the scale of CD, i.e., by the underlying word order. The limitations of the surface word order in English are related to the fact that a secondary placement of the intonation center occurs relatively often here. Consider (5b) for illustration. Also, in some cases, syntactic devices such as passivization are used to allow the surface word order to correspond to the underlying word order; consider (7b). These and similar examples have been analyzed with several series of tests (for Czech, German and recently also for English), with the result that SO differs from one language to the other. It appears that for some of the main complementations of English, the scale of SO is as follows:

Actor–Addressee–Objective–Origin (Source)–Effect–Manner–
Directional-1–Means–Directional-2–Locative

Czech, and probably also German, differ from English in that the positions of Objective and Effect in these languages are more to the right, after most of the adverbial complementations. This may be justified typologically, since in English the participants that are expressed without a function morpheme could not be easily recognized if separated from the verb by a series of prepositional groups. In German, the Means probably precedes the Objective under SO, so that (8a) below is ambiguous as for the position of the Means (CB or NB, i.e., contextually not bound), whereas (8b) lacks this ambiguity (the Objective always belongs here to the Topic):

(8) a. *Jim hat mit einer Hacke eine Rinne gegraben*
     lit. 'Jim has with a hoe dug a ditch'.
     b. *Jim hat eine Rinne mit einer Hacke gegraben*
     'Jim has a ditch with a hoe dug'.

That is, Indo-European languages differ from each other in the shape of SO. In consequence, it has to be noticed that SO changes during the development of a language. Because such changes are very slow, it may be assumed that there are transition periods in which the position of a given pair of complementations in SO of a language varies stylistically, locally, or with individual verbs.

It should be recalled that TFA is not only a matter of contextual positions of sentences, of pragmatics (or of stylistics), but that it is semantically relevant—even from the viewpoint of truth conditions. This is true not only of sentences with such overt complex quantifiers as those illustrated by (9) and (10), but also for other examples; see, for instance, (11) and (12).

(9) a. *Everybody in this room knows at least two languages.*
     b. *At least two languages are known by everybody in this room.*

(10) a. *John talked to a few girls about many problems.*
     b. *John talked about many problems to a few girls.*

(11) a. *English is spoken in the Shetlands.*
     b. *ENGLISH is spoken in the Shetlands.*

(12) a. *They smoke in the corridor.*
      b. *They SMOKE in the corridor.*

Moreover, the means for realizing TFA clearly belong into the grammar. They concern surface word order; in some languages such as Japanese, Tagalog, etc. specific morphemes; the difference between clitic and "strong" forms of pronouns (e.g., in Czech); and also syntactic constructions such as passivization, clefting, or such inversion verb constructions as the English *make into* vs. *make out of*. Furthermore, the placement of the intonation center within a sentence should be regarded as a phonologically relevant feature. Therefore, we consider TFA as one of the dimensions of the underlying structure of the sentence. TFA belongs to the system of language, not only to the functioning of language in communication.

4 Status of Underlying Structure

As already mentioned above, the underlying structure can be characterized as the level of linguistic (literal) meaning, i.e., as a pattern of the cognitive content that is determined by a particular language. The cognitive content itself is not directly accessible to the human observer. The underlying structure corresponds to the "naive ontology" that is based on the interpretation of the world as defined in terms of events, objects, properties, relations between events and properties, and so on. The underlying structure and its description can serve as a useful interface between linguistics in the narrow sense (the theory of language systems) on one side, and interdisciplinary domains such as that of semantic interpretation (logical analysis of language, reference assignment based on inferences using contextual and other knowledge, further metaphorical and other figurative meanings, discourse or text linguistics, etc.) on the other side. It should be noticed that only a small part of the information conveyed by a message is actually contained in the linguistic patterns of utterances. While interpreting a linguistic pattern, the Hearer has all his mental ability at his disposal, so that he understands much more than what he is actually told. Thus, for instance, in (13) it is understood only via inferences based on factual knowledge (general, in this case) that the door Jim closed was the one through which he came into the room where Jane was watching TV (in fact, a context can be imagined where he entered another room or closed another door).

(13) *While Jane was still watching TV, John entered the room and closed the door.*

This step in semantic interpretation (concerning reference assignment) does not belong to the system of language, although, of course, it constitutes an important object of linguistic (and interdisciplinary) studies.[6] The semantic (and pragmatic) interpretation also includes other "not-purely-linguistic" steps (the interplay between which is quite complex). One of them concerns checking the uttered sentence for absence of contradictions. In another one, the choice is made between possible figurative meanings and hyperbolic ways of speaking. The illocutionary force of the primary or secondary speech act is determined on this basis. Further steps in the process of interpretation include, for instance, the examination of the truth conditions of the (declarative) sentence and, after their confrontation with the situation spoken about, also the truth value of the utterance.

In several approaches based on syntactic dependency, as well as in approaches that are based on constituency, a level of surface syntax is used together with a level of underlying sentence structure. Certainly, this was useful in the first studies concerning grammatical ambiguity and synonymy in a framework using explicitly characterized levels. However, it is not certain whether strictly synonymous syntactic constructions exist. Examples such as the following were taken to be synonymous in some of the studies quoted above, including those of the Prague group:

(14) a. *After he arrived, we started to discuss this.*
b. *After his arrival we started to discuss this.*

(15) a. *She told them to sing.*
b. *She told them that they should sing.*

However, in (14b) the *after*-group does not express tense; the fact that the time point of *arrival* precedes that of the utterance is only inferred from the combination of the meanings of *after* and of (the Preterite in) *started*. On the other hand, for instance, in (16) such an inference cannot take place and the temporal relationship remains indistinct then. That is, (16) corresponds semantically either to (17a) or to (17b).

(16) *After his arrival we will start to discuss this.*

(17) a. *After he arrives, we will start to discuss this.*
b. *(Now,) after he has arrived, we will start to discuss this.*

Thus, synonymy is at least questionable here. This is similar to (15). In (15a), the coreference of *them* with the deleted Subject of the infinitive is grammatical (intrasentential control relationship). In (15b), the coreference is textual, expressed by a pronoun whose reference is, in general, indistinct. So that (as for restrictions determined by grammar) the referential identity in (15b) is not ensured. Compare (18), where in (b) *them* refers to *Mary and Paul*, whereas *they* refers to their children:

(18) a. *She told Mary and Paul that their children should sing.*
       b. (*Mary and Paul asked the hostess what their children should do.*) *She told them that they should sing.*

Equally, in the case of passivization, it is still not clear whether a really synonymous pair of constructions is given. In languages where, in contrast to English, an active sentence and its passive counterpart can display the same word order (so that they often share their TFA), it would be possible to look for synonymy between active and passive verb forms. However, if a sentence contains an adverbial that has a specific relationship to the Subject (as, e.g., *inadvertently* or *with great pleasure*), the underlying structures of the active and the passive sentences appear to differ again.

The concept of Subject (as opposed to Actor, or underlying Subject) is certainly necessary since, as we just have seen, the choice of the Subject is semantically relevant in certain cases. This choice is also relevant with respect to the control relation since the Subject of the infinitive (be it active or passive) is the controlee. Therefore, the notion of Subject seems to be necessary for underlying representations. This means that the usefulness of the notion of Subject does not support the assumed necessity of a level of surface syntax. Moreover, it seems that surface word order can be interpreted as belonging to the level of morphemics only, where the representation of the sentence is a string without parentheses, rather than a tree (or a more complex network) or its linearization. An immediate transition from the underlying level to that of morphemics would then offer a possibility to cope with the difficult issue of projectivity. Non-projective constructions are strictly limited and may be described as such by means of shallow rules that change the underlying projective order under certain specific conditions. In the output of these rules on the morphemic level, the condition of projectivity is absent. Thus, for instance, sentence (19) can be described by a shallow rule that brings the heavy relative clause to the end of the sentence in a similar way that (without involving projectivity) prepositions are brought to the beginning of their nominal groups (the projections). Such a rule also holds for the conjunction and the verbal group; for example in (20).

(19) *I met a man yesterday who asked me for your address.*

(20) *Jim visited Claire since he wanted to ask her for advice.*

The conjunction is derived from the underlying index (a part of a complex symbol) that characterizes the dependent verb; in this case as occupying the position of (the head of) an adverbial of Cause. Word order shifts concerning a marked position of the intonation center should be handled by similar shallow rules. Consider the difference between the primary morphemic shape of (4a) and (21), where the *to*-group belongs to the Topic in all readings of the sentence, similar to (4b).

(21) *They went by CAR to a river.*

In this way, even if a description with several levels of representation needs to be used, it would be possible to reduce the number of levels (a similar reduction can be found now in Chomsky's "minimalist program").

5 Lexical and Grammatical Information

As we have mentioned, a dependency-based approach meets the well-known requirement according to which much of grammatical information is found in the lexicon (especially in the valency frames or grids), i.e., according to which the word is understood as one of the central units of the language system. This point of view was reflected quite clearly in European classical linguistics, especially in the works of L. Tesnière and E.M. Uhlenbeck. Equally, the research on the relationship between lexical and grammatical issues carried out within MTT has always paid attention to the central role of the word. Recent developments of generative approaches also stress the significance of the lexicon. If valency is given priority over constituency in the description of the core of syntax, such a view can be even more outspoken. With valency frames and lists of free complementations, it is possible to specify the (underlying) structure of the sentence on the basis of properties of individual words and word classes (the latter being technically specified, e.g., by means of indices in the individual lexical entries).

In the Prague approach, a lexical entry consists of the following parts:

(i) The underlying representation of the lexical unit itself, i.e., of its lexical meaning. In case of ambiguity, there are several representations (in separate lexical entries), whereas in case of vagueness there is a single meaning.[3]

---

[3] Vagueness is a property of meaning. It is partially resolved during semantic interpretation by inferences based on contextual and other knowledge.

(ii) The specification of the values of relevant grammatical categories, i.e., of grammatemes that belong to the given word class. For example, number and definiteness for nouns; tense, aspect, different kinds of modalities, etc. for verbs; degrees of comparison for adjectives. Restrictions on the combinations of these values are listed for every word class as a whole; only exceptions have to be registered in individual lexical entries.

(iii) The valency frame of the given lexical unit. The basis of the frame is the list of its possible complementations (Actor, Addressee, Objective, Effect, Origin, Locative, Instrument, Manner, Cause, etc.). The complementations are ordered in accordance with SO as discussed in Section 3. Inner participants and obligatory complementations are indicated by specific indices. Since they may be either deletable (as Dir-2 with [to] *arrive*) or not deletable (as Objective with [to] *create*), it is denoted by a specific index whether a complementation is deletable with the given head. The optional or obligatory function of an item as controller is also specified here. For example, Actor is an obligatory controller in the case of [to] *try* and an optional one in the case of [to] *decide*; Addressee is an optional controller in the case of [to] *advise* and [to] *forbid*. Furthermore, indices of the individual complementations characterize them as being able to occupy certain specific positions in the clause (e.g., the position of the Subject, or of a *wh*-element) or to appear as barriers for movement.

(iv) Subcategorization conditions specified for the individual types of complementations in the frames. For instance, the Objective of a verb may (or may not) have the shape of a noun group, of a verb clause, etc.

Note that in some cases, different lexical entries share their lexical part proper, i.e. the lexical unit. Such lexical entries differ only in their frames, which provide different starting points for semantic interpretation. This concerns verbs such as [to] *swarm* (either with an obligatory Means as in *The garden swarms with bees*, or without it as in *Bees swarm in the garden*) and [to] *load* (either with an obligatory, though deletable, Means as in *They loaded the truck with hay*, or with an obligatory Dir-2 as in *They loaded hay on the truck*).

6 Specification of Underlying Representations

The class of underlying representations can be specified either by means of a generative procedure or by a corresponding declarative definition. Either of them can use a small number of general principles to describe the core of the grammar. The generative procedure for the specification of underlying representations is based on the following points (see Hajičová et al., 1990 for the first preliminary formulation):

(i) To generate a node n means

- To create the node n either as the root of a representation, or as a node that is dependent on another node, and is placed to the right of all its sister nodes.
- To choose n's lexical value and the values of its grammatemes. This is to be done taking into account the subcategorization conditions of the mother node and the restrictions on the combinations of grammatemes. As mentioned earlier, they are specified in the lexical entry of the head or in the data concerning the respective word class. The technique used to evaluate these conditions and restrictions is unification. For example, if n is the Objective of a verb that subcategorizes its Objective as a verb, the lexical unit in the label of n has to be accompanied by the symbol identifying its word class as verb.

If n is a root, the lexical part of its label is a verb, and its grammatemes determine it as a finite verb form of the main clause. Then n is specified either as CB (i.e., as belonging to the Topic) or as NB (i.e., as belonging to the Focus).

(ii) If the symbol of a complementation (inner participant or adjunct) is present in the frame of the node n, then it is possible to generate either a left or a right daughter of n:

- In case a left daughter is being generated, a CB marker and a complementation value chosen from the frame of n is assigned to it.
- If a right daughter is being generated, a NB marker and a complementation from the left end of the frame of n is assigned to it. Analogously to the primary values of the grammatemes, the NB marker can be interpreted as primary, i.e., as the absence of a marker.

Note

If the chosen complementation is an inner participant, it is deleted in the frame of n (as having been saturated). The choice of a complementation "from the left end" means that optional complementations can be skipped. The skipped complementations are deleted in the frame of n. If the last complementation in the frame has been deleted, no more daughter nodes can be currently generated, and point (iii) below is carried out.

(iii) If no complementation is present in the frame of n, the procedure goes back to the mother node of n, which now is to be considered as node n. If no mother node is available, the procedure is finished.

Only representations that contain a focus are understood as underlying representations of sentences; more precisely, only those in which a NB node is included in the branch that starts from the root and contains exclusively rightmost daughters.

A declarative specification of the class of the underlying representations of sentences can follow similar lines using unification. However, the notion of unification must be modified in order to allow the checking of the order of nodes and making a distinction between saturated and non-saturated items. The deletion of a saturated inner participant mentioned in the Note above ensures that an inner participant occurs at most once in a clause. This restriction does not affect free, adverbial complementations; compare the three temporal adverbials in *Yesterday she came in the morning late to the office.*

As was stated above, this specification of underlying representations covers only the core of sentence syntax. It has to be completed in a number of areas, especially with respect to coordinated structures (corresponding to a third dimension of the network) and the position of such syntactically specific items as the operator of negation and other focalizers (*only, even, also, ...*).

Thus using dependency syntax in combination with a "free" word order in the syntactic representation and including a large portion of grammatical information in lexical entries, it is possible to describe the core of syntax in a relatively economical way. In this way, a highly natural account of innate properties that allows for the acquisition of language as embedded in context may be gained.

Endnotes

[1] The development of MTT and FGD has been pursued in parallel. Both of them are based on a common, or at least similar, background—that of European structural linguistics. Even though in several specific issues the two models differ, I hope that the present brief characterization of the Praguian viewpoints will be understood as an offer of certain suggestions that might be suitable to stimulate further development in MTT, rather than as an argument against its core. For instance,

the definition of dependency we prefer (Sgall et al., 1969, 1986; Plátek & Sgall, 1978; Plátek et al., 1984; Petkevič, 1987) appears to have certain advantages in that it allows for an unlimited number of sister nodes and for a relatively free use of non-terminals in the derivations of sentence representations. It is important that the representations contain only terminal symbols.

Our main task is certainly to continue research on dependency-based linguistic description and to clarify its advantageous relationship with other approaches, finding out how seemingly weak points of dependency can be overcome.

[2] Combinations of dependency with constituency as proposed, e.g., by Fitialov and Robinson (see Goralčiková, 1974) are redundant. When combined properly with a treatment of coordination and apposition and a treatment of such relationships as control (grammatical coreference) and Topic-Focus Articulation (TFA), dependency covers the whole domain of sentence syntax. It has always been recognized in European linguistics that control and TFA correspond to a dimension that basically differs from syntactic dependency. For a formal treatment see (Petkevič, in press).

[3] Let us note that the "direction" of the dependency relation can also be specified on the basis of such a criterion. This can be done since one of the members is syntactically omissible—if not in a lexically specified pair of words, then at the level of word classes. Thus, e.g., in *very slow progress*, the syntactic combinability of the heads is clearly the same as that of the whole groups. In *Jim met Sally* nothing can be deleted. We know, however, from other cases that the verb can never be deleted in the sense of free syntactic combinability (without a specific context). In contrast, the Object can be absent in clauses with such verbs as, e.g., [to] *read*, and Subject is absent in clauses with such verbs as [to] *rain*.[4] Articles, prepositions, auxiliary verbs, etc. do not give rise to such problems since in the syntactic structure of the sentence, they do not occupy specific positions (see above). Other questions open to discussion are problematic for all kinds of syntactic descriptions. One such question is the boundary line between so-called *equi-* and *raising-verbs* in English. Such issues must be discussed in the context of individual languages, bearing in mind the specific relationships between their underlying structures and the outer shape of sentences.

[4] In a specific situation where, e.g., the question is whether the arrival means an arrival at a particular hotel or railway station in the given town, it should be noted that a deletion is present in the question already.

[5] Note that among the differences between underlying and surface word order, there are those which are treated by shallow rules involving the verb, the parts of noun groups, the function words, and the clitics. In a dependency grammar, Wackernagel's position is relatively easy to define as the second position in the uppermost part of the dependency tree. Furthermore, a secondary surface position of the intonation center of the sentence marks the most dynamic element of the sentence as being moved to this position from the end of the sentence. In such a case, the complementations to the right of the intonation center belong to the Topic, i.e., are CB.

---

[4]Since in clauses with [to] *rain*, [to] *snow*, etc. the English pronoun *it* cannot be replaced, it is just a morphemic filler with no semantic relevance.

[6] The question of how to find and describe a finite mechanism that allows the Hearer to decide which of the many possible reference assignments is meant by the Speaker, was discussed by Hajičová (cf. Hajičová & Vrbová, 1982; Hajičová et al., 1995). The proposed model is based on degrees of salience of the items in the stock of information shared by the Speakers and, as assumed by the Speakers, also by the Hearers. An account of the vagueness of linguistic meaning can be found in (Novák, 1993).

Bibliography

Firbas, J. 1957. "Some Thoughts on the Function of Word Order in Old English and Modern English". *Sbornik prací filosofické fakulty brněnské university A5.* 72–100. Prague.

Firbas, J. 1975. "On the Thematic and the Non-thematic Section of the Sentence". *Style and Text* ed. by H. Ringbom et al. 317–334. Stockholm: Skriptor.

Gaifman, H. 1965. "Dependency Systems and Phrase-Structure Systems". *Information and Control.* 8:304–337.

Goralčiková, A. 1974. "On One Type of Dependency Grammars". *Prague Bulletin of Mathematical Linguistics.* 21:11–26.

Hajičová, E. 1979. "Agentive or Actor/Bearer?". *Theoretical Linguistics.* 6:173–190.

Hajičová, E. 1983. "Remarks on the Meaning of Cases". *Prague Studies in Mathematical Linguistics.* 8:149–157.

Hajičová, E., T. Hoskovec & P. Sgall. 1995. "Salience and Topic-Focus Articulation". *Prague Bulletin of Studies in Mathematical Linguistics.* 64:5–24.

Hajičová, E. & J. Panevová. 1984. "Valency (Case) Frames of Verbs". *Contributions to Functional Syntax, Semantics and Language Comprehension* ed. by P. Sgall. 147–188. Amsterdam & Philadelphia/Prague: Benjamins Academic Publishers/Academia.

Hajičová, E., J. Panevová & P. Sgall. 1990. "Why Do We Use Dependency Grammar?". *Buffalo Working Papers in Linguistics 90-01, Special Issue for Paul Garvin* ed. by W. Walck. 90–93. Buffalo.

Hajičová, E. & J. Vrbová. 1982. "On the Role of the Hierarchy of Activation in the Process of Natural Language Understanding". *Proceedings* of the 9th International Conference on Computational Linguistics (Coling '82) ed. by J. Horecki. 107–113. Amsterdam, Prague: North Holland.

Novák, V. 1993. *The Alternative Mathematical Model of Linguistic Semantics and Pragmatics*. New York: Plenum Publishing Corporation.

Panevová, J. 1974. "On Verbal Frames in Functional Generative Grammar". *Prague Bulletin of Mathematical Linguistics*. 22:3–40.

Petkevič, V. 1987. "A New Dependency-Based Specification of Underlying Representations of Sentences". *Theoretical Linguistics*. 14:143–172.

Petkevič, V. in press. *Underlying Structure of Sentence Based on Dependency*. Technical report. Prague: Charles University.

Plátek, M. & P. Sgall. 1978. "A Scale of Context Sensitive Languages: Applications to Natural Language". *Information and Control*. 38:1–20.

Plátek, M., J. Sgall & P. Sgall. 1984. "A Dependency Base for a Linguistic Description". *Contributions to Functional Syntax, Semantics and Language Comprehension* ed. by P. Sgall. 63–98. Amsterdam & Philadelphia/Prague: Benjamins Academic Publishers/Academia.

Schnelle, H. 1991. *Natur der Sprache. Die Dynamik der Prozesse des Sprechens und des Verstehens*. Berlin: W. de Gruyter.

Sgall, P. 1980. "Case and Meaning". *Journal of Pragmatics*. 4:525–536.

Sgall, P., E. Hajičová & J. Panevová. 1986. *The Meaning of the Sentence in Its Semantic and Pragmatic Aspects*. Dordrecht: Reidel Publishing Company.

Sgall, P., L. Nebelský, A. Goralčiková & E. Hajičová. 1969. *A Functional Approach to Syntax*. New York: American Elsevier.

A Formal Look at Dependency Grammars and Phrase-Structure Grammars, with Special Consideration of Word-Order Phenomena

Owen Rambow and Aravind Joshi

1 Introduction

In the past, there has been little contact between those linguistic traditions working on the basis of dependency grammars (DGs), such as *Meaning-Text Theory* (MTT), and those linguistic traditions working on the basis of context-free phrase-structure grammars (CFGs), such as the various incarnations of Chomskyan *Transformational Grammar* (which we will henceforth refer to by a recent name, *Government and Binding Theory* or GB). The linguistic insights from one tradition have generally not been transferred to the other. While this fact has been discussed in the past (see, e.g., Nichols, 1979), the discussion has not specifically addressed the effect of the underlying formalisms on the linguistic theories that are developed in them. This is not to say that the formalisms themselves have not been compared (see Gaifman, 1965); however, while both MTT and GB developed out of formal and/or computational approaches, both theories have shed their original explicitly mathematical underpinnings. A mathematical comparison between the underlying formal systems will therefore not tell us much about the linguistics of the two theories. Instead, we must ask how the formalisms affect the linguistic theories which are expressed in them.

The formalisms that linguistic theories use for the purpose of expressing syntactic structure can differ in two ways. Firstly, the formalisms can differ in the type of representation they use. A phrase-structure grammar postulates the existence of non-terminal syntactic categories, while a dependency grammar does not. Secondly, the linguistic theories can differ in how they use the syntactic formalism they have chosen. Chomskyan approaches follow a generativist approach, while MTT does not. As has been pointed out previously (Kunze, 1972:10), these two issues—the definition of the formalism itself and how it is used by a linguistic theory—are orthogonal. It is perfectly possible to define a generative DG; see for instance (Hays, 1964). While the difference between a generativist and a non-generativist approach will have profound methodological (and perhaps philosophical) implications for the resulting linguistic theories, in this paper we will concentrate on the representational difference in the formalisms themselves.

It has often been observed that a key linguistic difference between MTT (and other dependency-based theories) on the one hand and GB on the other hand is the central role that the lexicon plays in MTT, but not in GB (see, e.g., Sgall, this volume). We claim that this difference is not coincidental, but due to a mathematical property of the underlying formalisms: context-free phrase-structure grammars *cannot* be the basis of a lexicon-oriented linguistic theory (in a technical sense, which we will define in the next section), while dependency grammars *must* be.[1] An attempt to "lexicalize" CFGs leads naturally to a more powerful phrase-structure system called *Tree Adjoining Grammars* (TAGs).[2] In Section 2, we will show that TAGs show many important similarities to DGs. These similarities have two beneficial results: firstly, we are able to apply formal results from the mathematical study of phrase-structure grammars to DGs; secondly, we are able to transfer linguistic analyses made in one framework to the other framework. In Section 3, we will illustrate these points by looking at two non-projective syntactic constructions.

Our major goal in this paper is to study the interaction between formal systems and linguistic theories, and to explore how results in the framework of one theory can be expressed in the particular formal context of other theories. Such work provides insights into those aspects, linguistic and formal, that appear to be invariant across a class of formalisms. The reader should not interpret our goal as suggesting that MTT needs to adopt a phrase-structure representation for whatever reason! We do not address the question of whether phrase structure is necessary for linguistic theory, and leave this issue to others.

---

[1] From a historical perspective, it presumably was the interest in developing a lexicon-oriented linguistic theory that led to the use of a dependency grammar for MTT. However, in this paper we take a synchronic view.

[2] TAG was originally introduced as a tree generating system on its own (Joshi et al., 1975). It was only recently shown that TAGs can lexicalize CFGs. In this paper, we will only be interested in lexicalized TAGs. For a general introduction to TAGs, see (Joshi, 1987a).

2 Dependency, Phrase Structure and the Lexicon

One of the most important features of MTT is the central role that the lexicon plays (see, e.g. Mel'čuk & Polguère, 1987; in fact, much of the MTT literature deals with the lexicon). For syntactic purposes, it contains information about the subcategorization frame of a lexeme, and how the arguments are realized (case assignment and function words). The importance of the lexicon for syntactic theories has also been increasingly recognized in the American linguistic traditions. We will take it as a given, and address the question how a phrase structure-based syntactic theory can be adapted to a lexical approach. It turns out that there are intrinsic, formal problems. These problems have been investigated in detail by Schabes (1989); for a summary of some of the mathematical properties of tree grammars including lexicalization, see (Joshi & Schabes, 1991). We will provide a brief discussion here.

If we want to analyze how formal systems can be used for linguistic theories, we must start by determining what sort of *elementary structures* the formalism provides, and how these elementary structures are combined using the *combining operations* defined in the formalism. We will illustrate these notions with some examples. First, consider CFGs. In a CFG, a grammar consists of a set of rewrite rules, which associate a single nonterminal symbol with a string of terminal and nonterminal symbols. Here is a sample context-free grammar:

(1) a. S $\longrightarrow$ NP VP
 b. VP $\longrightarrow$ really VP
 c. VP $\longrightarrow$ V NP
 d. V $\longrightarrow$ likes
 e. NP $\longrightarrow$ John
 f. NP $\longrightarrow$ Lyn

Each of these rules is an elementary structure in this grammar. We combine these elementary structures by using one rule to rewrite a symbol introduced by a previous application of some rule. For example, when we use rule (1a), we introduce the nonterminal symbols (or "nodes") NP and VP. We may rewrite the VP node by using rule (1b) or (1c). This grammar generates, among others, the following string:

(2) *John really likes Lyn.*

Derivations in CFGs can be represented as trees: for each nonterminal node in the tree, the daughters record which rule was used to rewrite it. The phrase-structure tree that corresponds to sentence (2) is given in Figure 1.

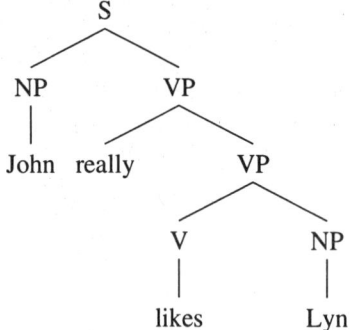

Figure 1: *Phrase-Structure Tree for* John really likes Lyn

Now consider a different type of mathematical formalism, *Tree Substitution Grammars* (TSG). In a TSG, the elementary structures are phrase-structure trees. A sample grammar is given in Figure 2. It consists of three trees, one of which is rooted in S, and two of which are rooted in NP. Note that even though from the point of view of a CFG, a tree is a derived object, not an elementary one, we have defined TSGs in such a way that a tree is now an elementary object of the grammar.

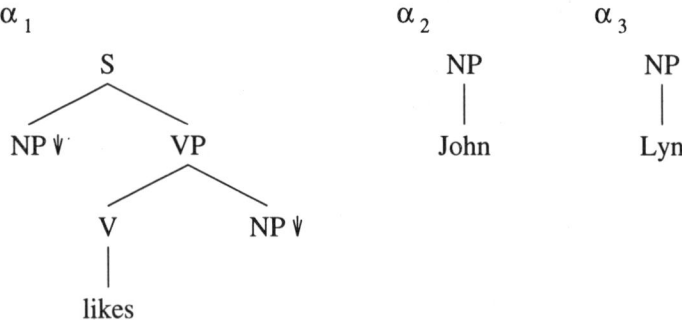

Figure 2: *A sample TSG*

We combine elementary structures in a TSG by using the operation of *substitution*, illustrated schematically in Figure 3. We can substitute tree β into tree α if there is a nonterminal symbol on the frontier of α which has the same label as the root node of β ('A' in Figure 3). We can then simply append β to α at that node. (Nodes at which substitution is possible are called "substitution nodes" and are marked with down-arrows ($\downarrow$).) A derivation in our sample TSG is shown in Figure 4. The trees representing the two arguments of the verb *like*, *John* (α_2) and *Lyn* (α_3), are substituted into the tree associated with the verb (α_1), yielding the well-formed tree α_4, from which the sentence *John likes Lyn* can be read off.

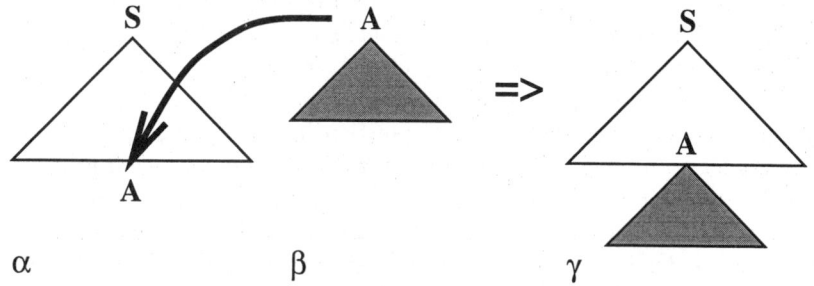

Figure 3: *The Substitution Operation*

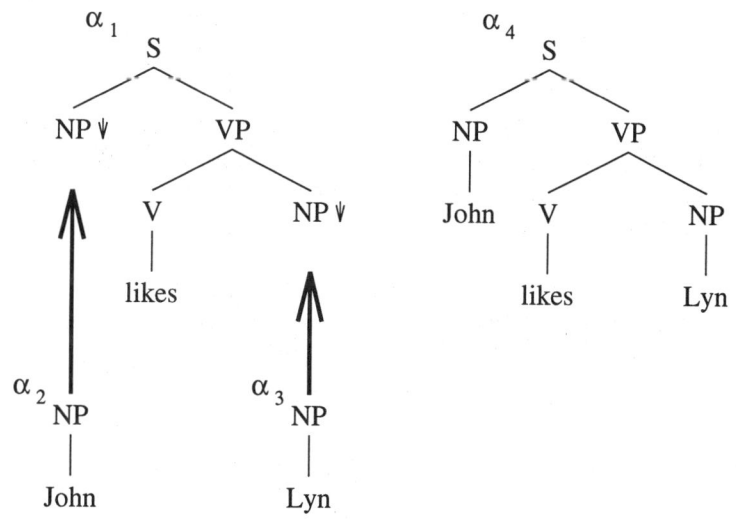

Figure 4: *Substitution of arguments into initial tree of* likes

Finally, compare the DG used for MTT to CFG and TSG. In DG, the elementary structures are simply nodes labeled with terminal symbols, i.e., lexical items. There are no nonterminal symbols. Nodes are composed by establishing dependency relations between them. The result is a dependency tree.

CFGs and TSGs are weakly equivalent (they generate the same languages). However, to a linguist, they look very different. A context-free rule contains a single "level", i.e., a phrase-structure node and its daughters; an elementary tree in a TSG may be of arbitrary height. Put differently, in TSG we have increased the "domain of locality" of the elementary structures of the grammar. This increased domain of locality allows the linguist to state linguistic relationships (such as subcategorization, semantic roles of arguments, case assignment and agreement) differently in a TSG. As an example, take agreement between Subject and verb in English. The linguist working in TSG can simply state (by using some feature-based notation) that the verb and the NP in Subject position in tree α_1 of Figure 2 agree with respect to number. The linguist working in CFG has a harder time: since the verb is in rule (1d), while the Subject NP is in rule (1a), he cannot simply state the relation directly, since it is impossible to state constraints that relate nodes in different elementary structures. Instead, the linguist must propose that the NP in fact agrees with the VP in rule (1a), and that the VP agreement features are inherited by its head in rule (1d). The notion that the VP (and not only the verb) agrees with the Subject is a meaningful linguistic proposition, and in fact the TSG linguist could have adopted it as well. However, the crucial issue is that the CFG linguist, because of his choice of formalism, was FORCED to adopt it, while the TSG linguist may choose to do so or not on purely linguistic grounds.

Now let us turn to our central concern, the role of the lexicon. We will call a grammar "lexicalized" if every elementary structure is associated with exactly one lexical item, and if every lexical item of the language is associated with a finite set of elementary structures in the grammar. Clearly, dependency grammars (including MTT) are naturally lexicalized in this sense, since the elementary structures simply are the lexical items.

The case is more complex for a CFG. Consider the sample grammar given above in (1). We can see that no lexical item is associated with rules (1a) and (1c); therefore, the grammar is not lexicalized. It would be possible to combine rules (1a), (1c), and (1d) into a single one:

(3)   S $\longrightarrow$ NP likes NP

However, it is now impossible to correctly place the adverb *really*, since a (lexicalized) rule of the form (1b) is no longer useful (the VP node having been eliminated). The adverb cannot be inserted between the Subject and the verb.

There is a second way of lexicalizing a CFG: instead of merging the two phrase-structure rules into a single rewrite rule, we can combine them and consider the result—a fragment of a phrase-structure tree—an elementary structure. Put differently, we move from CFG to TSG. For example, tree α_1

in Figure 2 is the result of combining rules (1a), (1c) and (1d). As desired, tree α_1 is associated with exactly one lexical item, the verb *likes*. Thus, we have now obtained a TSG from a CFG. We can derive the sentence *John likes Lyn* as shown previously in Figure 4.

It turns out that a TSG is not really what we want, either: we are again faced with the problem of getting the adverb in the right place, since there is no node into which to substitute it.[3] This problem is solved by the tree composition operation of *adjunction*, introduced in the framework of Tree Adjoining Grammars (TAG). Adjunction is shown in Figure 5. Tree α (called an "initial tree") contains a non-terminal node labeled A; the root node of tree β (an "auxiliary tree") is also labeled A, as is exactly one non-terminal node on its frontier (the "foot node"). All other frontier nodes are terminal nodes or substitution nodes. We take tree α and remove the subtree rooted at its node A, insert in its stead tree β, and then add at the footnode of β the subtree of α that we removed earlier. The result is tree γ. As we can see, adjunction can have the effect of inserting one tree into the center of another. Our linguistic example is continued in Figure 6. Tree β_1 containing the adverb is adjoined at the VP node into tree α_4. The result is tree α_5, which corresponds to sentence (2). Note that α_5 is composed of trees α_1, α_2, α_3 and β_1, each of which corresponds to exactly one lexical item, in contrast to the grammar given above in (1).

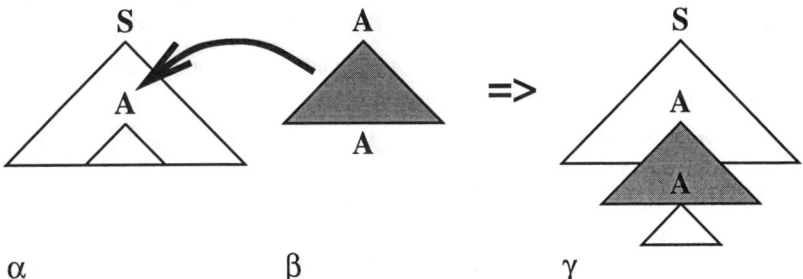

Figure 5: *The Adjunction Operation*

A formalism in which the elementary structures of a grammar are trees, and in which the combining operations are adjunction and substitution is called a TAG. Schabes (1989) has shown that a tree composition system is only lexicalizable if the composition operations include adjunction.[4] Thus,

---

[3] Having two verbs *like*, one of which also subcategorizes for an adverb, does not solve the problem, since it does not generalize to multiple adverbs (in addition to being linguistically unappealing).

[4] Schabes & Waters (1993) show that a restricted form of adjunction, in which the footnode of auxiliary trees is always in the rightmost or leftmost position on the frontier,

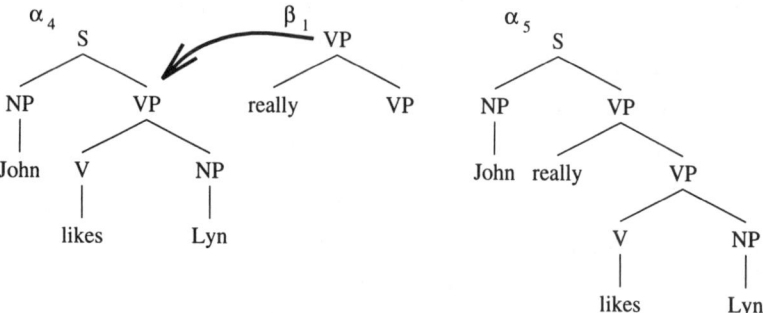

Figure 6: *Adjunction of* really *into initial tree*

the process of lexicalizing a CFG naturally leads to a TAG. TAGs are more powerful formally than CFGs, meaning that they can derive more complex languages than CFG. They are also more difficult to parse. Several other proposals have been made to adapt phrase-structure grammars to a lexical approach, including categorial formalisms such as *Context Categorial Grammar* (CCG) (Steedman, 1991), and non-transformational phrase-structure grammars such as *Lexical-Functional Grammar* (LFG) (Bresnan & Kaplan, 1982) and *Head-Driven Phrase Structure Grammar* (HPSG) (Pollard & Sag, 1987). Interestingly, the underlying formalisms of these frameworks are also more powerful than CFG. For a summary of mathematical and computational properties of TAGs and some related phrase-structure formalisms, see (Joshi et al., 1991); for a discussion of the relation between TAG and categorial systems, see (Joshi & Kulick, 1995).

Like a CFG, a TAG derives a phrase-structure tree, called the "derived tree". (The derived tree for our example is the right tree in Figure 6.) In addition to the derived (phrase-structure) tree, a second structure is built up, the "derivation tree". The derivation tree records how the derived tree was assembled from elementary trees. In this structure, each of the elementary trees is represented by a single node. Since the grammar is lexicalized, we can identify this node with the (base form of the) lexeme of the corresponding tree.[5] If a tree t_1 is substituted or adjoined into a tree t_2, then the node representing t_1 becomes a dependent of the node representing t_2 in the derivation tree. Furthermore, the arcs between nodes are annotated with the position in the "target tree" at which substitution or adjunction takes place. In the TAG literature, this annotation is in the form of the tree address of the node (using a formal notation to uniquely

---

can also lexicalize a CFG.

[5]This is not exactly what is done in the TAG literature, but the difference is purely notational.

identify nodes in trees, without reference to linguistic concepts). However, in analogy to the MTT notation, we can simply assign numbers to argument positions, and introduce the convention that all other positions are attribute positions, marked as ATTR. The derivation tree for the example derivation above is shown in Figure 7. We can see that the derivation structure is a dependency tree which closely resembles the *Deep-Syntactic Representation* (DSyntR) of MTT

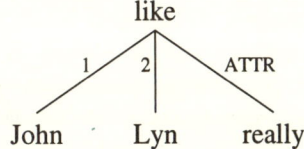

Figure 7: *Derivation Tree for* John really likes Lyn

The resemblance between the derivation structure and the DSyntR is not a coincidence. It is a direct result of lexicalization. We would like to summarize some striking similarities between a *Meaning-Text Model* (MTM) of a language and a TAG for that language:

1. As in the case of an MTM, a grammar in the TAG formalism consists of a lexicon, whose elementary structures are combined by some very simple rules of composition (substitution and adjunction in the case of TAG).

2. The function words are included in the elementary structures of the lexemes that require them in their subcategorization frame, i.e., they are represented in the lexical entries for content words, not separately. They are therefore not represented in the derivation structure, just as they are not represented in the DSyntR. (For an example of an elementary tree which includes a function word, see tree β_1 in Figure 9; also see the derivation structure in Figure 10.)

3. A verb subcategorizes for its arguments—there must be exactly one constituent for each of its obligatory arguments. Adjuncts are not subcategorized for and there is no (syntactic) limit on their number. In MTT, this is reflected by the fact that there may an unbounded number of ATTR subtrees, while there is only one subtree for each of the numeric arc labels. In TAG, this distinction is captured by the fact that arguments are substituted, a unique and obligatory step, while adjuncts are adjoined, a recursive but optional step.

4. In a TAG, the lexicon consists of one tree family for each lexeme, each tree family containing trees for the syntactic variants of the

lexeme (active/passive voice, *wh*-questions for each argument, "topicalization" (fronting) for each argument, etc.). As in the case of MTT, certain syntactic paraphrases can be handled by general rules ("metarules", Becker, 1993). Lexical Functions and syntactic paraphrases that use Lexical Functions have not yet been introduced in the TAG framework, but they could be integrated in a straightforward way.

5. Idioms (phrasemes) have been discussed both within the TAG framework (Abeillé & Schabes, 1989) and in MTT (Mel'čuk, 1988:60). Both frameworks can account for idioms in a natural and similar way, namely by postulating elementary structures that (non-compositionally) contain more than one lexeme.

However, there are some important differences between the two approaches:

1. In TAG, word order must be determined at the same time as dependency. This process cannot be separated into two steps, as in MTT.[6] This means that the lexicon in a TAG grammar for a specific language must contain more syntactic information than a lexicon in the MTT framework: not only must it contain information about subcategorization and function words, the trees themselves must also contain enough information so that the word order comes out right.

2. While substitution of a tree t_1 into tree t_2 corresponds to a dependency of the lexical item of t_1 on that of t_2, this need not be the case in adjunction. We will see later examples in which t_1 is adjoined into t_2, but the lexical item of t_2 depends on that of t_1. Thus, while adjunction corresponds to the establishment of a syntactic dependency relation, the direction of the relation cannot be determined from the direction of the adjunction alone. We return to this issue in more detail in Subsection 3.3.

The similarities between MTT and a TAG approach, both in the linguistic approach and in the resulting representations, allow us to use TAG as a way of relating MTT analyses to phrase structure-based analyses. While much of the work on the interface between syntax and semantics, on Lexical Functions and on syntactic paraphrases in the MTT framework can be reformulated in terms of a TAG analysis, we will concentrate in this paper on applying insights from TAG analyses to the MTT framework.

---

[6]There have been proposals for formal variants of TAG in which the linear precedence of nodes is stated independently from immediate dominance; see (Joshi, 1987b; Becker *et al.*, 1991).

3 Formal Aspects of Word Order Variation

In the previous section, we have argued that analyses using lexicalized TAG and dependency-based analyses bear striking resemblances. In this section, we will exploit these resemblances and discuss two types of non-projective constructions. Roughly, a dependency analysis of a sentence is "non-projective" if, when we draw projection lines down from the nodes in the dependency tree to a linear representation of the sentence, we cannot do so without having some projection lines cross one of the arcs of the dependency tree. A construction is non-projective if its dependency analysis is non-projective. For a more complete discussion, see (Mel'čuk, 1988:35f).[7] (We will only consider deep non-projectivity, i.e., non-projectivity which affects lexical items that are already present at the level of DSyntR.) There are two potential problems with non-projective constructions in a dependency-based theory:

(i) No parsing model for non-projective constructions is known that is computationally "well-behaved".

(ii) The syntax of non-projective constructions must be expressed differently from that of projective constructions, which is linguistically unmotivated.

We discuss the first point in more detail in Subsection 3.1, and the second in Subsection 3.2. Subsections 3.3 and 3.4 discuss two illustrative syntactic constructions. In Subsection 3.5, we present a proposal for handling certain non-projectivity within the MTT notion of "syntagm".

3.1 *Computational Properties of Dependency Grammars*

The principal reason for studying mathematical aspects of the syntactic formalism used by a linguistic theory is probably the need to explain the computational processes involved in the generation and understanding of language. While it appears that most syntactic constructions in most languages are projective (Mel'čuk & Pertsov, 1987:184), many languages do have syntactic constructions (often, but not always, pragmatically marked) that are not. It has been shown that a fully projective dependency grammar is weakly equivalent to a CFG (Gaifman, 1965), where "weak equivalence" means that for every DG, there is a CFG that generates exactly the same set of sentences, and *vice versa*. The equivalence of projective DGs and CFGs

---

[7]The definition given in (Mel'čuk, 1988:35f) can be shown to be equivalent to those discussed in (Marcus, 1965).

lets us transfer parsing results from CFGs to such grammars. In particular, we know that we can parse a string in a CFG in at most $O(n^3)$ time, i.e., in an amount of time proportional to the cube of the length of the input string. Though the parsing of non-projective DGs has been discussed (see Covington, 1990 and the references therein), to our knowledge no formal results have been published. There is reason to believe that in the worst case they can be parsed in a time proportional to an exponential function of the length of the input string ($O(2^n)$). If this worst case actually occurred in natural language parsing, then a DG would not be a very appealing candidate for a model of human language processing.

Why is this a potential problem for MTT? Humans appear to be quite good at parsing, i.e., constructing a syntactic representation for a linear string of language. If a linguistic theory wants to account for this process, then it must be able to provide an account of how the syntactic structures the theory postulates can be effectively and efficiently constructed from the input. Even if a linguistic theory does not aim at providing an account of human sentence processing (as in fact neither MTT nor GB do), then it must be the case that such an account can, in principle, be found, since otherwise the relation of the theory to observable human behavior is unclear. But an account of human sentence processing must be inherently computational. While a mathematical study cannot, of course, provide a computational theory of processing, it can provide useful guidelines for the elaboration of such a theory, and thus confirm the possibility of elaborating such a theory.

Of course, it could be argued that non-projective constructions are in fact much more difficult for humans to process than projective ones, and that therefore the lack of a processing account for non-projective trees is actually welcome, rather than a problem. However, data from psycholinguistic experiments suggests that processing difficulty does not pattern with the projective/non-projective distinction (or, equivalently, the distinction between CFGs and more powerful formalisms). For example, Bach *et al.* (1986) show that the non-projective Dutch cross-serial dependencies (which we discuss in Subsection 3.4 below) are in fact easier to process than German projective nested dependencies. Joshi (1990) gives a TAG-based account of these differences that crucially relies on the fact that both constructions can be handled by the same mathematical formalism.

3.2 *Word Order Rules and Non-Projectivity*

Non-projectivity also has an unappealing effect on linguistic description. In MTT, word order is not stated at the deep-syntactic level of representation, but is introduced by the *Surface-Syntactic Component*. The basic rules for stating linear order are the "syntagms", local rules which linearly order two nodes linked by a dependency relation. As discussed in (Mel'čuk & Pertsov, 1987:180), word-order rules for unbounded non-projective constructions cannot be stated as syntagms, or as conditions on syntagms. (Here, "unbounded non-projectivity" means that there is no limit on the number of lexical items simultaneously in violation of projectivity.) Instead, they must be stated in separate global rules. The existence of two types of word-order rules to specify the POSSIBLE word orders in a language is not fully satisfactory:[8] it is motivated not by any linguistic considerations, but only by the mathematical properties of the underlying dependency formalism; and it contradicts the spirit of Mel'čuk's *Principle of Maximal Localization* (Mel'čuk, 1988:383). One may therefore ask whether the syntagms can be expanded in some manner to handle certain types of (linguistically relevant) non-projectivity as well.

We will illustrate the problem in the following two subsections. In Subsection 3.5 we present a proposal, derived from TAG, for handling certain types of deep non-projectivity using syntagms.

3.3 Embedded Wh-Words in English

Like in many other languages, *wh*-words in English generally must appear in sentence-initial position. This is also true in the case that the *wh*-word is an argument of an embedded verb. Strikingly, there is no bound on the depth of the embedding:

(4) Who do you think that Mary claimed that Sarah liked?

In (4), the *wh*-word is an argument of the most deeply embedded verb *like*, thus causing non-projectivity, as can be seen in Figure 8.

A TAG can capture the long-distance dependency naturally, since the recursive adjunction operation allows an unbounded number of clauses to intervene between directly dependent lexemes. An analysis of *wh*-movement in the TAG framework has been proposed by Kroch (1987); our analysis (Figure 9) is a slight variation of his analysis. We first substitute all nominal arguments into their respective verbal trees, and then adjoin the intermediate *claim*-clause (β_2) into the most deeply embedded *like*-clause (α_1) at the S node immediately below the root node. This has the effect of separating the *wh*-word from its verb, even though they originated in the same

---

[8]Mel'čuk (1988:85) lists global word order rules which determine the *best* word order among many possible ones. This is quite a different matter, and the use of a different type of rule is linguistically motivated.

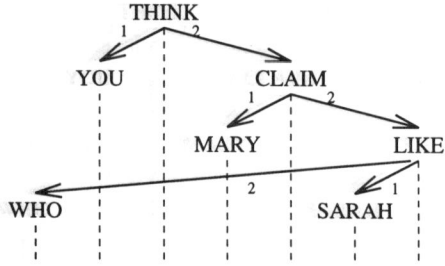

Figure 8: *DSyntR for Sentence (4)*

structure. We then subsequently adjoin the matrix *think*-clause (β_1) into the intermediate *claim*-clause.

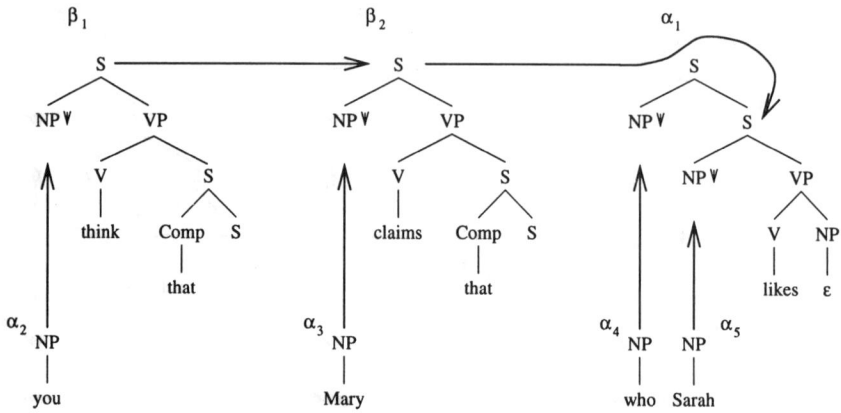

Figure 9: *TAG derivation for Sentence (4)*

The derivation leads to two structures: the derivation tree in Figure 10, and the derived tree in Figure 11. The derivation structure records the sequence of adjunctions and substitutions that leads to the derived tree, while the derived tree in Figure 11 shows the phrase structure and thus the word order of the final sentence. These two structures exist in parallel; we do not have to determine the word order from the dependency-based derivation tree as a separate step.

The reader will observe that, contrary to the example of sentence (2), the derivation structure (given in Figure 10) does not correspond directly to the DSyntR: the direction of adjunction between the verbs (more precisely, the trees anchored in verbs) does not correspond to the direction of

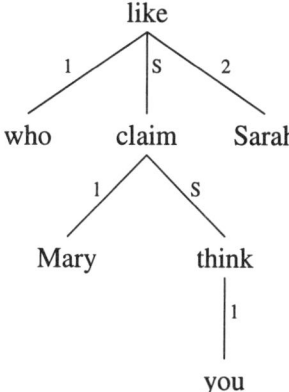

Figure 10: *TAG derivation tree for Sentence (4)*

the dependency.[9] Why is this? We have seen that nominal arguments are substituted into verbal trees, and that adjuncts are adjoined into trees they modify. In both instances, the derivation structure corresponds to the dependency structure (as in Figure 7). However, in the analysis for embedded clauses we have given here, we adjoin the matrix clause into the dependent clause at its S node. Thus, in the derivation structure, the node for the embedded verb dominates the node for the matrix verb. We annotate the arcs between such nodes in the derivation tree (Figure 10) with an 'S' rather than with an MTT-style annotation. This difference, however, does not affect the point we would like to make in this paper: what is central to this exposition is that a derivation in a TAG is like a dependency analysis in that it establishes direct relation between lexical items. The direction of adjunctions need not correspond to the direction of the dependency, as long as the latter can be retrieved from the former by some linguistically motivated simple procedure. For example, in our case, the actual dependency structure can be derived trivially: arcs marked 'S' are simply inverted.[1]

We can make two observations. First, because the construction can be represented by a TAG, we can parse this type of non-projectivity in $O(n^6)$ time. Second, we can state the word-order rules locally in the elementary tree associated with one clause: in tree α_3 in Figure 9, the *wh*-word has been moved to the front of the clause. This local operation becomes a non-projective one through adjunction. In MTT, we need a global rule (as opposed to a syntagm) to place the *wh*-word in sentence-initial position.

---

[9]For many constructions, the exact dependency analysis is often a matter of discussion. However, in the case at hand, the issue is quite uncontroversial.

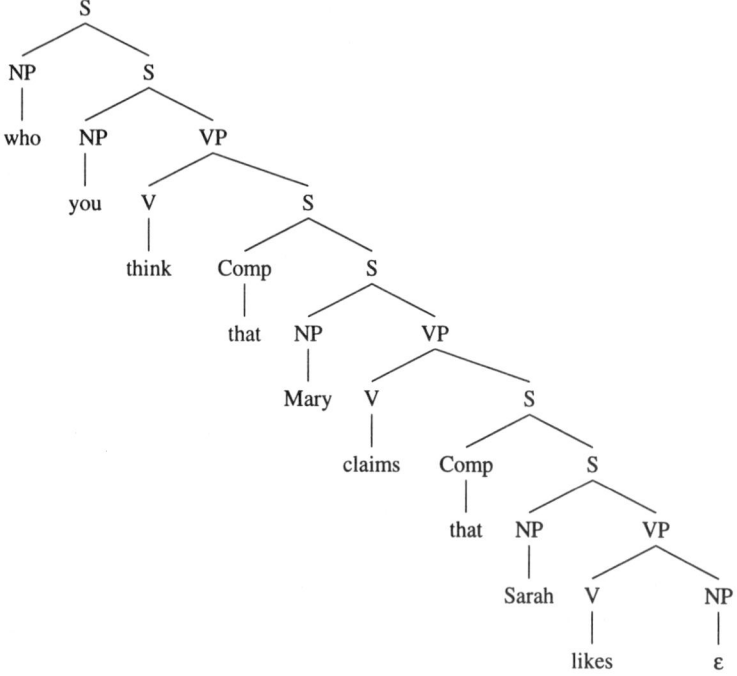

Figure 11: *TAG derived tree for Sentence (4)*

3.4 Embedded Clauses in Dutch

As in German, embedded clauses in Dutch can occur before the (clause-final) verb in a recursively embedded construction. However, the order of the verbs in the two languages differ: while in German the dependencies between the verbs and their arguments are nested, they are cross-serial in Dutch. Consider the following sentence:[10]

(5)   ... *omdat Wim Jan Marie de kinderen zag helpen leren zwemmen*
      ... because Wim Jan Marie the children saw to help to teach to swim
      ' ... because Wim saw Jan help Marie teach the children to swim'

This construction is one of the well-known non-projective constructions (see e.g., Mel'čuk, 1988:38), as can be seen in Figure 12.[2] Our TAG analysis

---

[10]We would like to thank Hotze Rullmann and Marc Verhagen for helping us with this example.

A FORMAL LOOK AT DEPENDENCY GRAMMARS

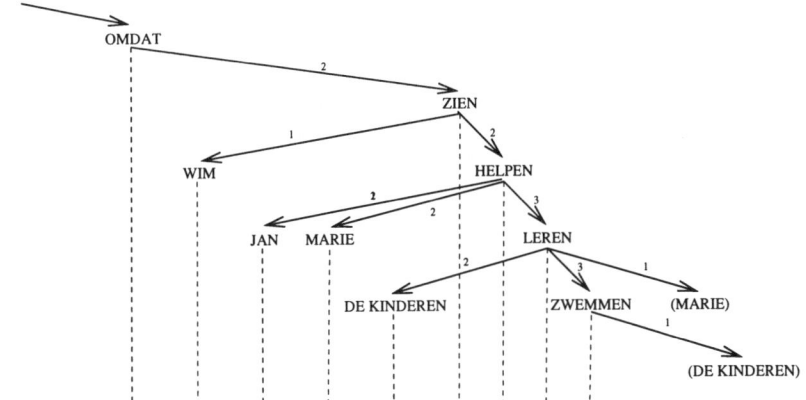

Figure 12: *DSyntR for Sentence (5)*

in Figure 13 is based on those proposed in (Joshi, 1987a; Kroch & Santorini, 1991). The main verb of each clause is "raised", an analysis proposed independently of the TAG analysis in the GB literature. We then adjoin each clause into its immediately dependent clause at the S node immediately below the root node. This "pushes" both verbs away from their nominal arguments, even though they originate in the same elementary structure. The order of the verbs in the final sentence simply follows from the way the elementary structures are adjoined; no global word-order rules are necessary.

Again, we can make two observations. First, this type of non-projectivity can be parsed in $O(n^6)$ time. Second, in the TAG analysis, the word-order rules can be expressed as local constraints on elementary clause-sized structures, while in the MTT analysis, we need to resort to non-local rules to describe the word order of the construction.

3.5 *Localizing Syntactic Rules*

As we have seen, in the case of *wh*-words and Dutch embedded clauses, MTT's syntagms cannot express the syntax of the constructions (though, of course, they can express the SOV order found in a single clause), while the TAG approach lets us localize the word-order rules within the elementary structure for a verb (just as the SOV order is localized in elementary trees). Can we transfer the TAG approach to MTT? We propose to associate *pairs* of strings (i.e., the *Deep-Morphological Representation*, or DMorphR, which is composed of linearized sequences of SSyntR nodes), rather than just single strings, with nodes of the dependency tree. This approach is inspired

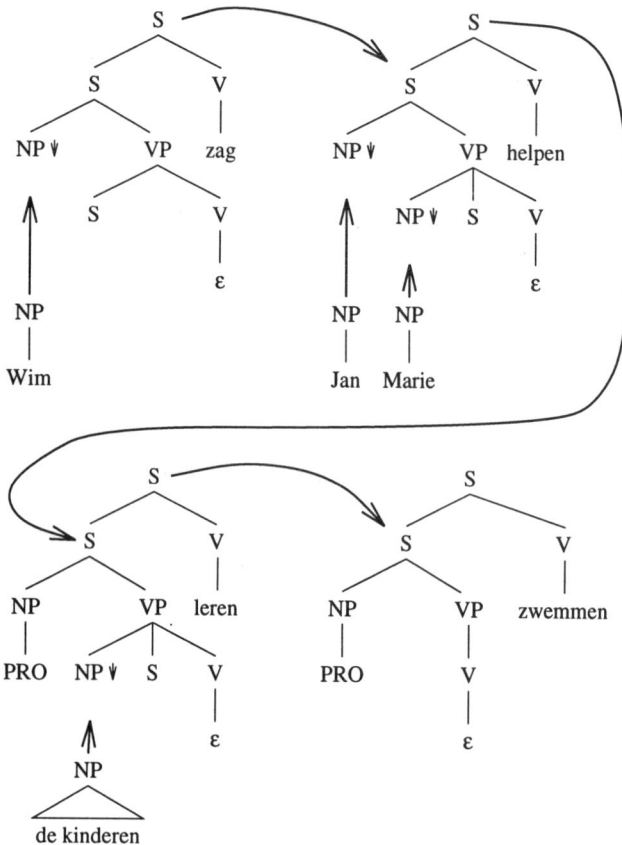

Figure 13: *TAG Derivation for Sentence (5)*

by a generalization of CFG, called *Head Grammar* (HG) (Pollard, 1984), which has been shown to be formally equivalent to TAG (Weir *et al.*, 1986). Basically, a HG provides a dependency tree and rules how to compute the final string (or "yield"). This string is computed bottom-up; with each node is associated a pair of string segments. As we go up the dependency tree, we compute the yield for each new node, based on the yields of its daughter nodes. The segments can be shifted around according to certain rules, and new terminal symbols added, but the segments may not be broken up. We see that this is exactly how the syntagms of MTT operate (see, e.g., Mel'čuk, 1967), except that in the syntagms, each node is associated with one string, while in the case of HG, there are two strings.

Our proposal can best be illustrated by giving two syntagms (hopefully in the spirit of Mel'čuk & Pertsov, 1987) in which we use two strings associated with one node to deal with the Dutch cross-serial dependencies (Figure 14).

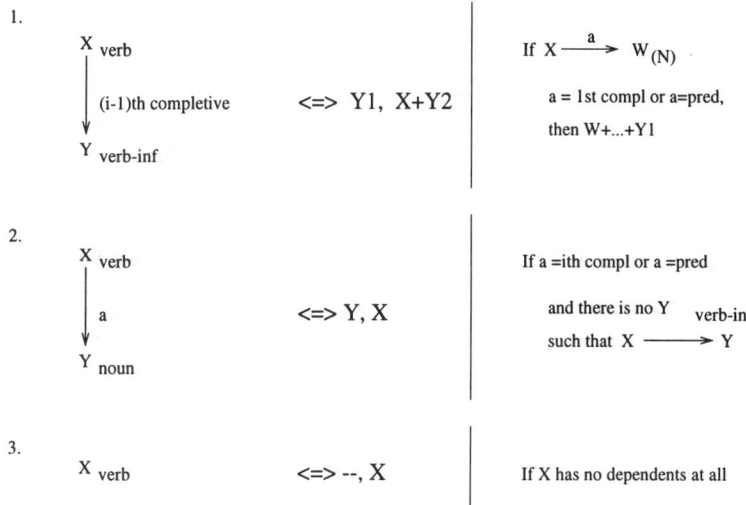

Figure 14: *Syntagm for Dutch Embedded Clauses*

A dependency relation is now linearized not as one string, but as two, which are represented as a pair, separated by commas (e.g., Y1, Y2). Syntagm 2 takes care of the most deeply embedded clause: the verb X is put in the second segment, while all the overt nominal arguments are put in the first segment. Syntagm 3 applies when the most deeply embedded verb has no dependents at all. Syntagm 1 applies to verbs that subcategorize for clauses. The DMorphR associated with the embedded clause, Y, is in two segments, called Y1 and Y2. The governing verb of Y, X, is added to the left of Y2. Any nominal arguments (the Subject or Object) of X are added to the left of Y1. As an example, consider Dutch sentence (5) discussed previously. We give the SSyntR in Figure 15.[11]

The noun phrase rooted in *kinderen* is of course linearized as *de + kinderen* (where we use '+' to denote concatenation). The clause rooted in *zwemmen* has no dependents (verbal or nominal). Therefore, syntagm 3 applies, and we get a DMorphR consisting of two strings, — (the empty string) and *zwemmen*. We then need to linearize the clause rooted in *leren*. Since *leren* does have a verbal dependent (namely *zwemmen*), syntagm 1 applies. We have Y1 = — (the empty string) and Y2 = *zwemmen*.

---

[11] The exact details, in particular the arc labels, are not of interest here. We also omit all features in the both the syntactic and morphological representations.

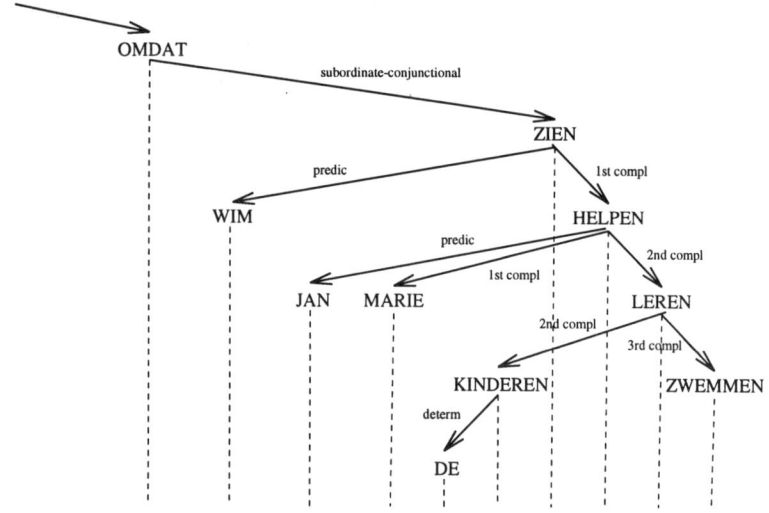

Figure 15: *SSyntR for Sentence (5)*

The verb *leren* is added to the left of Y2. Furthermore, the condition in syntagm 1 specifies that the nominal arguments of *leren* must precede Y1. We therefore obtain:

(6) DMorphR for subtree rooted in *leren*:
 de + kinderen,   leren + zwemmen

Now consider the subtree rooted in *helpen*. Again, syntagm 1 applies, this time with Y1 = *de + kinderen* and Y2 = *leren + zwemmen*. Again, the head verb is added to the left of Y2, while its nominal arguments are added to the left of Y1. We obtain:

(7) DMorphR for subtree rooted in *helpen*:
 Jan + Marie + de + kinderen,   helpen + leren + zwemmen

Finally, we apply syntagm 1 one more time for verb *zien*, and then the syntagm for the SUBORDINATE-CONJUNCTIONAL SSyntRel. This latter syntagm, not given here, will append the two parts of the DMorphR of its dependent *zien* node and append the *omdat* node, giving us the desired result:

(8) DMorphR for subtree rooted in *omdat*:
 omdat + Wim + Jan + Marie + de + kinderen + zien + helpen + leren + zwemmen

Thus, we do not need to have recourse to global rules: the word-order of the sentence is fixed in syntagms, despite the existence of unbounded deep non-projectivity. We can deal with embedded *wh*-words in a similar manner; for space limitations, we refrain from giving the details here.

Note that our proposal does not replace the notion of syntagm as defined in the Surface Syntactic-Component of MTT. Instead, it extends it, and it does so only in those cases where non-projectivity occurs (the other syntagms need not be changed). What is replaced is the notion of global ordering rules to handle cases such as English *wh*-movement and Dutch verb raising.

4 Conclusion

In this paper, we have argued that the crucial difference between a CFG-based analysis and a DG-based analysis is that the latter, but not the former, can be lexicon-based. We have described TAG, a phrase-structure grammar which can be lexicalized, and we have shown some similarities in linguistic analyses expressed in DGs and in TAGs. In considering non-projective word order phenomena, we have shown that two important results can be transferred from the TAG analysis to the MTT analysis: first, we can give attractive upper bounds on processing complexity for specific constructions; second, we do not need to have two types of word-order rules, syntagm-based rules and global rules. Instead, if we extend the definition of a syntagm, all rules can be expressed locally.

Acknowledgements

The authors would like to thank Richard Hudson and three anonymous reviewers for very helpful and insightful comments and suggestions. This work was partially supported by the following grants: ARO DAAL 03-89-C-0031; DARPA N00014-90-J-1863; NSF IRI 90-16592; and Ben Franklin 91S.3078C-1.

Endnotes

[1] It is also possible to define a new phrase-structure tree-rewriting system based on TAG so that the derivation *exactly* reflects dependency. Such a system, called *Dependency Tree Grammar* (DTG), is defined in (Rambow et al., 1995). The derivation structure in DTG is exactly the DSyntR of MTT. To our knowledge, DTG is the first phrase-structure system whose definition is directly and explicitly motivated by considerations of dependency.

[2] In this and other DSyntRs, actants that are deleted at subsequent stages (i.e., at the Surface-Syntactic Representation, SSyntR) are represented in parentheses. Furthermore, in DSyntR trees we follow the common practice of labeling nodes with the infinitives of verbs, while for TAG trees we will label nodes with the fully inflected form. Note that the non-projectivity of the construction is independent of the particular analysis chosen for "control" verbs of various types.

Bibliography

Abeillé, A. & Y. Schabes. 1989. "Parsing Idioms in Tree Adjoining Grammars". *Proceedings of the 4th Conference of the European Chapter of the Association for Computational Linguistics.* 1–9. Manchester.

Bach, E., C. Brown & W. Marslen-Wilson. 1986. "Crossed and Nested Dependencies in German and Dutch: A Psycholinguistic Study". *Language and Cognitive Processes.* 1.4:249–262.

Becker, T. 1993. *HyTAG: A New Type of Tree Adjoining Grammars for Hybrid Syntactic Representation of Free Word Order Languages.* PhD thesis. Saarbrücken: Universität des Saarlandes.

Becker, T., A. Joshi & O. Rambow. 1991. "Long Distance Scrambling and Tree Adjoining Grammars". *Proceedings of the 5th Conference of the European Chapter of the Association for Computational Linguistics.* 21–26. Utrecht.

Bresnan, J. & R. Kaplan. 1982. "Lexical-Functional Grammar: A Formal System for Grammatical Representation". *The Mental Representation of Grammatical Relations* ed. by J. Bresnan. Cambridge: MIT Press.

Covington, M. 1990. "Parsing Discontinuous Constituents in Dependency Grammar". *Computational Linguistics.* 16.4:234–236.

Gaifman, H. 1965. "Dependency Systems and Phrase-Structure Systems". *Information and Control.* 8:304–337.

Hays, D.G. 1964. "Dependency Theory: A Formalism and some Observations". *Language.* 40:511–525.

Joshi, A.K. 1987a. "An Introduction to Tree Adjoining Grammars". *Mathematics of Language* ed. by A. Manaster-Ramer. 87–115. Amsterdam & Philadelphia: Benjamins Academic Publishers.

Joshi, A.K. 1987b. *Word-Order Variation in Natural Language Generation.* Technical report. Philadelphia: Department of Computer and Information Science, University of Pennsylvania.

Joshi, A.K. 1990. "Processing Crossed and Nested Dependencies: An Automaton Perspective on the Psycholinguistic Results". *Language and Cognitive Processes.* 5.1:1-27.

Joshi, A.K. & S. Kulick. 1995. "Partial Proof Trees as Building Blocks for Categorial Grammars". *Presented at the MOL4 Workshop.* A revised version has been submitted for publication to *Linguistics and Philosophy.*

Joshi, A.K., L. Levy & M. Takahashi. 1975. "Tree Adjunct Grammars". *Journal of Computer Systems Science.* 10:136-163.

Joshi, A.K. & Y. Schabes. 1991. "Tree-Adjoining Grammars and Lexicalized Grammars". *Definability and Recognizability of Sets of Trees* ed. by M. Nivat & A. Podelski. North Holland: Elsevier.

Joshi, A.K., K. Vijay-Shanker & D. Weir. 1991. "The Convergence of Mildly Context-Sensitive Grammatical Formalisms". *Foundational Issues in Natural Language Processing* ed. by P. Sells, S. Shieber & T. Wasow. 31-81. Cambridge: MIT Press.

Kroch, A. 1987. "Subjacency in a Tree Adjoining Grammar". *Mathematics of Language* ed. by A. Manaster-Ramer. 143-172. Amsterdam & Philadelphia: Benjamins Academic Publishers.

Kroch, A. & B. Santorini. 1991. "The Derived Constituent Structure of the West Germanic Verb Raising Construction". *Principles and Parameters in Comparative Grammar* ed. by R. Freidin. 269-338. Cambridge: MIT Press.

Kunze, J. 1972. *Die Auslaßbarkeit von Satzteilen bei koordinativen Verbindungen im Deutschen.* Berlin: Akademie Verlag.

Marcus, S. 1965. "Sur la notion de projectivité". *Zeitschrift für mathematische Logik und Grundlagen der Mathematik.* 11:181-192.

Mel'čuk, I.A. 1967. "Ordre des mots en synthèse automatique des textes russes". *T. A. Informations.* 8.2:65-84.

Mel'čuk, I.A. 1988. *Dependency Syntax: Theory and Practice.* Albany: State University of New York Press.

Mel'čuk, I.A. & N. Pertsov. 1987. *Surface Syntax of English.* Amsterdam & Philadelphia: Benjamins Academic Publishers.

Mel'čuk, I.A. & A. Polguère. 1987. "A Formal Lexicon in the Meaning-Text Theory (or How to Do Lexica with Words)". *Computational Linguistics.* 13.3-4:276–289.

Nichols, J. 1979. "The Meeting of East and West: Confrontation and Convergence in Contemporary Linguistics". *Proceedings of the Fifth Meeting of the Berkeley Linguistics Society.* University of California.

Pollard, C. 1984. *Generalized Phrase-Structure Grammars, Head Grammars and Natural Language.* PhD thesis. Stanford: Stanford University.

Pollard, C. & I. Sag. 1987. *Information-Based Syntax and Semantics. Volume 1: Fundamentals.* Stanford: CSLI.

Rambow, O., K. Vijay-Shanker & D. Weir. 1995. "D-Tree Grammars". *Proceedings of the 33rd Meeting of the Association for Computational Linguistics.* 151–158. Cambridge, MA.

Schabes, Y. 1989. *Computational and Mathematical Studies of Lexicalized Grammars.* Technical report. Philadelphia: Department of Computer and Information Science, University of Pennsylvania.

Schabes, Y. & R.C. Waters. 1993. "Lexicalized Context-Free Grammars". *Proceedings of the 31rd Meeting of the Association for Computational Linguistics.* 121–129. Columbus, OH.

Steedman, M. 1991. "Structure and Intonation". *Language.* 68.2:260–296.

Weir, D., K. Vijay-Shanker & A. Joshi. 1986. "The Relationship between Tree Adjoining Grammars and Head Grammars". *Proceedings of the 24th Meeting of the Association for Computational Linguistics.* New York.

Subject Index

↓ s. substitution node
achievement, 66, 71
act, momentary, 71
actant, xiii, 3, 8
    deep-syntactic (DSyntA), 121
    direct, 97, 102, 104
    elision
        in Lushootseed, 96
    peripheral, 97, 102, 105
    referential characteristics of, 147
    semantic, 8, 29, 83
    syntactic, 8
action, 62, 67–69
    intentional, 68, 69
    result-oriented, 66, 71
    taxonomic category of, 62
Actor, 151, 152, 159, 161
Addressee, 80, 83, 152, 161
adjunction, 173, 176, 179
Adv_i, 28
Adv_1, 28
Adv_2, 28
Agent, 69
Aleut, 101
allophone, 5
ambiguity, regular, 67, 68
American Sign Language, 131
Appurtenance, 151, 152
argument, xiii, 3, 5, 8, 11
    deep-syntactic, 122
    semantic (SemA) 1,2, 119
    type of, 48
    typed, 48

Artificial Intelligence, 50
asserted component (of a definition), 47
assertion, 13
assertion vs. presupposition, 13

background, 13
Backgrounding, 108
Beja, 101
Bella Coola, xvi
Buriat, 101

Case Theory, 149
category
    lexical, xvi, 94
    taxonomic, xiv
causation, xiii–xv, 62
    controlled, xv, 62, 63, 67–69
    direct, 64
    guaranteed, xv, 64, 70, 71
    indirect, 64
    intentional, xv, 63
    non-controlled, xv, 63, 65–69
        unfolding, 68
    non-intentional, xv, 63
        accomplished, 72
        as happening, 72
        unfolding, 72
    partially controlled, xv, 69
causative expression
    conjunctive, 79, 87
    verbal, 79, 87
Cause, 161
causer, 62
    internal, 61

CB s. complementation, lexically
   bound
CCS predicate s. 'change or
   conservation of state'
   predicate
CD s. dynamism, communicative
'change or conservation of state'
   predicate, xvii, 138–140,
   146
class, aspectual, xv, 62
clause
   canonical
      structure of, 95
   conditional, 31
clitic, pronominal, 101
Coeur D'Alene, 115
Cognitive Psychology, 50
comment, 103
complementation, 162
   classification of, 152
   contextually bound (CB), 154,
      162, 164
   deletion of, 152, 163
   free, 150–152, 160
   inner, 150, 151
   not bound (NB), 156, 162, 163
      marker of, 162
   obligatory, 152, 153, 161
component
   semantic, xii
      'attempt', 70
      'damage', 66
      'success', 70
   surface-syntactic, 113, 178,
      187
compositionality principle, 38
conatives, 70
concept, 50, 51
   linguistic 2, 4, 6, 14
Conj$_2$, 29
Conj$_i$, 29

conjunction, 58
   coordinating, 41
   description of (in the ECD),
      40
   descriptive, 40, 41
   illocutionary, 40, 51
   non-illocutionary, 40
   rhetorical, 40, 41, 51
   subordinating, 41
connector, 9
   causative, 62
   logical, 30
Consequence, 63, 64, 66
constituency, 149, 160
constituency grammar, 111
constituent (immediate)
   structure, xviii, 149
construction
   non-projective, xix, 159, 182
   projective, xix, 159
   syntactic, synonymous, 158
content
   cognitive, 153
   descriptive, 45
   of a lexeme
      denotative, 50, 52, 53
      semantic, 50, 52
   ontological, 153
Context Categorial Grammar
   (CCG), 174
context-free phrase-structure
   grammar (CFG), xviii,
   167–169, 171, 177, 187
   derivation in, 170
control
   complete, 64
   non-complete, 64, 69
   partial, 69
   usual, 69
controller, 161
Conv$_{21}$, 28

SUBJECT INDEX

Conv, 28, 56
conversives, 28, 53
coordination, 151
copular construction, 101
coreferentiality
    distributive, 140, 141, 143, 145
    generalized, 140, 142, 143, 145
    of classes, 146
    of individuals, 146
    of noun phrases, 138, 140
correspondence
    SemR $\Longleftrightarrow$ DSyntR, 15

Deep Case, 49, 150
definition, 55
    lexicographic, xiv, 19, 61
        categorial component of, 62
        format of, 62
        scheme of, 62
        semantic component of, 62
DG s. dependency grammar
deictic
    as phrasal head, 115
    as syntactic governor, 116
    enclitic
        demonstrative, 110
        non-demonstrative, 110
    hypothetical, 109
    non-contrastive, 109
    proclitic
      distal, 109, 110
      middle, 110
      proximal, 110
    pronominal, 115, 117
    proximal, 109
      indefinite, 110
    remote, 107, 109, 110, 125
    spreading, rule of, 113
    unique, 109, 110
    unreal, 107, 109, 110, 125

deictics
    in Bella Coola, 112
    in Lushootseed, 112
deixis, in NPs, 109
dependency, xvii, 149, 151, 176
    communicative, xvi, 20, 90, 108
    cross-serial, 185
    long-distance, 179
    morphological, 4, 90
    non-projective, 177
    projective
        nested, 178
    semantic, 4, 5, 19
    serial (in Dutch), 178
    syntactic, 4, 111, 151, 158
dependency grammar (DG), xii, xix, 110, 111, 167, 171, 172, 187
    fully projective, 177
    generative, 168
dependency structure, 181
dependency tree, 108, 183
    top of, 128
Dependency Tree Grammar (DTG), 187
dependent of a predicate, 11
derivation structure, 175
derivation tree, 174, 180
description
    lexicographic, 147
    notional, 48
determiner phrase (DP), 110
determiner, in Salish, 110
dialogue test, 152
dictionary, notional, xiv, 53, 55
Dir-1, 151, 152, 155
Dir-2, 151, 155, 161
discourse
    presupposition, 108
    structure, 98

topic, xvi, 104
dislocation, 39
DMorphR s. representation, deep-morphological
domain of locality, 172
dominance, communicative, 108, 117, 118
double implication, 35
DP s. determiner phrase
dynamism, communicative, 151, 154
  scale of, xviii, 154

ECD s. Explanatory Combinatorial Dictionary
Effect, 152, 156, 161
element, deictic, 122
elementary structure, 172
Emphasis, 108
enclitic, 110, 112, 114, 115, 131
entailment, 31
entry node, xvi, 109
  rhematic, 128
entry, lexical, 160
equi-structures (in English), 164
equivalence
  semantic, 27
  weak, 177
Even, 101
event, 62
exhaustivity law, 58
Existential Negative, xvi, 94, 106, 125
Explanatory Combinatorial Dictionary (ECD), xii–xiv, 2, 6, 19, 26–28, 38, 40, 47, 49, 53–55, 58
  definition in, 2, 6, 13, 18, 19
  definition zone in, 28, 30–32, 47
  of French, 15
exposition. 66

expression, causative
  conjunctive, 75–79
  verbal, 75–79
    lexical, 87, 88, 90
    syntactic, 87, 88, 90

focalization, xv, 78, 79, 82, 84, 86
focalizer, 163
focus, xii, 151, 154
  proper, xviii, 154
foot node, 173
force, illocutionary, 45, 46, 158
foreground, 13
Foregrounding, 108, 130
Functional Generative Description (FGD), 149, 163
functor, xiii, 3, 8, 12, 30, 48
  communicative, dominant, 128, 129

gender
  grammatical, 131
  in Bella Coola, 131
Generative Grammar, 76
Generative Lexicon, xi
Generative Semantics, 76
genericity, 137
  meaning of, xvii, 144, 147
  quantifier of, 144–147
given, xv, 13, 78, 79, 81, 83, 107
given vs. new, 75, 153
Giveness, 108
Government and Binding Theory (GB), 167, 168, 178
governor, 150
  semantic, 11
  surface-syntactic, 112, 113
  syntactic, 118
grammar, lexicalized, 172
grammateme, 150, 161, 162
grammeme, 144

Halkomelem, 131
happening, 62, 65, 67–69
   with an acting Subject, 66
head, 111, 150, 151, 162
   surface-syntactic, 111
   syntactic, 77
Head Grammar (HG), 184
Head-Driven Phrase Structure
     Grammar (HPSG), 174
homosemy, xv, 75, 76

idiom, 176
Imperfective, 68
initial tree, 173
Inner Object, 61
inner scope, xvii, 137
Instrument, 69, 161
intentional
   accomplished, 72
   guaranteed, 72
   unfolding, 72
interpretation, resultative
   of Imperfective, 68
intonation center, 157, 164
invariant
   Jakobson's, 153
   semantic, 55
inverse, 130

Kalmyk, 101
Ket, 101

L-meaning, xiii, 3, 4, 6, 8, 10, 19
   decomposed, 16
   dominant, 7, 15
   non-decomposed, 7
L-presupposition, xiii, 13, 14
La Presse, 90
language
   generation, 78
   of linguistics, 1
     Type I, 2

Type II, 2
Type IV, 3
Types I – IV, 1
level
   conceptual, 83
   semantic, 83
   surface-syntactic, 111
   syntactic, 83
lexeme
   denotation of, 53
Lexical Function (LF), xi, 28,
     54–57, 137, 176
   Adv$_i$, 28
   Adv$_1$, 28
   Adv$_2$, 28
   Conj$_i$, 29
   Conj$_2$, 29
   Conv$_{21}$, 28
   Conv, 28, 56
   Syn, 28, 56
Lexical Functional Grammar
     (LFG), 150, 174
lexical unit
   complements of, 161
   negation of, 137
lexicalization, 108
LF s. Lexical Function
LFG s. Lexical Functional
     Grammar
licensing, 111
Lillooet, 110
lingua mentalis, 19
link, semantic, 4
Locative, 161
Locutionality, 108
logics, modal, 31
Lushootseed, xvi

Magn, 137
Manner, 152, 161
meaning, xii, 3, 7
   contextual, 54

decomposition of, 55
focalized, 78
generic, 145
linguistic
    vagueness of, 165
linguistic1, 1, 17
    taxonomy of, 3
linguistic2, 2
non-focalized, 78
non-unitarized, 87
proximity of, 27
situational, 75, 76
unitarized, 87
Meaning-Text (MT)-network, xii, 2, 3, 6, 7, 9, 10, 15, 20
    communicative structure of, xiii, 3
    formalism, 19
    semantic structure of, xiii, 3
Meaning-Text Model (MTM), 16, 61, 68, 175
Meaning-Text Theory (MTT), xi–xiii, xvii, xix, 1, 6, 15, 25, 28, 40, 55, 56, 58, 94, 108, 111, 129, 130, 149, 154, 160, 163, 167, 168, 172, 178, 181, 183
    meta-model of, 18
Means, 156, 161
metarule, 176
mismatch, deictic, 124
modality, epistemic, 47
modifier, 150
Mongolian, 101
MTT s. Meaning-Text Theory

Nanay, 101
negation
    existential, 107
    in Russian, 143
        scope of, 144
network, semantic, 1

language of, 1
new, xv, 13, 78, 79, 81
Nivkh, 101
node
    communicative, dominant, xvi, 7, 9, 10, 15, 17, 117, 118, 121, 128
    entry, 126, 128
        lexical, 126
        rhematic, 129
nominalization
    morphological, 102, 105, 131
    sentential, 131
    syntactic, 102, 111
non-projectivity, 178, 179, 181
    unbounded, 179
notion, xiv, 48, 49, 55, 58
    theoretical status of, 50
noun phrase
    generic, xvii, 141, 144
    non-generic, 141
noun/verb distinction, 94

object name, xiii, 3, 12, 19
Objective, 151, 152, 156, 161, 162
ontology, naive, 157
operation
    logical, 21
    para-logical, 21
operator, xiii, 3, 8, 19
    higher, 10
    linguistic1, 9
opposition, communicative, xv, 87, 108
    Backgrounding, 108
    dominance, communicative, 108
    Emphasis, 108
    Foregrounding, 108
    Giveness, 108
    Locutionality, 108
    Presupposedness, 108

Thematicity, 108
Unitariness, 108
Optimality Theory, 128
Origin, 152, 161
overstatement, the semantic component of, 38

parameter
    illocutionary, 58
    non-illocutionary, 58
    of interest, xv, 78, 83
    pragmatico-communicative, 40, 41
    strictly semantic, 40
    syntactic, 40, 41
paraphrase, 19, 26, 176
    linguistic, 26
    non-linguistic, 26
    semantic, 26, 29, 32
    syntactic, 26, 176
participant
    construal of, 98
    inner, 152, 153, 161
    peripherality of, 98
partition, thematic, 122, 129
passive, 130
Patient, 65
Perfective, 68, 70
perspective, on an event, 98
phoneme, 5
phrase-structure, xviii, 149
    representation, 168
phrase-structure grammar, 110
Prague school (of linguistics), xii, xviii, 84, 149, 160, 163
predicate, xiii, 3, 5, 10, 19
    actants of, 11
    deep-syntactic, 109, 120, 122, 125
    scope of, 143
    semantic, 93, 120
    syntactic, 94, 98, 99, 102, 103, 107
presentation
    emphatic, 13
    neutral, 13
Presupposedness, 108
presupposition, xiii, 3, 12–14, 18, 48, 53, 78
    grammatical, 13
    lexical, 13
primitive, semantic, 19, 31, 47, 150
Principle of Maximal Localization, 179
process, 62
    non-agentive, 61
    with an inherent limit, 65
proclitic, 110, 112, 113, 131
program, minimalist, 160
Progressive, 68
projection, 159
projectivity, 159
pronoun
    emphatic, 98
proposition
    final, 138
    initial, 138
proximity, semantic, 28, 76
Puget Salish, 93
Purpose, 62, 63

quantification, 10
quantifier, xiii, 3, 9, 10, 19, 137
    generic, 137, 145–147
    of genericity, 144
    scope of, 10, 137, 146

radical
    adjectival, 99, 116
    deictic, 116
relation
    causative, xii, 61

arguments of, 62
surface-syntactic, 115
D⟶N, 115
Relational Grammar, 150
Relationship, General, 151
representation
    conceptual, 50, 56
    deep-morphological
      (DMorphR), 183, 185
    deep-syntactic (DSyntR), xii,
      2, 8, 16, 56, 108, 113, 115,
      117, 175, 177, 180, 187,
      188
    semantic (SemR), xii, xiii, 2,
      8, 12, 13, 16, 19, 25, 56,
      75, 77, 78, 83, 108, 116,
      118, 126, 127
    surface-syntactic (SSyntR),
      113, 183, 188
residue, 104, 106
Result, 62–64
rewrite rule, 169, 172
rhematicity, 98
rheme, xv, 13, 78, 82–84, 93, 103,
    105, 106
    deep-syntactic, 124
    semantic, 108, 119–122, 125,
      127–129

salience, 97, 165
    relative, 97
Salish, 93, 94, 97, 110
semanteme, xiv, 48, 50, 51, 55,
    58, 77, 82, 116
SemCommS s. structure,
    semantic-communicative
seme, 31
SemR s. representation, semantic
SemRhetS s. structure,
    semantic-rhetorical
SemS s. structure, semantic
sentence

    narratively focused, 103
    verbless, xvi, 93, 94, 98, 102,
      104, 106, 112, 119
      communicative structure of,
        94
shift, categorial, 67
sign, linguistic1, 21
signified, 6
situation, 75, 88
specification, xv, 78, 79, 84
speech act, 41, 45, 46
    negative, 108
Squamish, 130
SSyntR s. representation
    surface-syntactic
SS-valency s. valency,
    surface-syntactic, passive
state, 62
    deontic, 71
    epistemic, 70, 71
    perceptive, 71
    volitive, 70
Straits Salish, 110
structure
    cognitive, xviii
    communicative, 12, 56, 77,
      79, 93, 94, 103, 104, 108,
      119, 120, 129
    deep (of causative verbs), 61
    deep-syntactic (DSyntS), xvi,
      109, 120, 121, 129
    dislocated, 39
    presuppositional
      of MT-networks, 13
    semantic-
      communicative
      (SemCommS), xii, xv,
      xvi, 25, 76–78, 82, 87,
      108, 120, 121, 128, 129
    rhetorical (SemRhetS), xii,
      25, 56, 78

SUBJECT INDEX

semantic (SemS), xii–xiv, xvi,
    13, 25, 56, 78, 83, 87, 108,
    109, 118, 119, 138
  coreferentiality in, 138, 140
  thematic, 93
  thematization, 83
  underlying, xviii, 151, 153
subcategorization condition, 161,
    162
subcategorization frame, 175
Subject, 69
  animate, 65
  concept of, 159
substitution, 170
substitution node, 170
suffix
  agent-orienting, 96
  applicative, 96
  middle, 96
  patient-orienting, 96
supposition, 46, 47
Syn, 28, 56
synonymy, xv, 76
syntactic role, 94
syntacticization, 108, 109, 118,
    119, 122, 125, 128
  communicatively-driven, 129
  lexically-driven, 130
syntagm, xix, 177, 179, 183
Systemic Ordering (SO), xviii,
    154, 156, 161
  scale of, 155

term, subjective, 53
TFA s. Topic-Focus Articulation
The American Heritage
    Dictionary, 4
thematicity, 108, 127, 129, 130
thematization, xv, xvi, 78, 79, 84
  secondary, 122
theme, xii, xv, 13, 75, 78, 82–84,
    93, 103–105

sub-, 84
deep-syntactic, 124
semantic, 108, 120, 128
theme/rheme partition, 122
Theory of Principles and
    Parameters, 150
theta
  grid, 150
  role, 150
topic, 103, 154
  proper, xviii, 154
Topic-Focus Articulation (TFA),
    xviii, 153, 154, 156, 159
topicality, 130
Transformational Grammar, 167
transitive
  primary, 61
  secondary, 61
tree
  auxiliary, 173
  derived, 174, 180
  elementary, 172, 174
Tree Adjoining Grammar (TAG),
    xii, xviii, xix, 168, 173,
    187
  combining operations in, 169
  elementary structure of, 169
  lexicalized, 168
Tree Substitution Grammar
    (TSG), xviii, 170, 171
truth
  evaluation of, 30
  linguistic, 30
  logical, 30
truth condition, 158
typology of language, 130

U-meaning, xiii, 3, 6, 7, 9, 10, 19
U-presupposition, xiii, 13, 14
Udeg, 101
Ul'ch, 101
unification, 162, 163

Unitariness, 108
unitarization, xv, 78, 89
   block, 89
      indivisibility of, 89
unity
   of space, 87
   of time, 87
utterance, 6

$VAL^{SS}_{pass}(L(w))$, 111
valency, 149, 151, 160
   active, 111
   filling, 137
   frame, xviii, 152, 160, 161
   grid, xviii, 160
   surface-syntactic, passive, 111–114
      of a PP, 112
      of an NP, 112
   syntactic, 151
verb
   control, 188
   raising, 183
      (in English), 164
   taxonomic category of, 62
voice, choice of, 83

Wh-
   element, 93, 106, 161
   movement, 179
   question, xvi, 93, 104, 121, 183, 187
      in English, xix, 179
word order, 176, 181, 183
   free, 155
   surface, 164
   underlying, 164
   unmarked
      in Bella Coola, 95
      in Lushootseed, 95

X-Bar Theory, 150

Name Index

Abeillé, 176
Abney, 110
Apresjan, 61, 67, 68, 70, 144, 149, 151

Bach, 178
Bates, 95
Beck, xii, xv, 93, 94, 97, 99, 100, 102, 113, 115, 130
Becker, 176
Bloomfield, 149
Boguslavsky, xii, xvi, 137
Bresnan, 174
Bulygina, 69

Chomsky, 76, 149, 150, 160, 167
Cornulier, De, xiv, 33, 34, 38, 58
Coseriu, 153
Covington, 178
Culioli, 48

Davis, 93–95, 97, 103, 110, 111, 124, 131
Demers, 93, 94, 115
Dostie, 16
Dowty, 82
Ducrot, 31, 45, 46, 58

Eijk, van, 94
Escalier, xii–xiv, 25

Fillmore, 48, 69, 149, 150
Firbas, 154
Fitialov, 164
Fodor, 76
Fournier, xii–xiv, 25

Gaifman, 150, 167, 177
Garde, 4
Gavrilova, 61
Gerdts, Donna, 131
Givón, 108
Goralciková, 164

Hajičová, 151, 162, 165
Halliday, 79, 83, 93
Hays, 168
Hellwig, 149
Hess, 94, 95, 109, 110, 130, 131
Heylen, xi
Hjelmslev, 153
Hudson, 101, 110, 114, 149

Iordanskaja, xiv, 8, 28, 32, 40, 41, 44, 51, 79, 83, 84, 126
Ioup, 137

Jacobs, 130
Jakobson, 153
Jelinek, 93, 94, 98, 115
Joshi, xii, xviii, 167–169, 174, 176, 178, 183

Kaplan, 174
Kerbrat-Orecchioni, 53
Kinkade, 93, 94, 97, 115
Kroch, 179, 183
Kroeber, 93, 100
Kuipers, 94
Kulick, 174
Kunze, 149, 168

Langacker, 116

Langendonck, van, 110
Lyons, 61

Marcus, 177
Martin, 30
Maslov, 70
Matthewson, 94, 111
McCarthy, 128
McKeown, 79
Mel'čuk, xi, 1–3, 5–8, 13, 15, 16,
    18, 26, 27, 56, 61, 76, 78,
    79, 84, 93, 108, 110, 111,
    117, 122, 126, 130, 137,
    149, 151, 169, 176, 177,
    179, 182, 184
Mørdrup, 14

Nater, 95, 103, 131
Nichols, 167
Nicodemus, Lawrence, 115
Novak, 165

Paducheva, xii, xiv, 61, 69, 82
Panevová, 151, 152
Pertsov, xi, 16, 177, 179, 184
Petkevic, 164
Platek, 164
Polguère, xii, 1, 2, 7, 8, 17, 20,
    117, 126, 169
Pollard, 174, 184
Poppe, 101
Prince, 128
Pustejovsky, xi

Radford, 110
Rambow, xi, xii, xviii, 167, 187
Robinson, 164
Rozencvejg, 151
Rullmann, 182
Ruwet, 75, 87

Saarinen, 137
Sag, 174

Sandmann, 93
Santorini, 183
Saunders, 93, 95, 97, 103, 110,
    124, 131
Saussure, de, 49, 153
Schabes, 169, 173, 176
Schnelle, 153
Sgall, xii, xvii, xviii, 79, 84, 149,
    151, 154, 164, 168
Skorik, 101
St-Germain, xii, xv, 6, 75, 87
Starosta, 149
Steedman, 174

Tarski, 35
Tesnière, 160
Tommola, 70

Uhlenbeck, 160

Vendler, xv, 62, 66, 71, 82
Verhagen, 182

Wackernagel, 164
Wanner, xi
Waters, 173
Weir, 184
Wierzbicka, xv, 6, 7, 19, 61–65,
    71, 75, 76, 82, 87
Woods, 10

Zalizniak, 70
Zholkovsky, xi, 61, 137

In the STUDIES IN LANGUAGE COMPANION SERIES (SLCS) the following volumes have been published thus far or are scheduled for publication:

1. ABRAHAM, Werner (ed.): *Valence, Semantic Case, and Grammatical Relations. Workshop studies prepared for the 12th Conference of Linguistics, Vienna, August 29th to September 3rd, 1977*. Amsterdam, 1978.
2. ANWAR, Mohamed Sami: *BE and Equational Sentences in Egyptian Colloquial Arabic*. Amsterdam, 1979.
3. MALKIEL, Yakov: *From Particular to General Linguistics. Selected Essays 1965-1978. With an introd. by the author + indices*. Amsterdam, 1983.
4. LLOYD, Albert L.: *Anatomy of the Verb: The Gothic Verb as a Model for a Unified Theory of Aspect, Actional Types, and Verbal Velocity*. Amsterdam, 1979.
5. HAIMAN, John: *Hua: A Papuan Language of the Eastern Highlands of New Guinea*. Amsterdam, 1980.
6. VAGO, Robert (ed.): *Issues in Vowel Harmony. Proceedings of the CUNY Linguistics Conference on Vowel Harmony (May 14, 1977)*. Amsterdam, 1980.
7. PARRET, H., J. VERSCHUEREN, M. SBISÀ (eds): *Possibilities and Limitations of Pragmatics. Proceedings of the Conference on Pragmatics, Urbino, July 8-14, 1979*. Amsterdam, 1981.
8. BARTH, E.M. & J.L. MARTENS (eds): *Argumentation: Approaches to Theory Formation. Containing the Contributions to the Groningen Conference on the Theory of Argumentation*, Groningen, October 1978. Amsterdam, 1982.
9. LANG, Ewald: *The Semantics of Coordination*. Amsterdam, 1984.(English transl. by John Pheby from the German orig. edition *"Semantik der koordinativen Verknüpfung"*, Berlin, 1977.)
10. DRESSLER, Wolfgang U., Willi MAYERTHALER, Oswald PANAGL & Wolfgang U. WURZEL: *Leitmotifs in Natural Morphology*. Amsterdam, 1987.
11. PANHUIS, Dirk G.J.: *The Communicative Perspective in the Sentence: A Study of Latin Word Order*. Amsterdam, 1982.
12. PINKSTER, Harm (ed.): *Latin Linguistics and Linguistic Theory. Proceedings of the 1st Intern. Coll. on Latin Linguistics, Amsterdam, April 1981*. Amsterdam, 1983.
13. REESINK, G.: *Structures and their Functions in Usan*. Amsterdam, 1987.
14. BENSON, Morton, Evelyn BENSON & Robert ILSON: *Lexicographic Description of English*. Amsterdam, 1986.
15. JUSTICE, David: *The Semantics of Form in Arabic, in the mirror of European languages*. Amsterdam, 1987.
16. CONTE, M.E., J.S. PETÖFI, and E. SÖZER (eds): *Text and Discourse Connectedness*. Amsterdam/Philadelphia, 1989.
17. CALBOLI, Gualtiero (ed.): *Subordination and other Topics in Latin. Proceedings of the Third Colloquium on Latin Linguistics, Bologna, 1-5 April 1985*. Amsterdam/Philadelphia, 1989.
18. WIERZBICKA, Anna: *The Semantics of Grammar*. Amsterdam/Philadelphia, 1988.
19. BLUST, Robert A.: *Austronesian Root Theory. An Essay on the Limits of Morphology*. Amsterdam/Philadelphia, 1988.
20. VERHAAR, John W.M. (ed.): *Melanesian Pidgin and Tok Pisin. Proceedings of the First International Conference on Pidgins and Creoles on Melanesia*. Amsterdam/Philadelphia, 1990.

21. COLEMAN, Robert (ed.): *New Studies in Latin Linguistics. Proceedings of the 4th International Colloquium on Latin Linguistics*, Cambridge, April 1987. Amsterdam/ Philadelphia, 1991.
22. McGREGOR, William: *A Functional Grammar of Gooniyandi*. Amsterdam/Philadelphia, 1990.
23. COMRIE, Bernard and Maria POLINSKY (eds): *Causatives and Transitivity*. Amsterdam/Philadelphia, 1993.
24. BHAT, D.N.S. *The Adjectival Category. Criteria for differentiation and identification*. Amsterdam/Philadelphia, 1994.
25. GODDARD, Cliff and Anna WIERZBICKA (eds): *Semantics and Lexical Universals. Theory and empirical findings*. Amsterdam/Philadelphia, 1994.
26. LIMA, Susan D., Roberta L. CORRIGAN and Gregory K. IVERSON (eds): *The Reality of Linguistic Rules*. Amsterdam/Philadelphia, 1994.
27. ABRAHAM, Werner, T. GIVÓN and Sandra A. THOMPSON (eds): *Discourse Grammar and Typology*. Amsterdam/Philadelphia, 1995.
28. HERMAN, József: *Linguistic Studies on Latin: Selected papers from the 6th international colloquium on Latin linguistics, Budapest, 2-27 March, 1991*. Amsterdam/ Philadelphia, 1994.
29. ENGBERG-PEDERSEN, Elisabeth et al. (eds): *Content, Expression and Structure. Studies in Danish functional grammar*. Amsterdam/Philadelphia, 1996.
30. HUFFMAN, Alan: *The Categories of Grammar. French lui and le*. Amsterdam/ Philadelphia, 1997.
31. WANNER, Leo (ed.): *Lexical Functions in Lexicography and Natural Language Processing*. Amsterdam/Philadelphia, 1996.
32. FRAJZYNGIER, Zygmunt: *Grammaticalization of the Complex Sentence. A case study in Chadic*. Amsterdam/Philadelphia, 1996.
33. VELAZQUEZ-CASTILLO, Maura: *The Grammar of Possession. Inalienability, incorporation and possessor ascension in Guaraní*. Amsterdam/Philadelphia, 1996.
34. HATAV, Galia: *The Semantics of Aspect and Modality. Evidence from English and Biblical Hebrew*. Amsterdam/Philadelphia, 1997.
35. MATSUMOTO, Yoshiko: *Noun-Modifying Constructions in Japanese. A frame semantic approach*. Amsterdam/Philadelphia, 1997.
36. KAMIO, Akio (ed.): *Directions in Functional Linguistics*. Amsterdam/Philadelphia, 1997.
37. HARVEY, Mark and Nicholas REID (eds): *Nominal Classification in Aboriginal Australia*. Amsterdam/Philadelphia, 1997.
38. HACKING, Jane F.: *Coding the Hypothetical. A Comparative Typology of Conditionals in Russian and Macedonian*. Amsterdam/Philadelphia, n.y.p.
39. WANNER, Leo (ed.): *Recent Trends in Meaning-Text Theory*. Amsterdam/Philadelphia, 1997.
40. BIRNER, Betty and Gregory WARD: *Information Status and Noncanonical Word Order in English*. Amsterdam/Philadelphia, n.y.p.